Literature in the Classroom

NCTE Yearbook Committee

Literature in the Classroom

Readers, Texts, and Contexts

Edited by
Ben F. Nelms

National Council of Teachers of English
1111 Kenyon Road, Urbana, Illinois 61801

"January Chance" is reprinted from *Collected and New Poems: 1924–63* by Mark Van Doren. Copyright © 1963 by Mark Van Doren. Reprinted by permission of Farrar, Straus and Giroux, Inc.

Interior Book Design: Tom Kovacs for TGK Design

NCTE Stock Number 30054

Library of Congress Cataloging-in-Publication Data

Literature in the classroom.

    (NCTE forum series)
    Includes bibliographies.
    1. Literature — Study and teaching (Elementary) — United States. 2. Literature — Study and teaching (Secondary) — United States. 3. Reading — United States. 4. Literature — History and criticism — Study and teaching — United States. I. Nelms, Ben F. II. Series.
LB1575.5.U5L57 1988   372.6'4   88-1689
ISBN 0-8141-3005-4

Contents

Foreword

This volume is the second in a series planned by the NCTE Yearbook Committee at the request of NCTE's Executive Committee during the term of former president Stephen Tchudi. The first volume was published as a yearbook to celebrate NCTE's Diamond Jubilee in 1986. *Consensus and Dissent* ranged over broad issues that have stirred discussion and debate during the Council's seventy-five-year history. The subsequent books planned by the Yearbook Committee will address specific topics of concern to teachers of English and will constitute the beginning of the NCTE Forum Series.

That literature should be the subject of the present volume was a consensus arrived at without dissent. The Yearbook Committee readily agreed that the book should address a single issue and that its purpose should be to reassert the central place of literature in the English curriculum. As committee members expanded upon that purpose, they agreed that *Literature in the Classroom* should meet several objectives:

Present examples of varied approaches to the teaching of literature in elementary and secondary schools.

Relate the teaching of literature to current modes of literary criticism and to reader-response theory.

Examine recent research in reading as it relates to the teaching of literature.

Give attention to the social and cultural contexts that surround the teaching of literature.

As the nature of the volume began to take shape in the committee's discussions, it soon became clear that an articulate, knowledgeable, committed editor, one who would move quickly to enlist writers and give them essential guidance, was already on board. Ben Nelms, then chair of the Yearbook Committee, willingly took on this assignment because of his commitment to literature. He is well aware that the teaching of literature is a major concern of classroom teachers and that this concern is not frequently addressed these days in professional journals or at conferences, where reading, writing, and "thinking skills" seem to have taken over.

From the committee's cheerful brainstorming, through the sticky tasks of writing, editing, revising, and rewriting, through group decision making and conflicting editorial opinions, through all the mishaps of production, Ben Nelms has been persistent and patient, tactful and tenacious. And ultimately successful — although that is a judgment for the readers to make.

Anyone with experience in writing and editing knows that the hazards of collaboration are magnified tenfold when a manuscript must emerge from a committee — and in this case not one committee but three, counting the contributors and the Editorial Board. With the same investment of time, talent, and energy, Ben Nelms might have written his own definitive text on the teaching of literature. But his book would have spoken with a single voice, not with the many voices of a forum. This volume happily joins the voices of first-grade teachers, seventh-grade teachers, high school teachers, college English professors, teachers of teachers, and, less directly, the voices of researchers and theorists. What emerges, we believe, is a comprehensive record — of course not an exhaustive one — of what was happening during 1987 in the teaching of literature.

Margaret Early, Chair
NCTE Yearbook Committee

Literature in the Classroom

1 Sowing the Dragon's Teeth: An Introduction in the First Person

Ben F. Nelms
University of Missouri

As an undergraduate, I learned to think of the literary text as an edifice. Almost as a temple. Complete, autonomous, organically whole, sacrosanct. We approached it with reverence. We might make temple rubbings, and we were encouraged to explain how its arches carried its weight and to speculate on the organic relationship between its form and function. But it was an edifice and we were spectators before its splendors.

As a practicing teacher, I have learned that it is sometimes better to think of the text as a construction site — or as the blueprint around which all the activity at a construction site is centered, or the excavation and foundation work upon which the building is to be erected. As Octavio Paz writes, "The poem is just this: a possibility, something that is only animated by the contact with a reader or a listener. There is one note common to all poems, without which it would never be poetry: participation" (1973, p. 14). So it is with all literature.

If the text is simple and direct, each of us may succeed without much ado to erect a house and, as in many American subdivisions, all of the houses built by readers from the same blueprint may look pretty much alike. But if the text is more demanding and if the resulting structure is to be more imposing, the construction site may prove to be a beehive of communal activity, with crane operators, steeplejacks, bricklayers, carpenters, plumbers, interior decorators, landscape artists, and window washers all contributing their bit: an insight here, a relevant piece of information there, and occasionally a sense of direction or an organizing principle.

The edifices I most admire and return to year after year, those called *Hamlet* and *Jane Eyre* and "Ode on a Grecian Urn" and *The Hobbit* and the Ananse stories, consist of more than literary texts. They comprise my repeated readings and experiences, the questions and insights of hundreds of my students, and the information and inter-

1

pretations provided by a whole community of scholars and critics. These works also comprise dozens of renderings on stage, in film, by readers and storytellers, in satires and parodies, in my own silent reverie, and in the halting voice of yet another student approaching the text with yet another claw hammer or bulldozer. For the edifices are still a-building. The *Hamlet* that I read with my daughter for her senior English class a few weeks ago had a different Ophelia than I had seen before, younger and prettier, more vulnerable and possibly a bit more like my daughter than I could have imagined twenty-seven years ago when I first taught *Hamlet*. As Paz writes, "The poem is a work that is always unfinished, always ready to be completed and lived by a new reader" (p. 174), or, one might add, remodeled and lived again by her father.

Looking back, I can admit from the safe distance of middle age that I probably became an English major not so much because of my reverence for literary texts as because of my fascination with this construction business. I thought then that I had been won over from history (or speech or religion or whatever my major was that particular month) to English by Keats's "Ode on a Grecian Urn." I now realize that I was won over by the probing questions of my teacher Miss Jennie Pittie Brown, by my joint struggles with two or three perceptive classmates to make sense of words on the page, and by a book I discovered during that sophomore year, Earl Wasserman's *The Finer Tone*, which reproduced the similar struggles of an enormously erudite scholar and critic to make sense of those same words. I now realize, too, that it was not his interpretation of Keats's work that attracted me, though his reading of the great odes is still the most persuasive I have encountered, but it was the clarity with which he revealed his own handling of disparate bits of data and his obvious zest in the undertaking.

But like most of my generation, I was brought up on *Understanding Poetry* by Brooks and Warren, and I became an advocate. I subscribed, at least in my pronouncements, too ardently to the vision of the individual psyche standing naked before an autonomous text, unaided and unhampered by intentional fallacies and affective fallacies and pathetic fallacies — just me and my objective correlative.

When, as a doctoral student, I discovered the work of Northrop Frye and under the gentle but insistent tutelage of Murray Krieger took a hard look at the presuppositions of the New Criticism, I hardly wavered. From a broader perspective, I admitted, one could substitute Literature or the whole universe of discourse for the individual text and apply the concept of organic unity to all the works of the human imagination. Thus the search for mythic patterns, archetypes, and genre might prove interesting and illuminating. But at the heart of the enterprise still stood the inviolate text and the inquisitive reader, and the reader was still more or less a spectator at the Grand Exhibition.

That was my stance as a scholar-critic. Teaching was a different matter. College sophomores could be persuaded to watch patiently for fifty minutes at a time while the skyscraper I called *Hamlet* slowly took shape before them. On my better days, I fancy they were rather like pedestrians peering through the wire fence at a construction site, mildly interested in what a skillful construction worker can do, but convinced they never could do the same thing nor would want to, soon walking on toward their real destinations. But eighth graders, I discovered, were not so patient, nor were those eighteen-year-olds who in those days were called "terminal" twelfth graders, the non-college-bound sons and daughters of plumbers and carpenters and bricklayers, often anxious to get on with the real business of the world. They wanted to be in on the action. They liked stories and plays, songs and funny sayings. They liked to talk about people and motives and happenings and what it all meant to them. But they did not much care for archetypes, themes, and organic unity (not in those terms). And they could smell a symbol a mile away.

The literary community from which I came and to which I aspired was an oligarchy with a recognized social and political hierarchy and some well-established conventions of behavior. The literature class-room, I discovered, had to be a participatory democracy. The terminal twelfths could be persuaded to act out even the most dramatic scenes from *Macbeth* and compare Lady Macbeth and her husband to their own relatives and local demagogues, more than you would believe, and recurring motifs be damned! Eighth graders could enter with blood-curdling gusto into the most bizarre stories of Edgar Allan Poe or the craziness of *A Midsummer Night's Dream* and respond with imitations, graphic drawings, eerie oral readings, and wildly imaginative alternative endings. They identified in assorted verbal and nonverbal ways with Adam Cooper in *April Morning*, True Son in *Light in the Forest*, and Anne Frank, and they could stand aside and critique the worlds of Ray Bradbury and Susie Hinton alike. But dwell for long on plot-setting-character or symbol-image-theme and they withdrew into their collective shell like tortoises in a thunderstorm.

Good teachers of literature, especially working with younger and less experienced students, have always had to be reader-response critics. They have had to live in or near the buildings their students erected. They have had to be patient with structures that deviated slightly or monstrously from the blueprints they saw in the texts. They have had to content themselves with questioning, probing, and occasional shoving to get doors and windows and stairs and pipes in reasonable spots. Mostly they have helped students find texts that they could build upon and in which they could live fuller lives.

This book had its impetus in the struggle of those good teachers to reconcile the needs and interests of student-readers in their classrooms and the promises and expectations of the literary community in which they themselves had taken residence. More specifically, this book grew as a response to John Gerber's (1970) wise and helpful essay written in the heyday of new critical zeal, an essay called "Varied Approaches to 'When Lilacs Last in the Dooryard Bloom'd.' "

"I have done a small bit of research on how we prepare to teach Whitman's 'When Lilacs Last in the Dooryard Bloom'd,' " he begins, tongue only partly in cheek, "and have found that the majority of us follow some such agonizing procedure as this:

1. Look to see if there are any notes in the anthology.
2. Go back to the old college notebooks to see what old Professor Smedley in American Lit had to say.
3. Ask other teachers what they do.
4. Read a brief biography or two of Whitman, the one in the anthology and possibly one in an encyclopedia.
5. Read the poem itself.
6. Pray for guidance, and go to class." (p. 353)

Many things have changed in the teaching of literature in the more than twenty years since this essay was first published, but I suspect that many teachers recognize the ritual. Gerber goes on to describe in some detail common approaches to the study of literature ranging from the analytic to the mythical.

When Gerber wrote the essay, it embodied a number of widely held assumptions about the teaching of literature. Some of these were explicit, some implicit in his clear and cogent discussion of the practical problems of the classroom teacher of literature. He assumed, for example, that English teachers — he addressed high school teachers primarily — were well versed in the periods, genres, and major authors of British and American literature, but were ill-prepared to undertake independent analyses of many of the texts they were expected to teach.

Further, Gerber assumed that at least one of the purposes of the teaching of literature should be to engage students in critical analysis of received texts. The teacher should therefore be able to present varied critical analyses to students and probably induct them into critical activity by having them imitate those analyses. It is also clear, in spite of Gerber's title, that those would be formal analyses of autonomous texts. Though he expounded, for example, historical, psychological, sociological, and ideological approaches to criticism, these were always used in the service of a close reading of the text. The text was seen as an object that deserved and would reward close reading and that clearly had a life of its own beyond its author's intentions or its readers' responses.

Finally, Gerber probably assumed that the body of works to be studied would be drawn from an informally recognized canon of literature, a list of great books, for which relevant background information and critical apparatus would be readily available. As long as the works studied were drawn from the major works of major authors in the mainstream of British and American literature, teachers and their students would have no great difficulty in finding the information they would need to apply the critical approaches he surveyed.

One of the great values of Gerber's essay is that, based on these assumptions, it presented such a sound and workable tool for the classroom teacher. One purpose of this volume is to present similarly sound and workable tools for English language arts teachers today, but in a very different context. Today's teachers might have difficulty accepting any of the assumptions I attribute to Gerber. Their undergraduate preparation may have emphasized critical analysis more than historical periods, traditional genres, or major authors. They are likely to have given serious attention to long-neglected works by women, ethnic minorities, and writers of the non-Western world, and in subclassical genres such as science fiction and fantasy. Among the outcomes that today's teachers might expect of literary study are personal satisfaction, developmental values, social awareness, and the articulate expression of response as well as skill in critical analysis. Literary critics of several different persuasions have challenged the primacy of formal analysis in the repertoire of critical strategies, and in fact some have mounted an outright attack on the notion that the text is an independent, autonomous object for interpretation. Attention has shifted to readers' responses, to the act of reading, and to the "text" in the reader's head.

Perhaps the assumption underlying all of Gerber's other assumptions — one that the contributors to this yearbook share — is the centrality of literature in the English language arts curriculum. Even that assumption is less widely held today. At least less attention in professional meetings and journals has been given to the teaching of literature in recent years. Emphasis on writing, on reading, and on thinking skills has inevitably led to less attention to the teaching of literature per se. In general, the emphasis in contemporary schools on practical and useful life skills may be contributing to a decline in interest in the humanities in elementary and secondary schools as well as in colleges and universities. Even the excitement and ferment within the literary establishment itself may be contributing to a decline in interest and confidence in the teaching of literature, for the debates among critical schools and over the literary canon may have engendered a sense of laissez-faire in the teaching of literature, leaving inexperienced teachers confused and ill at ease.

As you read the somewhat disparate essays in this book and try to see them as a coherent whole, it may prove helpful to think of the experience of literature as a process involving four recursive stages or activities. (Ten years of talk about the composing process in our profession has conditioned us to think of all language processes as recursive.) I like to think of the process as a series of Chinese boxes, each one opening up the possibility of yet another one, each one reflecting upon and enriching the others.

The first box is what I call *evocation*, or what Wolfgang Iser (1974) calls passive synthesis. It is the silent and personal process of reading and imaging a story or poem. Evocation is the stage at which we give ourselves up to the story. For the moment, we become what we read. We say that we lose ourselves in a good book or that we forget ourselves. The more successful we are as readers, the more likely we are to be unconscious of the reading process itself. Hence, we may speak of this stage as being essentially inarticulate, for we are not called upon to supply language, only to embody the language we receive with mental images.

This does not mean, of course, that the mind is passive during the process. For that reason, I am not particularly fond of Iser's term *passive synthesis,* for it implies that one simply lets the words and images wash over one, exerting no influence over the development of the story, either conscious or unconscious. As a matter of fact, all readers create their own stories and each one is different. They draw upon their memories, linguistic repertory, previous experiences with literature, and their own momentary moods and expectations. What anyone sees or finds or remembers in a story will be different from what another sees or finds or remembers. Some reading specialists have called this evoked text the real text and refer to the printed page as text potential. That terminology seems unnecessarily cumbersome to me, but it is true that these evoked texts furnish the raw materials for the teacher of literature. In the classroom we deal not with the printed texts, but with whatever has emerged from the students' individual interactions with those printed texts. Thus, after the story has been read as homework or the poem read aloud in the classroom, the teacher of thirty confronts thirty different versions of that story or poem.

As soon as we begin to talk about the story or poem with our friends, or even when we begin to talk to ourselves about our experience of the work, we enter a new phase, which I shall call *response* (though dialogue or conversation might be better words for the kind of response I have in mind). For the minute we begin to articulate our feelings, ideas, and judgments about a piece of literature, it begins to take another shape. We see things we had not seen before, and we begin to forget those things that do not relate to the account we are giving of the story. This is true whether we are simply retelling the story to a friend, asking a question of a trusted colleague, expressing our opinions to a stranger on the street, or pausing a moment to talk silently to ourselves about what we have just read. A distancing process begins. The focus is still on the interaction of text and reader, but the emphasis moves from the text itself to the reader.

My research with adult readers leads me to think that this articulation is likely to involve what Purves and Rippere call engagement-involvement and perception, but also to make certain beginnings toward interpretation, especially the raising of significant questions, the expression of confusion, the formulation of tentative hypotheses, and extrapolation from the text of disconnected inferences not yet coherent enough to justify the term *interpretation*. With most readers and most texts, this may be where the experience of literature ends: an evoked text followed by almost random conversation, private or public.

Where the general public leaves off, the critical and scholarly community is likely to begin, sometimes leaving the impression (and not always innocently, especially in performances before uninitiated students) that those inchoate and unimpressive stages never existed, that a full-blown and coherent interpretation emerged in the critic's mind without benefit of gloss or intercession by others. In actual practice, of course, even the most astute critic's interpretation evolves with a certain amount of personal groping, verifying of hunches, and interacting with others. Most of us, especially when we work with complex texts, are likely to consult sources ranging from scholarly varioria, to previous critical commentary, to Professor Smedley, or to Cliffs Notes.

Whatever the critic's interpretive predisposition, the critic's work begins with *interpretation,* with the pursuit of significance in the literature or an explanation of the breakdown of significance. New critics and archetypal critics, post-structuralists and deconstructionists alike are interested in a reading of the work that convinces others, in an explanation of the significance of a work that synthesizes its most disparate elements and persuades other readers to discover and accept the same formulation. True, for the last fifty years at least, critics have been suspicious of the reductive interpretation that anatomizes the work or summarizes it in a prose paraphrase separate from the experience of the work itself. Even so, the critic's business is to produce texts about the text, hence to give an account of what the text means or to describe how the experience of the text is achieved.

Thus the focus moves from the text and the individual reader to a broader community of readers attempting to assist and influence one another in a fuller realization of the text. The distancing from the work becomes more pronounced. What had been essentially a non-verbal or inarticulate evocation of the work and then became a discussion or dialogue with another trusted individual now becomes public discourse or debate. Willing suspension of disbelief and emotional involvement in the work make way for rational analysis, susceptible to the canons of logic and empirical evidence.

The last phase of the experience of literature may be called true *criticism.* It attempts to place the work in larger contexts — to define its place in its social milieu or the history of ideas, to evaluate its significance according to any number of established or newly proposed criteria, to test the world view it embodies (at least according to the critic as interpreter), to use it as a focal point for questioning one's assumptions about human experience or the sense of values prevalent in one's society, to analyze the adequacy of its language and literary devices to achieve effects deemed appropriate for its genre or theme.

Clearly, the pleasures and perils of interpretation and criticism are quite different from the pleasures and perils of evocation and response. Students tend to resist them; literature teachers tend to impose them. Given the reluctance of students to interpret and criticize and the limited background they have for doing either, it is not surprising that harried teachers either content themselves with testing comprehension (the evoked text) and sometimes promoting personal response (dialogue or conversation), or press their students to accept their own preformulated interpretations and critical judgments.

The attempt to bridge the gap is, in part at least, what this book is about. Most of the teachers represented herein seek to promote analytical thinking and critical judgment without denying the pleasure of evocation or the importance of personal response. They want their students to lose themselves and find themselves in good books. But they also want their students to question the texts rather than blindly react to them and to use texts to question the world around them rather than precipitately reject what they read when it calls their own predispositions into question.

In the first section of this book, "Readers: Student Responses to Literature," we focus on evocation and response — the initial interaction between readers and texts — and on ways to encourage students to open themselves to the literary experience. In the second section, "Texts: Interpretive Approaches to Literature," the focus is largely on the act of interpretation. These essays presuppose students with a strong sense of the text and a willingness to respond, but they also invite students to join in interpretive communities, to explore possibilities of meaning and significance in the texts. In the third section, "Contexts: Social Dimensions of Literature," we focus finally on criticism, on the use of literature to broaden our students' world view and to question their unexamined values. Thus we return to our responsibility to lead students in questioning the literary texts and the literary canon. Our original intention in planning the organization of this book was to present critical and pedagogical theory and classroom practice in separate sections. As the essays materialized, it became clear that such a distinction would be artificial, that essays on classroom experience should be grouped with the theoretical essays with which they were most closely aligned.

However, neither the organization nor my arbitrary division of the experience of literature into discernible parts should imply that we think these parts are independent. As the essays in part II make abundantly clear, interpretation at whatever level implies evocation and personal commitment, and evocation and commitment may be enhanced and clarified by the act of interpretation. At least they will almost certainly be changed. Likewise, the distancing that is involved in critical judgment — whether of the literary work or through it — does not require a sacrifice of either the pleasure of evocation or the passion of personal commitment. One's childhood delight in the adventures of Huck Finn and one's identification with his physical and moral struggles need not be displaced by an interpretation that sees the novel as embodying larger social and moral issues. This genuine response and active involvement in a search for meaning may lead to, and even be enriched by, a critical view that uses the book to judge the society which produced it and our own society as we read it. Our response may of course be changed by a critical view that finds the novel itself ultimately wanting in its own commitment to the values it has espoused, but even so our conscious delight in character and incident will not be supplanted. Indeed, with the great texts our initial pleasure may grow and deepen with each successive effort at interpretation and criticism.

You should be forewarned that not all of the essays in this book are perfectly consistent with one another. There are tensions, as we think there should be. The decision to divide the book into three separate sections, focusing respectively on readers, texts, and contexts — a decision that was not originally intended and did not come easily — at first simply recognized the unique pitfalls and promises of each emphasis, but ultimately came to throw them in clear relief. Even in their differences, however, the authors in all three sections agree in pursuing the goals of authenticity, flexibility, and pluralism in the study of literature.

Robert Probst strikes the keynote in chapter 2, when he argues for the selection of literature that evokes authentic responses from student readers and the presentation of literature in such a way that encourages the celebration and sharing of such responses. He anchors the study of literature upon students' direct response to texts. In chapter 3 Margaret Early and Bonnie Ericson explore the act of reading itself, synthesizing what recent research offers teachers eager to facilitate successful interactions among students and literary texts. They marshal an impressive array of strategies that teachers can use to make possible authentic reading and response. Likewise, in his consideration of classroom discourse — both writing and talk — James Marshall in chapter 4 wrestles with the teacher's recurring problem: How does one encourage growing sophistication in the use of language and at the same time protect the authenticity of the individual's ideas and concerns? He analyzes the discourse in a high school literature classroom with a view toward discovering how it impedes or supports students' active engagement with texts. In demonstrations of the reading of literature in classrooms, Dorothy Watson, Nancy Knipping, and their colleagues in chapters 5 and 6 allow their students freedom in selecting and discussing books. They are at some pains not to impose teacherly ideas and ideals prematurely. Their respective essays show what happens in a year-long program in which children choose their own literature texts and respond to them freely in small reading communities. Though the emphasis in part I is on the authenticity of reader responses, the goal already is to provide opportunities for flexibility of response and a plurality of ideas.

It might appear that in moving from the evocation and response emphasized in part I to the interpretation and criticism envisioned in the final two sections, one must move from engagement toward detachment, from indulgence in psychological projection toward commitment to social action, from attention to the internal needs of Self toward attention to the external pressures of Society. Indeed, there is a sense in which these are polar extremes that must inevitably be balanced in the study and teaching of literature. One moves back and forth — not always easily — between the inner worlds of experienced texts and the outer worlds to which those texts apparently refer.

On the one hand, it is not so much that we make literature a Rorschach inkblot. Literature, as all other experiences, *is* a Rorschach blot, for it triggers in our conscious and subconscious mind a myriad of associations, memories, images, purely idiosyncratic flights of fancy. They come unbidden, the more so the more engaging the literature proves to be to any given reader. The dialogue and discussion in which readers express their responses to literature simply raise these to consciousness, allow us to examine these inner worlds as we attempt to put them into words, and give us the opportunity to compare our own silent projections with those of our peers — not to be judged, challenged, or measured, but to begin negotiating a communal reading, to extend ourselves toward tolerance, toward flexibility and pluralism.

On the other hand, as we move toward the conscious application of interpretive and critical strategies, we need not transform literature into moral and social documents, with ideologies and agendas for action. Literature comes to us with "messages," with apparent statements about life and the world. We may label these as themes, world views, underlying assumptions, or what have you. One cannot read the simplest adolescent novel without inferring its views of an outer world — a world of parents, peers, siblings, personal freedom, and personal responsibility — any more than one can read the work of Dostoevsky or Dickens without inferring a model of human nature and human experience.

The writers in part II do not advocate the imposition of a single interpretive method or the exposition of a single archetypal theme. Rather, they aim toward flexibility by providing a variety of schemata, interpretive approaches, and vocabularies to use in confronting questions of meaning and value that emerge during the period of evocation and response. Because several of the essays in this section apply one interpretive schema to one particular work, it may appear that the writers are advocating a monolithic approach. This appearance, however, arises from the organizing convention that we used in these essays, the application of a single approach to a single work. As a matter of fact, all these writers would agree that the most serious mistake one could make, as students move from personal response to communal interpretation, would be an exclusive reliance on one overarching method or theme. Therefore, we chose to begin this section with an essay (chapter 7) by Eugene Garber, one of John Gerber's students some years ago. He essentially updates Gerber's essay, substituting a Hawthorne short story for the Whitman poem and cataloguing several critical approaches, all of which enjoy some currency now. Garber is at pains to make clear that he is not recommending this as a model for student writing about literature or for teachers' presentation of literature. His rather exhaustive analysis of one story is simply a device to capsulize a variety of current interpretive approaches.

Patricia Hansbury's companion piece (chapter 8) to Garber's essay demonstrates the movement from response to interpretation through the application of the various interpretive approaches in her classroom. The section continues with the work of six of Garber's colleagues in junior and senior high schools who consciously use interpretive paradigms to sustain and inform class discussions of such authors as Ray Bradbury, John Steinbeck, Arthur Miller, and Charlotte Brontë, moving as Hansbury says from response to interpretation. All of these works were chosen because they are frequently taught in secondary schools and would be familiar to readers of this book at all levels. James Butterfield in chapter 9 shows how he begins to ground the thinking of his seventh graders in a sense of historical context. Doris Quick in chapter 10 translates fairly sophisticated structuralist tools into meaningful activities for ninth graders. Carol Decker Forman in chapter 11 explores a variety of sociological vocabularies as she moves toward the consideration of social context in the reading of *Death of a Salesman*, thus demonstrating how one basic approach, informed by sociology, may yield varied insights when the viewpoints of certain sociologists are invoked. Thus even a single method results in multiple meanings. Roseanne DeFabio, likewise, applies categories of thought and judgment from feminist criticism to *Jane Eyre* (chapter 12). In so doing, she finds that the applications of these insights not only raise students' consciousness, but also contribute to more satisfying interpretations of the novel.

There is no hidden, critical orthodoxy at work here. Rather, these teachers provide some sense of flexibility for student readers, leaving them free to pick and choose among interpretive devices or to question, perhaps ultimately reject, them all. Students are led not to supplant their original authentic responses, but to question their unexamined assumptions and critical predispositions. The effort to enlist alternate interpretive categories to make meaning of various texts may be seen not as antithetical, but as complementary to the freedom of response advocated in part I. The point is that the students make meaning; they do not simply absorb it from the text or from a teacher's explication. They are given tools for managing texts, but more important they are given responsibility — the responsibility that comes with a sense that texts are open, not invulnerable, that they require and reward readers' scrutiny.

Nevertheless, as will be abundantly clear to the reader, there is still a certain amount of tension between part I and part II. Many of the writers in the first section would undoubtedly be skeptical about the kind, degree, and directness of the teachers' involvement in the lessons depicted in the second section. Likewise, the teachers represented in part II would probably be unwilling to grant students the kind of autonomy sometimes suggested in part I, especially if such autonomy did not ultimately result in their moving beyond personal responses to something approaching critical interpretation. What this book as a whole envisions is an approach that would capitalize on the greater authenticity of response envisioned in part I and the greater flexibility of approach demonstrated in part II.

We think most of the writers would agree on the need for a judicious mixture, but would be unlikely to agree on the exact mix. For example, Watson says, "The teacher can teach. . . . It may be appropriate, even crucial to the thinking process of some students, for the teacher to spend five or ten minutes with a single group or with the entire class, talking about [matters of literary form and genre]." And Hansbury admits, "The idea of letting the lesson go in the direction of student response can be a little unsettling to any teacher like me who relies on a moderately structured, ordered, planned-to-the-last-detail kind of approach," but finally she argues that "response to a work is a way into that work. When discussion begins with students' questions instead of the teacher's questions, the direction of study begins to take shape."

In moving toward social conscience, the last two essays in part II and the essays in part III insist upon pluralism — first, pluralism within the literature, the depiction of the multiethnic and multivalued nature of the real world. But finally, the essays insist upon the pluralism of visions that only literature can provide with its hypothetical worlds and hypothetical renderings of the real worlds to which it may refer. Mary Sasse in chapter 13 details her struggle to find ethnic diversity in the literature she teaches in high school. In charting her personal evolution as a teacher of ethnic literature, she mirrors our profession's struggle to broaden the canon of American literature. Eileen Tway and Mary Lou White, using books for young readers as their starting point in chapter 14, celebrate the possibility of international diversity and indirectly condemn the parochialism that so often characterizes reading choices in American schools. The authors challenge us to expand our horizons beyond national boundaries and select literature that will give our students an international perspective.

Regina Cowin working in an elementary school and Sylvia White and Ruie Pritchard working with high school students describe their efforts to focus readers' attention on social and personal values and thus to heighten social sensitivity. At the same time, however, they encourage students' independence in responding to literary texts. In chapter 15 Cowin briefly describes an experiment in which fifth and sixth graders arrive at a sense of ethnic diversity through the reading of novels. White and Pritchard exercise a good deal of guidance both in selecting the text for consideration and in providing strategies to empower students to derive and articulate their own responses in the context of their society's values. In their teaching of *Huckleberry Finn* (chapter 16), they take some pains to raise questions and facilitate meaningful exchanges rather than to provide answers and impose thinking. In chapter 17 Elizabeth Nelms and I attempt to show how the classroom study of literature relates to the culture from which adolescents come and can broaden their perspective, rendering them more responsive and responsible in their interaction with their environment.

All of these essays in part III suggest a didactic purpose in the conscious reference of literary texts to social contexts from which they were derived or in which they are read. The contributors argue for a diversity of texts and pedagogical approaches to match the diversity of interpretive approaches introduced in part II, and they all maintain firm footing on the diversity of personal responses encouraged and celebrated in part I. But the contributors do seem to belabor a single point: the social relevance of literary experience.

That point brings us squarely into contact with perhaps the clearest challenge to the integrity of literary education in today's schools: the challenge of censorship. Part III, and the book, conclude with Deanne Bogdan's case study of a well publicized and rigorously contested censorship case (chapter 18). Her balanced and insightful analysis of the arguments by both the would-be censors and their opponents culminates in a defense of literature that recognizes its capacity to provoke both immediate personal experience and ultimate critical judgment, what I have called evocation and response on the one hand and interpretation and criticism on the other. Bogdan uses the arguments elicited in the censorship imbroglio to examine the nature of literature and the purpose of literary study. She faces squarely the problem of the "referentiality" of literature, a claim naively used in the defense of disputed books when its proponents say, "It pictures life the way it is in the real world." Almost incidentally in her careful argument, she acknowledges the claims for what I have called authenticity of response ("[Literature] engages the reader in a true and real world, as anyone who has been entranced by a book will testify"), flexibility in interpretation ("Providing a plurality of critical approaches to the text helps further the movement away from indoctrination"), and pluralism in social vision ("The more varied the texts, the broader the base of reader identification and the greater the likelihood that literary experience will eventuate in a balanced view of the world"). Although she challenges a naive view of the moral dimension of literature, she finally argues staunchly for "literature's potential for human development."

After all, we trust that nothing in the presentation of these essays denigrates the literary texts themselves, those well-wrought urns that tease us out of thought. Whether we conceive of them as edifices to be admired, or construction sites upon which we build, or blueprints that we attempt to realize, none of us would deny their power to charm, to involve, to illuminate, and to provoke. Some of the texts have become vast cathedrals rewarding our patient attention time and time again. Some serve as pleasant bungalows, offering momentary respite and insight. Some are baroque, some are gothic, some are neoclassical, some are sleekly modern, some are just comfortable. Most are probably row houses or suburban family dwellings or condominiums, not destined for the ages, but good for a heap o' living for those who help build them and return to them for homecomings every now and then.

Neither this homely metaphor nor the new emphasis on readers' participation in the literary text itself should detract from our sense of the power of the printed word. In this the censors are right after all, for the printed word has power to change minds and to move hearts, to inspire visions and to instigate revisions. Having just celebrated the two-hundredth anniversary of the United States Constitution, teachers of the English language should remember that power. What Northrop Frye called "the educated imagination" includes the ability to imagine possibilities far beyond those available in the world around us. Inevitably, then, it fosters our capacity for expressing dissatisfaction with the status quo and for acting upon otherwise unimaginable possibilities. It is therefore fitting that this volume conclude with an essay that urges us to combat censorship not with facile arguments that belie the power of the literary text to influence or disturb readers, but with a celebration of the freedom that active engagement with literature bestows.

John Milton, that great defender of the freedom to read, begins his famous argument in the *Areopagitica* with an acknowledgment of the power of books:

> For books are not absolutely dead things, but do contain a potency of life in them to be as active as that soul whose progeny they are. . . . I know they are as lively, and as vigorously productive, as those fabulous dragon's teeth [in the legend of Jason and Medea]; and being sown up and down, may chance to spring up armed men.

Whether we are prepared to deal with the fact or not, we teachers of literature are sowing the dragon's teeth. The texts we share with our students have a life of their own. Unless our students are totally passive, when they read these texts they will recreate works, works that will be new and different from what we might have expected. In our classes we confront these "armed men" that spring up from the seeds we have sown in the minds of our students. Whether we planned to be or not, teachers have to be reader-response critics. We have no choice in the matter. That thought is somewhat unnerving, but it makes our task exciting. Construction sites tend to have more life about them than edifices.

References

Gerber, J. C. 1970. Varied Approaches to "When Lilacs Last in the Dooryard Bloom'd." In *English Education Today*, ed. L. S. Josephs and E. R. Steinberg. New York: Noble and Noble.

Iser, W. 1974. *The Implied Reader.* Baltimore: The Johns Hopkins University Press.

Paz, O. 1973. *The Bow and the Lyre: The Poem, the Poetic Revelation, Poetry and History.* Trans. R. L. C. Simms. Austin: University of Texas Press.

I Readers:
Student Responses to Literature

2 Readers and Literary Texts

Robert E. Probst
Georgia State University

Conceptions of Literature

To enliven her handwriting lesson, a first-grade teacher asked her students to copy — neatly — a sonnet she had put on the board. A third-grade teacher asked his students to read a poem for the "facts" it had to teach them. A twelfth-grade teacher instructed her students to read "The Rape of the Lock," searching for the ten characteristics of Pope's poetry that he had given them in a brief introductory lecture. And a college professor teaching Hawthorne encouraged his class to begin reading the critical essays about the stories rather than the stories themselves.

Different as they are, these four lessons have some common elements. Most important, they all transform the act of reading into something other than literary experience, at least as that experience has been described by many writers. Consider, for instance, Wordsworth on poetry:

> All good poetry is the spontaneous overflow of powerful feelings. . . .
> . . . Poetry is the most philosophic of all writing: . . . its object is truth, not individual and local, but general, and operative; not standing upon external testimony, but carried alive into the heart by passion; truth which is its own testimony, which gives strength and divinity to the tribunal to which it appeals, and receives them from the same tribunal. Poetry is the image of man and nature. . . . The poet writes under one restriction only, namely, that of the necessity of giving immediate pleasure to a human Being possessed of that information which may be expected from him, not as a lawyer, a physician, a mariner, an astronomer or a natural philosopher, but as a Man. (Preface to the *Lyrical Ballads*)

Or, to broaden our discussion from poetry alone to include other genres, consider John Gardner's (1985) description of the experience offered by fiction:

> In great fiction, the dream engages us heart and soul; we not only respond to imaginary things — sights, sounds, smells — as though they were real, we respond to fictional problems as though they were real: We sympathize, think, and judge. We act out, vicariously, the trials of the characters and learn from the failures and successes of particular modes of action, particular attitudes, opinions, assertions, and beliefs exactly as we learn from life. Thus the value of great fiction, we begin to suspect, is not just that it entertains or distracts us from our troubles, not just that it broadens our knowledge of people and places, but also that it helps us to know what we believe, reinforces those qualities that are noblest in us, leads us to feel uneasy about our faults and limitations. (p. 31)

There is little of Wordsworth's passion and truth, little of Gardner's fictive dream, in any of the four lessons cited above. The handwriting practice needs no comment at all; the "facts" to be exhumed by those sad little third graders have nothing to do with Gardner's conception of knowledge; the unearthing of ten characteristics has little to do with Pope's vision; and those preeminent critics may arouse uneasiness about our faults and limitations as students but not as human beings. In each case, the literature has been offered as an exercise, one devoid of either passion or knowledge.

In none of the lessons is there any interest in the emotions aroused by the literature, the experience it offers, or the sort of knowledge — as Gardner has characterized it — toward which it might lead. The closest we come, perhaps, is in the third-grade lesson, where the poem is a source of facts, but the difference between collecting facts and creating knowledge is too obvious to mention. In the high school and college lessons, the literature is not even a source of facts, much less of knowledge. Rather, the student is asked to learn facts *about* the text, facts that come in the one lesson from the teacher and in the other from the critics. But the literature itself is not treated as a source either of experience and emotion or of knowledge. It is something *about* which we may know, but not something *through* which we come to know.

It is not difficult to see why the literature curriculum at all levels, from elementary school through the university, has tended toward the sort of instruction represented by these four lessons. The conception of literature that they exemplify is much more manageable than that suggested by Wordsworth and Gardner. Literature conceived of as a set of skills — handwriting at the most absurd level, and comprehension skills such as extracting facts from texts at a slightly less absurd level — is reasonably easy to organize on the scale of the lesson and on that of the course. The organizing principles for literature conceived of as information about a set of important texts are also fairly obvious. If we choose to arrange courses historically, as we often do in the upper grades of high school and in the universities, we may quarrel over which texts are the most important and over dates and characteristics of periods, but essentially we progress chronologically, considering such matters as influence, evolution of styles and genres, relationships between the literature and other historical events. If we prefer to emphasize not historical sequence but critical comment, then we may arrange the study around certain critical texts, as the Hawthorne scholar arranged his course. But the organizing principles of a course or curriculum based on the conception of literature that Wordsworth and Gardner offer are not quite so self-evident.

The Relationship of Reader and Text

And yet much of modern critical theory suggests that Wordsworth and Gardner are addressing fundamental elements in literary experience and that consequently the patterns in literature classrooms illustrated by these four examples are ill-founded. Those critics roughly grouped together under the rubric "reader-response criticism" all emphasize that the role of the reader must be considered in any discussion of literature. As Slatoff (1970) said about literary works,

> The objects we study . . . assume their full or significant form and being only in active conjunction or interaction with the human mind. To some extent, of course, this is true of all objects. Whatever one's theory of perception, one has to agree that some qualities of any object are dependent on human perception. But works of literature have scarcely any important qualities apart from those that take shape in minds. (p. 23)

We might argue, more rashly perhaps, that literature can scarcely be said to have any existence at all outside the mind of the reader. A book as physical entity, ink on paper, is simply an object for heaving at the ill-behaved child. Its literary existence is as symbol, and items become symbols only when processed by the mind. The physical particulars of a symbol — its size, shape, and substance — are important only insofar as they contribute to or detract from that processing by the reader's mind.

A stop sign can be large or small, metal or wood, on a post or hanging from a wire, but none of those physical details is of great significance since the sign does not physically stop us. Rather, we stop ourselves because we treat the object as sign and respond accordingly. As physical object it is inert and powerless; only as sign does it have any strength, and it becomes a sign only when it enters the mind of a reader. It is the same with literary works. *Hamlet*, printed on cheap paper, shabbily bound in paperback, beaten and torn by weeks in a twelfth grader's hip pocket, remains *Hamlet. Sweet, Savage Love*, gilt-edged and bound in leather, remains . . . whatever it is. The physical characteristics of those texts are of no significance in our judgment of their literary quality. What matters to us is the possibility that we may engage in some rewarding transaction with the text as we read.

Bookstores using the curious shelving system that gives one section to "Literature" and another to "Fiction" show deference, in a primitive way, to this notion. They make the distinction among books not on the basis of physical characteristics, but rather in terms of the works' symbolic potential. "Literature" is the material judged to have the greater potential for processing in the mind, the more challenging and difficult material — the works people want to have read. "Fiction" is the material with less potential, lighter and less challenging, but entertaining — the works people want to read.

A text, then, is only potentially a literary experience. It is the experience — imaginative, intellectual, and emotional — that the work may enable us to have, by which we judge its literary merits. It is the book as it takes shape in our minds that matters — not the book as it lies there on the table. But to judge those merits, that experience, we must take into account not only the text, but also the mind in which that text will take shape.

Rosenblatt (1982) makes the point clearly:

> A Shakespeare text, say, offers more potentialities for an aesthetic reading than one by Longfellow. We teachers know, however, that one cannot predict which text will give rise to the better evocation — the better lived-through poem — without knowing the other part of the transaction, the reader. (p. 269)

She restricts the use of the term *poem* to refer to the transaction itself. What resides on the paper is simply a text; it does not become a poem until a reader makes it one. And the reader cannot make it a poem by treating it as a handwriting exercise, an encyclopedia, or a scavenger hunt.

In the schools, though, we have often talked about literary works and taught them as if they existed as things apart from us, as if they had an existence independent of our reading. Not that we have been interested in their bindings and typeface — that example is too extreme — but we have often focused our attention on features of texts and on information about texts as the four lessons illustrate. Applebee (1974) remarked many years ago that "teachers of literature have never successfully resisted the pressure to formulate their subject as a body of knowledge to be imparted" (p. 245), and the remark seems still to be true.

That knowledge has usually been of an objective, verifiable sort that a scientific, mathematical age would be likely to value. It consists of information about authors, their lives and times; about literary periods, their characteristic styles and concerns; about genres, their unique problems and possibilities. It consists, in other words, of information about texts and writers that scholarship has provided for us. Furthermore, if our curriculum has been influenced by the reading establishment as well as by literary scholarship, as it almost inevitably has been, then we deal with all of those texts and all of that information as exercises in comprehension.

Understandable as is the pressure to formulate the literature curriculum as a body of knowledge, much current criticism encourages us to consider it in other ways, perhaps to view it more as Wordsworth and Gardner view it. Rosenblatt would have us focus our attention on the literature's potential for functioning symbolically, which is to say, the potential for triggering responses in a reader's mind. Iser (1978) seems to concur:

> The significance of the work, then, does not lie in the meaning sealed within the text, but in the fact that that meaning brings out what had previously been sealed within us. (p. 157)

Jauss (1982b) would ground even literary history itself in the experience of readers:

> The historicity of literature rests not on an organization of "literary facts" that is established *post festum*, but rather on the preceding experience of the literary work by its readers. (p. 20)

If we accept the significance of the reader's experience with the text, agreeing with Rosenblatt that the poem is in the reader rather than on the page, with Iser that texts initiate performances of meaning rather than contain meaning, with Jauss that even literary history should take into account the experiences of people reading, then our literature curriculum should reflect that conception. These contemporary critics suggest alternatives to the literature curriculum conceived in terms of information about literary works, authors, genres, techniques, historical periods. They suggest that such information is not the most important consideration in reading or teaching literature and that to seek in it the organizing principles of a curriculum may distract us from what is central to the literary experience. The organizing principles for a literature curriculum might be derived from the notion that meaning is not located in the text, but in the reader, as so much contemporary criticism asserts.

One way to begin might be to look at the form that literary meaning thus conceived might take. It seems that there might be a number of possible outcomes for the act of reading literary texts — meaning made in the act of reading might be of several different kinds, and thus we may need to teach a variety of strategies for dealing with literature.

Meaning in Literary Experience

To see if any ideas for those organizing principles suggest themselves, consider briefly the kinds of meaning that might emerge from a reading of one poem:

> January Chance
>
> All afternoon before them, father and boy,
> In a plush well, with winter sounding past:
> In the warm cubicle between two high
> Seat backs that slumber, voyaging the vast.
>
> All afternoon to open the deep things
> That long have waited, suitably unsaid.
> Now one of them is older, and the other's
> Art at last has audience; has head,
>
> Has heart to take it in. It is the time.
> Begin, says winter, howling through the pane.
> Begin, the seat back bumps: what safer hour
> Than this, within the somnolent loud train,
>
> A prison where the corridors slide on
> As the walls creak, remembering downgrade?
> Begin. But with a smile the father slumps
> And sleeps. And so the man is never made.
>
>   Mark Van Doren

What kind of knowledge results from reading a poem like this one? What sorts of reflections does it promote; what private and personal memories does it awaken for a reader; to what ideas, what thoughts, does it lead?

Readers might find themselves reflecting upon a relationship with child or parent, perhaps becoming aware of what they themselves have not yet said or what was not said to them by someone important in their own lives. Out of that reflection may come something that amounts to knowledge of self. The text clearly has the potential for provoking such reflection. Anyone who has thought about a relationship with parents or children, or even with good friends, is likely to have some memory called to mind by the text.

So the reading might result in a statement about the self rather than one focused on the text itself, a statement that is not an interpretation or explanation of the sort the literature classroom has often demanded, but one that nonetheless constitutes knowing, perhaps very important knowing, for the reader.

Similarly, the reading might lead to reflection about that other person, the one to whom the reader might wish to have spoken or from whom he or she might wish to have heard. Again, the thought elicited by the text might lead to a kind of knowledge, here knowledge of another person. It might enable the reader to comprehend his or her own parent's inability to address those difficult issues of the sort the father in Van Doren's poem contemplated discussing with his son. Or, on the other hand, it may cause the reader to try to articulate the sorts of questions one might wish to raise with a parent.

If reading the text might lead to knowledge of others in the reader's prior experience, it might also lead to knowledge of others present. Discussion of the text should reveal different responses, different senses of the work that might awaken readers to the uniqueness of the others in their class. Discussion that invites students to share their readings — the feelings aroused, the thoughts and ideas suggested, the interpretations proposed, the judgments offered — will inevitably reveal differences and similarities among the readers. That socializing effect, the understanding of one another, is surely one of the valid objectives for instruction in literature.

Explicit attention to that kind of knowledge suggests to the students the important function of literature in society: it constitutes a way of thinking about experience. Gardner (1978) speaks explicitly of that function:

> In a democratic society, where every individual opinion counts, and where nothing, finally, is left to some king or group of party elitists, art's incomparable ability to instruct, to make alternatives intellectually and emotionally clear, to spotlight falsehood, insincerity, foolishness — art's incomparable ability, that is, to make us understand — ought to be a force bringing people together, breaking down barriers of prejudice and ignorance, and holding up ideals worth pursuing. (p. 42)

Obviously, the knowledge of self or of others to which readers come will depend upon who they are, what experiences they have had, what memories rise to consciousness as they read. What they make of their encounter with the text must take into account all of those variables. The results of attending to those matters cannot be predicted with precision. They are not the stuff of which neat and orderly curricula are made, and they do not lend themselves to tests and measures. But they may be important results nonetheless.

Students might also find themselves learning something about the text and how it works. They may note that the image of the train, a "warm cubicle" rolling along, isolating the father and son from other people, ringing phones, daily routines, suspends time and invites lazy, relaxed discourse on "the deep things." The image — the situation depicted — may suggest to the readers the kinds of thoughts forming in the father's mind before he drifts off. They may see that the poem works by implication: it does not specify what "the deep things" are; it does not list them explicitly, nor can they be deduced by careful examination of the text. Van Doren has offered details about the circumstances, perhaps inviting us to allow the deep things in our own experience to shape our reading and reflection.

Readers may notice also that the text invites participation by leaving so much unanswered and ambiguous. Does the last line, for instance, with the ominous "never," imply that there is in life one and only one opportunity for this sort of intimate talk between father and son? Does it suggest that such dialogue *never* really takes place, that the intimate father-son talk is simply a fantasy? And which man is it that is "never made"? Is it the son, who now must go on without his father's wisdom, or is it the father who, by failing to instruct his son, fails to discharge one of the obligations of manhood and thus remains less than a man, remains unmade himself? The text works in devious ways to invite the reader into the making of meaning.

Students may also come to see the importance of context in any reading. They may realize, for instance, that the reading of the text will differ depending on whether the reader is a parent or a child. They may see also that the circumstances in which the text is encountered may shape reactions to it. A reader who has recently lost a parent or a child will read it differently from one who has not.

And students may come to realize that there are various ways of dealing with the text. That is to say, they may come to some knowledge about the processes of making meaning. They may observe that readers differ in the ways they prefer to deal with texts. Some readers may be perfectly comfortable dealing with the text in the open discourse of the classroom. For others, that social situation may be too public;

the text may awaken thoughts they can deal with only in the privacy of a journal or in talk with a close friend or a small, trusted group.

Readers might also differ in the focus and mode of their work. Some might pursue meaning by analyzing the elements of the text, others by exploring the sources of ideas and emotions in the text and in their own histories, and still others by investigating the biography of the author or the culture of the author's time. In contemplating the text, they may write journal entries, reflective pieces, analyses, or they may write literary works of their own — poems or stories inspired by the text. Rosenblatt (1986) suggests that we might profitably investigate

> the transaction between author and text, or artist and artifact. We can at least recall that the author is the first reader of the text.
> The potential role of the production of such artifacts in the education of the student of literature or art is another of the many implications of the transactional theory to be explored. (p. 128)

Surely if the reading of literature is a way of learning, so too is the writing of the literary works.

The analysis of the potential transactions with "January Chance" suggests that we might conceive of the meaning that derives from literary experience as falling into these categories:

1. Knowledge of self

2. Knowledge of others

3. Knowledge of texts

4. Knowledge of contexts

5. Knowledge of processes (of making meaning)

6. Pleasure — not a kind of knowledge, perhaps, but nonetheless a significant goal for the curriculum

Could a literature curriculum be devised that grows out of this conception of literary experience and meaning, rather than out of the principles of literary history or New Criticism? It might be possible — by examining what we know of adolescent development, of adolescent reading interests, and of the literary heritage — to design a curriculum that would encourage students to create knowledge in each of these forms. Such a curriculum could respect the uniqueness of individual response, the developmental characteristics of adolescence, and the patterns of reading interest during those years, as well as the literary heritage. It could, consequently, have more psychological validity than curricula devised solely on the basis of chronology, genre, or some sequence of reading skills. And it could involve students more intimately in the ongoing dialogue about major issues that our literature represents.

Such a curriculum would recognize that literary transactions might yield knowledge about one's self and others, as well as about texts and authors; it would accept a much wider range of modes of discourse about literature; it would encourage the exploratory and expressive as well as the analytical and rational; and it would invite the creation as well as the reception of literary works. Finally, and perhaps most important, it would build a society in the classroom devoted to the making of meaning, the creating of knowledge, and thus might contribute significantly to the improvement of the human condition.

References

Applebee, A. N. 1974. *Tradition and Reform in the Teaching of English: A History.* Urbana, Ill.: National Council of Teachers of English.

Bleich, D. 1975. *Readings and Feelings: An Introduction to Subjective Criticism.* Urbana, Ill.: National Council of Teachers of English.

―――. 1978. *Subjective Criticism.* Baltimore: The Johns Hopkins University Press.

Cain, W. E. 1984. *The Crisis in Criticism: Theory, Literature, and Reform in English Studies.* Baltimore: The Johns Hopkins University Press.

Favat, F. A. 1977. *Child and Tale: The Origins of Interest.* Urbana, Ill.: National Council of Teachers of English.

Gardner, J. 1985. *The Art of Fiction: Notes on Craft for Young Writers.* New York: Vintage Books.

―――. 1978. *On Moral Fiction.* New York: Basic Books, Inc.

Holland, N. 1968. *The Dynamics of Literary Response.* New York: Oxford University Press.

―――. 1975. *5 Readers Reading.* New Haven: Yale University Press.

―――. 1973. *Poems in Persons: An Introduction to the Psychoanalysis of Literature.* New York: Norton.

Iser, W. 1978. *The Act of Reading: A Theory of Aesthetic Response.* Baltimore: The Johns Hopkins University Press.

―――. 1974. *The Implied Reader: Patterns of Communication in Prose Fiction from Bunyan to Beckett.* Baltimore: The Johns Hopkins University Press.

Jauss, H. R. 1982. *Aesthetic Experience and Literary Hermeneutics.* Minneapolis: University of Minnesota Press.

―――. 1982b. *Toward an Aesthetic of Reception.* Trans. T. Bahti. Minneapolis: University of Minnesota Press.

Kintgen, E. R. 1983. *The Perception of Poetry.* Bloomington: Indiana University Press.

Nilsen, A. P., and K. L. Donelson. 1985. *Literature for Today's Young Adults.* 2d ed. Glenview, Ill.: Scott, Foresman.

Probst, R. E. 1987. *Response and Analysis: Teaching Literature in Junior and Senior High School.* Upper Montclair, N.J.: Boynton/Cook.

Rosenblatt, L. M. 1986. The Aesthetic Transaction. *Journal of Aesthetic Education* 20, no.4: 122–28.

———. 1982. The Literary Transaction: Evocation and Response. *Theory into Practice* 21, no. 4: 268–77.

———. 1983. *Literature as Exploration.* 4th ed. New York: Modern Language Association.

———. 1978. *The Reader, the Text, the Poem: The Transactional Theory of the Literary Work.* Carbondale: Southern Illinois University Press.

Scholes, R. 1982. *Semiotics and Interpretation.* New Haven: Yale University Press.

———. 1974. *Structuralism in Literature: An Introduction.* New Haven: Yale University Press.

———. 1985. *Textual Power: Literary Theory and the Teaching of English.* New Haven: Yale University Press.

Slatoff, W. J. 1970. *With Respect to Readers.* Ithaca: Cornell University Press.

Suleiman, S. R., and I. Crosman, eds. 1980. *The Reader in the Text: Essays on Audience and Interpretation.* Princeton: Princeton University Press.

Tompkins, J. 1980. *Reader-Response Criticism: From Formalism to Post-Structuralism.* Baltimore: The Johns Hopkins University Press.

Van Doren, M. 1963. *Collected and New Poems, 1924–63.* New York: Hill and Wang.

3 The Act of Reading

Margaret Early
University of Florida

Bonnie O. Ericson
California State University–Northridge

Reading used to be the primary channel for the intake of literature. Today, film and television challenge the primacy of reading in the lives of many adults. In school, however, reading remains the chief medium through which teachers and students engage literature. How students read is therefore a major concern for all teachers of literature.

About fifteen years ago, spurred by developments in cognitive psychology and studies of language acquisition, reading researchers shifted their attention from the results of reading instruction to the act of reading itself. They asked how readers at different levels comprehend texts of various kinds. Readers' answers to questions became less important to researchers than tracing the thought processes that led to these answers. Sometimes readers' answers, especially unexpected ones, gave researchers clues that they might pursue further or provided support for notions or theories about what happens when readers understand written messages. Painstaking and expensive, this new research in reading is more likely to yield detailed case studies than to amass solid statistical "proof." Naturally, many gaps need to be filled when studies concentrate on individuals' thought processes. Nevertheless, even at this stage, research examining the reading process has freshened teachers' understanding of how their students read literature even as it has affirmed inferences and intuitions stemming from their own experiences and from their knowledge of literary theory.

Teachers of literature find that the new research in reading supports many ideas they have long subscribed to. At the same time, it renews and refreshes, suggesting altered emphases, variations, even changes in direction. Nor is this surprising, since reading researchers and

31

teachers of literature frequently hold ideas in common, although they label them differently. For example, where reading teachers talk about "structured overviews," teachers of literature may talk of "setting up points of connection" or "imaginative entry." Yet both groups are concerned with helping students bring what they already know (prior knowledge) to bear upon a new reading task.

As reading researchers learn more about how readers comprehend, they become more aware, too, of the writer's share in the act of reading. "Text" becomes an integral factor in the complex process of reading, and researchers ask how "considerate" the text is of the reader. Today's teachers, too, are careful to avoid statements about how well Johnny reads. Reads *what* is the issue. And under what conditions. Researchers have therefore added the issue of *context* to the study of readers and texts. In what kinds of classrooms, schools, communities and with what kinds of instruction are readers learning? How do teachers' explanations, directions, expectations affect how readers comprehend?

In this chapter, then, we organize our comments around three pivots of current reading research: reader, text, and context. This is not a review of that research, however; citations will be eclectic and sparse. Instead, we shall present research-based generalizations, widely accepted by scholars in reading in this decade, that influence how we teach literature.

1. Readers make meanings. To do so they use (1) their knowledge of the world and (2) the cues supplied by the text.

Of all the new, or renewed, insights coming out of recent reading research, the impact of prior knowledge on comprehension is the one that speaks loudest to teachers of literature. More than other kinds of text, literature draws on the reader's prior knowledge: of people and places, of historical periods and cultures, of spoken and written language, of human nature, of story grammar and literary forms, to name but a few categories.

The concept of prior knowledge derives from schema theory, which hypothesizes that a person's knowledge of the world is stored in interconnected structures called schemata (Rumelhart 1980). Readers use their schemata in comprehending what they are reading, in making predictions during reading, and in remembering what they have read. What readers of *To Kill a Mockingbird* understand about the courtroom scenes depends to a large degree on what they know about — that is, their schema for — court trials. Similarly, readers of Steinbeck's *The*

Red Pony rely on schemata for ranch life, parent-son relationships, and horses.

Schema theory hypothesizes two complementary processes: readers fit new information from the text into existing schemata (they "fill in the slots"), and they modify their existing schemata to accommodate information in the text that otherwise would not fit. How well readers manage these processes of assimilation and accommodation determines how closely their reconstruction of the text's meaning corresponds to that of other readers and perhaps to the meanings intended by the writer of the text. Thus the teacher's role is to activate students' prior knowledge of, say, a particular time and place or of how people act under certain circumstances. The teacher has two reasons for prereading discussions: first, to help students marshal their resources; second, to test out gaps in prior knowledge that might better be filled before reading than after confusion sets in.

A teacher in middle school, anticipating the reading of *My Brother Sam is Dead*, invited her students to talk about life in colonial America on the eve of the Revolution. She found that many of them peopled that era with cowboys, Indians, and gunfighters seen on television. Colonial New England was a long way from contemporary Kansas, and eighth-grade social studies had not modified existing schemata as much as the English teacher had assumed. She had, however, identified gaps she could fill with pictures, maps, a timeline, filmstrips, and films; with short, easy books she could recommend to individuals; and with essential information she herself could present. Even more important than knowledge of the setting in understanding this short novel is sensitivity to the feelings engendered by family relationships. The teacher focused attention on these feelings by introducing brief role-playing sessions. For some readers, this novel's chief value is its information on the American Revolution; for others, the novel provides a strong emotional and aesthetic experience. Most young readers would place themselves variously on Louise Rosenblatt's continuum from aesthetic to efferent if they were to define their purposes in her terms (Rosenblatt 1978, pp. 22–47).

An important aspect of prior knowledge is the students' familiarity with language patterns and modes of discourse. Good readers anticipate words and phrases because they are familiar with how twentieth century language works, as well as with many of the ideas conveyed in that language. (Research into comprehension processes using *cloze* techniques — having students supply words systematically deleted from statements — confirms that skillful readers add to their prior knowledge as they read, picking up clues that lead them to make accurate predictions of what is coming next.) Texts from another century, however, may limit even good readers' ability to predict and thus slow down their rate of comprehension.

In addition to schemata for vocabulary and concepts, readers also have schemata, or sets of knowledge and expectations, for literary forms (Applebee 1978; Ericson 1985; Galda 1982; Mauro 1984) and for the role of the reader. For example, students' expectations for fiction develop from their earliest experiences with stories heard, seen on television, and read on their own. Similarly, they have expectations for poetry, some of them negative and erroneous. Expectations for literary form and attitudes toward authors' purposes and the students' own purposes in reading influence the quality of comprehension.

Frank Smith's description of the reading process (1978) distinguishes two sources of information, visual and nonvisual. Visual information is what a reader's eye can see and send to the brain — the words printed on a page. Nonvisual information is what a reader already knows and relates to the material being read. If a reader has more of one type of information, less of the other is needed for comprehension — within limits. Too little of either visual or nonvisual information results in the breakdown of comprehension. (This is one explanation of the varying success the same student may have in reading contemporary and historical texts.)

We have all seen students struggle with sentences such as these from Edgar Allan Poe's "The Cask of Amontillado": "I must not only punish, but punish with impunity. A wrong is unredressed when retribution overtakes its redresser." With such sentences, difficulties in decoding the unfamiliar vocabulary may force students to attend primarily to visual information to such an extent that they are unable to use the nonvisual at the same time. What can the teacher do to prevent or remedy such bottlenecks? One tactic, of course, is to choose texts that match as closely as possible either students' present level of vocabulary development or their willingness to struggle for meaning. Another is to preteach essential vocabulary before assigning essential reading and to bolster students' perseverance through interest-inducing prereading activities. Even more effective over the long term will be carefully paced and invigorating instruction in vocabulary keyed to students' needs and interests. Both recent and long-familiar research studies have shown that excellent teaching of vocabulary can facilitate comprehension. Literature offers rich sources for vocabulary development, more so than do most other subjects in the curriculum, to the extent that the vocabulary is nontechnical and widely applicable.

2. *The best way to learn to read is by reading.*

Reduced almost to a slogan, this finding from research on beginning reading is a powerful reminder to teachers of literature in the upper grades of the importance of wide reading. Like any slogan, this one oversimplifies, but its truth is self-evident when we examine profiles of students who demonstrated mastery of higher order reading skills on the National Assessment of Educational Progress (1981). These students were the ones who read widely, choosing books of fiction and nonfiction beyond those required in school.

The impact of prior knowledge on comprehension tells us why students learn to read by reading. To acquire sufficient prior knowledge to read new texts easily, students must read widely because only a fraction of knowledge about the world can come from other experiences in their short lives. Since prior knowledge includes familiarity with varying modes of discourse as well as with concepts and their labels, we realize why students who do not read (even though they have no trouble with decoding words) are severely handicapped when required to approach literature (especially that selected by others) through reading on their own.

The implications for teachers of literature are obvious. Particularly in the middle grades and early secondary years, the balance between in-common reading and individualized reading must favor the latter. In-common reading selected by the teacher and directed toward familiarizing students with literary concepts and forms and with developing literary sensibilities must be relatively brief. Personal reading, guided by a teacher who knows the student's reading abilities, attitudes, and interests, must occupy a large share of time in class and out of class. Organized around themes, such reading contributes to common goals and is by no means unstructured and random. What is being argued for here, of course, is the thematic unit, supported in research and theory for more than sixty years and still widely ignored by teachers, publishers, and curriculum makers.

Because children and adolescents learn to read by reading, a literature program that embraces wide reading is most likely to lead to goals long cherished by teachers. That students enjoy reading is prerequisite to establishing lifetime reading habits that include literature. But beyond acquiring a habit of turning to books, students who read widely go on learning how to interpret literary works reasonably. They may also learn to respond fully to a range of literature. Without the experience of reading widely throughout their school years, students are unlikely to reach any of these three interlocking goals.

3. To make meanings, readers need to experience the whole text.

This insight from research on beginning reading also has implications for teachers at later stages. To reading teachers in primary grades, it is an injunction against too much attention to isolated skills and too little attention to the holistic process that combines many skills and strategies. To literature teachers, who are also concerned with the way their students make meanings, this research finding says: Focus on the whole text whenever possible. It is more nearly possible to respect the wholeness of a short text than a long one. So, especially with immature readers of literature whatever their age or grade level, literature teachers prefer the *short* story, poem, or play. After an appropriate introduction, students can read a short selection independently all the way through for the pleasure of the first impact. They can then reread it in whole or in part as they examine why or how the author has made them respond as they did on first reading.

Not every literary text can be treated holistically. Sometimes, as we note below, teachers want to emphasize how predicting and self-questioning affect comprehension. They also want students to experience a long, intricate novel or a five-act Shakespearean drama. With longer works they make reasonable study assignments, introducing each part with prereading activities. But they come back regularly to shorter pieces. Teachers avoid asking too many questions directed to small sections of a whole text, except where necessary to demonstrate particular strategies.

4. Good readers understand how they make meanings and are aware of breakdowns in the process.

Much recent research in reading has been concerned with monitoring comprehension. Good readers know when their reading makes sense and when it does not. When their understanding appears adequate, they simply read on, but when their understanding is unclear, they employ corrective strategies (Brown 1980; Olshavsky 1977; Wagoner 1983).

Comprehension monitoring is said to have two aspects. The first is awareness of adequacy of comprehension or assessment of inadequacy. When reading a Shakespearean sonnet, for instance, students may comment: "I don't get it," or "He couldn't mean *that,*" or "Oh, now I see what this is about." Assessment of comprehension assumes that readers have established, however unconsciously, a purpose for reading. If students elect to read *The Pearl* only to find out what happens to Kino, Juana, and Coyotito, they will be satisfied with understanding the story line, which they may accomplish quickly, paying scant attention to details. On the other hand, if their purpose is to understand the motivations of various characters or to examine the symbolic meaning of the pearl, their self-assessment will question their inferences and judgments.

The second aspect of monitoring comprehension, applying corrective strategies, should follow awareness that comprehension is inadequate. Research has identified the value of strategies such as rereading or looking back, reading ahead, using context to figure out word meanings, making inferences, referring to personal experience, and making predictions. Research documents our assumption that fluent readers use a greater variety of corrective strategies than poor readers do and tend to use them more often (Garner and Reis 1981; Olshavsky 1977).

Poor readers are often unaware of their lack of adequate understanding, or if they do recognize their failure to comprehend, they are unable to apply an appropriate corrective strategy. Such students cannot be told to "figure it out" because they do not know how to go about it. And teachers often have trouble describing how to "figure it out" because they themselves are so skilled in monitoring comprehension that they are unconscious of the process.

How teachers can facilitate appropriate comprehension-monitoring strategies (as well as other aspects of the reading process) has been the object of much recent research, which brings us to our next generalization.

5. *Modeling, direct explanations, and questioning are teaching strategies that improve comprehension.*

How can we teach students to monitor their comprehension? Research points to two strategies that many teachers tend to neglect. One is modeling the process; the other is explaining or describing what students should do. These strategies are also used to teach students how to make inferences, since failure to do so is frequently the cause of faulty comprehension.

From time to time teachers talk about their own misreading of words or phrases, speculate on why a particular miscue has occurred, and estimate the distortion in understanding that may result. Students, too, share their own miscues and thus raise their level of consciousness about this aspect of the reading process. Since it is easier to monitor miscues, that is a good place to begin, but monitoring the assimilation of ideas is more important. A teacher might begin by reading aloud a poem, short story, or essay, interrupting the text to insert his or her own interpretations and queries. (This must be a genuine first reading on the teacher's part.) Modeling the process, the teacher makes predictions and corrects them as new data are gathered from the text.

Good choices for introducing students to monitoring (and thinking aloud as they do so) are short stories that begin by withholding all the clues, or poems that compress much meaning into a few lines. Some teachers find May Sarton's *Poems to Solve* particularly effective for this type of demonstration; one of them is the widely anthologized "Southbound on the Freeway."

One suggestion from research is to model the inference process when answering questions (Gordon 1985; Roehler and Duffy 1984). The teacher defines what an inference is, then reads a portion of text, asks an inference question, gives the answer, and explains the reasoning involved. Gradually students take over the successive phases of the procedure. When given this type of instruction, students improve in their ability to draw inferences.

Another strategy is to teach students that answers to questions have different sources. Teachers classify inference questions as "think and search" (putting together information from several different places in the text) and "author and me" (combining what the reader knows with what the author tells) (Raphael 1984).

Questions have long been the staple of teachers' techniques for promoting comprehension. What is new in the research investigating teacher intervention in the comprehension process is that students are taught to ask their own questions. A reciprocal questioning strategy aimed at helping students to adopt a question approach to their reading is the ReQuest procedure (Manzo 1969). Working with individuals or small groups, the English teacher and students take turns asking each other questions following the reading of segments of a poem, short story, or essay. The teacher may ask, "What is the significance of the character's age?" or "What do you think will happen next?" or "What would you do now if you were she?" These questions require inferences based on details from the selection as well as from the reader's prior knowledge. Through teachers' modeling, students may be led to produce inference questions in class and when they read independently.

Questions may be presented in an "anticipation guide" in which students are asked to agree or disagree with four or five statements before reading a selection. For example, before reading Ray Bradbury's "The Flying Machine," students might ponder the following statements: (1) Two people could use the same invention in very different ways. (2) Advances in technology usually have more potential for good than harm. (3) Progress can be stopped. Discussion of students' responses before reading may inform the teacher as to their depth of knowledge, intensity of beliefs, and misconceptions. Discussion of the same statements after reading can strengthen students' ability to support inferences and analyze generalizations.

The success of modeling, direct explanations, and questioning depends to a significant degree on timing. Sensitive teachers plan *brief* demonstrations of processes; they know when a modeling session loses its audience. Likewise, they carefully time students' demonstrations of thinking aloud and their discussions of miscues and misapprehensions. Through experience, intuition, trial and error, teachers learn when to transfer responsibility for questioning from themselves to their students. They interrupt discussions from time to time to assess the significance of students' questions and the purpose of their own or textbook questions. They provide many examples of high level questions in discussion guides that they design themselves, borrow from others, and get their students to make.

All of these strategies for reading literature are necessary and planned for, not left to chance. But they must never be allowed to get in the way of the story. They are means to an end — the enjoyment of literature.

6. *Good readers use cues in the text and knowledge in their heads to make predictions. Predicting strengthens comprehending.*

Literature teachers at every level have made creative use of this research finding. Primary grade teachers share lists of "predictable books" that they read aloud. As children catch on to the story line or to repetitive phrases, the teacher invites them to finish the sentence or to predict what will happen next. A middle school teacher might duplicate and cut up a "short short" story, giving students one segment at a time to read silently. In discussion at the end of each section, students speculate on what will happen next and point out the cues in the text that support the prediction. Science fiction, mysteries, and surprise-ending stories are good choices for this kind of exercise. The author's conclusions may or may not be predicted accurately. In either case, the readers retrace the author's steps, looking for planted clues (foreshadowing). They judge whether the author's conclusion is inevitable or the surprise ending fair.

With mature students at any grade level, teachers ask them to read carefully the first half or two-thirds of a story. The students are then invited to write an ending that uses the author's clues and is in keeping with the style. An instructor in freshman composition uses Kate

Chopin's "The Story of an Hour" in this fashion and finds that it stimulates precise reading as it instructs students in the writer's craft.

7. *Analysis of inferences supports teaching strategies that focus on how to read literature.*

Inferences are at the very heart of the comprehension process and never more so than when readers are making meanings of literature. Authors can never state explicitly and entirely what characters look like or think or do, nor do they want to. Instead, they call on readers to elaborate on details, drawing upon their own experiences (that is, prior knowledge). Imaginative literature especially places demands on the reader's ability and willingness to draw inferences and thus to integrate information about characters and their motives, events and their sequence, about setting, conflict, and theme.

Several means of helping students to draw inferences have already been described in this essay, since so much of comprehending is inferring. Predicting, for instance, is a form of inferring. In addition to examining how (and if) students draw inferences and what teaching strategies affect the process, recent research has examined the nature of inferences. One study categorizes the inferences needed for comprehending narratives as (1) informational inferences (about characters, setting, things); (2) logical inferences (about motivations and causes); and (3) value inferences (readers' evaluations of aspects of a story). Logical inferences seem to be more difficult for readers than informational inferences.

Hillocks and Ludlow (1984) identify an order of increasing difficulty: (1) simple implied relationships (can be identified from cues close to each other in the text); (2) complex implied relationships (cues are scattered); (3) author's generalizations ("implied by the whole fabric of the literary work as it reflects some conception of the human situation as it exists outside the limits of the work" [p.12]); and (4) structural generalizations (inferences about how aspects of the work achieve their effect). The hierarchical order of these categories is affirmed by studies showing that students who are unable to draw type 2 inferences, for example, also fail with types 3 and 4.

Such categorizing is helpful to teachers. They can build that necessary platform of success with poor readers by pitching them questions that require them to put together details about character, setting, and things. As readers develop, teachers move gradually toward discussions requiring inferences from several sources of information within the text and drawn from the reader's prior knowledge.

Moreover, awareness of "levels of inferences" guides teachers in judging the difficulty of texts they select for in-common reading and the objectives they aim for in literature study with different members of their class.

8. *Inferences depend on apprehension of details.*

Research on the inferential dimension of the reading process, whether it is based on examination of readers or texts, underscores the importance of attending to or catching details. Generalizations are derived from details. How much emphasis, and what kind, teachers put on detail is a matter of crucial importance and complexity, but as yet research offers little guidance. Experience suggests, however, that teachers' strategies with respect to details must vary according to readers' achievement.

The naive teacher is likely to ask questions aimed only at details and to hit too many too fast. The teacher who is a sophisticated reader may aim first at the broad generalizations (inference types 3 and 4 in the Hillocks and Ludlow scheme), assuming that the students have assimilated the right details and have enough prior knowledge to recognize their significance. Both kinds of teacher may confuse or bore some of their students. With mature readers, it may be a good idea to begin with higher order inferences, referring only as necessary to the details that support them. With poor readers, the focus on details should be discriminating, but should precede asking for generalizations based on them.

Reading for details (facts) has received a bad press over the years, largely because some teachers quizzed students *only* on details and often on insignificant ones. These teachers stopped short of the reason for attending to details — that is, to use them for arriving at larger meanings. The reaction against this kind of poor teaching led many to discount the importance of details. The new attitude toward teaching higher order skills promises to reinstate the value of apprehending and assessing details. In literature as in other arts, details create the effect; we want students to realize both the effect and its sources.

9. *The range of students' reading achievement grows wider at each successive grade level until dropouts occur.*

That students differ in their reading potential and achievement is no news to teachers. The new research, however, offers more detailed descriptions of these differences. As current and future research documents how differences among readers are affected by texts and contexts, especially by teaching strategies, teachers will know more about why and how to individualize instruction. In the meantime, they can act upon two well-established and gross research generalizations that are often overlooked in spite of pious respect for individual differences.

First, students in every class, even "homogeneous" ones, read at different rates. (A very wide range of reading rates is often observed in gifted classes.) Teachers can help students estimate their rates of reading and can then take them into consideration when planning in-common reading and homework assignments. To prevent an experience with a novel from stretching beyond an optimal two to three weeks, teachers abridge and skip some chapters, while still encouraging their best readers to absorb every word. Similarly, in assigning different works to individuals and clusters, teachers can easily consider length; complexity is a more difficult criterion.

Second, cultural diversity, which is increasing in many schools, accounts heavily for differences in comprehension. Students who read English as a second language constitute a large part of our school population. Their proficiency in reading varies greatly. In spite of significant advances in the teaching of beginning reading, many students, native as well as immigrant, arrive in junior and senior high school with very limited comprehension skills and negative attitudes toward reading for nonutilitarian purposes.

For students of low reading ability, whatever the reason, the best approach to literature may be through nonreading channels. But literature, because it is the stuff of human experience, can be a highly motivating vehicle for learning how to read. So teachers supplement listening and viewing with reading-based literature lessons. The best first step they can take is to broaden their view of what literature is (tolerate a little trash!). The second step is to think very carefully about the variability of prior knowledge and its impact on comprehension. Thinking should lead to creative prereading activities: previews or synopses (advance organizers), semantic mapping or highlighting words and concepts, interest-arousing questions, films, role playing, and improvising.

For all students, the ultimate goal must be: "I can read it myself — and I will." The "it" of that goal statement represents literature of the widest diversity in content and quality, appropriate to the reading levels of those who make the declaration.

Bibliography

Applebee, A. N. 1978. *The Child's Concept of Story: Ages Two to Seventeen.* Chicago: The University of Chicago Press.

Brown, A. L. 1980. Metacognitive Development and Reading. In *Theoretical Issues in Reading Comprehension,* ed. R. J. Spiro, B. C. Bruce, and W. F. Brewer. Hillsdale, N.J.: Erlbaum.

Ericson, B. O. 1985. A Descriptive Study of the Individual and Group Responses of Three Tenth-Grade Readers to Two Short Stories and Two Textbook Selections. *Dissertation Abstracts International* 46, no. 2: 388-A.

Galda, L. 1982. Assuming the Spectator Stance: An Examination of the Responses of Three Young Readers. *Research in the Teaching of English* 16: 1–20.

Garner, R., and R. Reis. 1981. Monitoring and Resolving Comprehension Obstacles: An Investigation of Spontaneous Lookbacks among Upper-Grade Good and Poor Comprehenders. *Reading Research Quarterly* 16: 569–82.

Gordon, C. J. 1985. Modeling Inference Awareness Across the Curriculum. *Journal of Reading* 28: 444–47.

Hillocks, G., and L. H. Ludlow. 1984. A Taxonomy of Skills in Reading and Interpreting Fiction. *American Educational Research Journal* 21: 7–24.

Manzo, A. V. 1969. The ReQuest Procedure. *Journal of Reading* 13: 287–91.

Mauro, L. H. 1984. Personal Constructs and Response to Literature: Case Studies of Adolescents Reading about Death. *Dissertation Abstracts International* 44, no. 7: 2073-A.

National Assessment of Educational Progress. 1981. *Three National Assessments of Reading: Changes in Performance, 1970–1980.* Report 11-R-01. Denver: Education Commission of the States.

Olshavsky, J. E. 1977. Reading as Problem Solving: An Investigation of Strategies. *Reading Research Quarterly* 12: 654–74.

Olson, M. W. 1985. Text Type and Reader Ability: The Effects on Paraphrase and Text-Based Inference Questions. *Journal of Reading Behavior* 17: 199–213.

Raphael, T. E. 1984. Teaching Learners about Sources of Information for Answering Comprehension Questions. *Journal of Reading* 27: 303–11.

Roehler, L., and G. G. Duffy. 1984. Direct Explanation of Comprehension Processes. In *Comprehension Instruction,* ed. G.G. Duffy, L.R. Roehler, and J. Mason. New York: Longman.

Rosenblatt, L. 1978. *The Reader, the Text, the Poem.* Carbondale, Ill.: Southern Illinois University Press.

Rumelhart, D. E. 1980. Schemata: The Building Blocks of Cognition. In *Theoretical Issues in Reading Comprehension,* ed. R. J. Spiro, B. C. Bruce, and W. F. Brewer. Hillsdale, N.J.: Erlbaum.

Smith, F. 1978. *Understanding Reading.* 2d ed. New York: Holt, Rinehart and Winston.

Wagoner, S. A. 1983. Comprehension Monitoring: What It Is and What We Know About It. *Reading Research Quarterly* 18: 328–46.

Warren, W. H., D. Nicholas, and T. Trabasso. 1979. Event Chains and Inferences in Understanding Narratives. In *New Directions in Discourse Processing,* ed. R. Freedle. Norwood, N.J.: Ablex.

4 Classroom Discourse and Literary Response

James D. Marshall
University of Iowa

As teachers of both writing and literature, we have for many years overseen a comfortable if somewhat passionless marriage between the two. From book reports to interpretive essays, our students' writing has often centered on their reading of literature and, for better or worse, this curricular arrangement has endured. If one of our major goals in teaching writing has been to familiarize students with the conventions of written discourse, then literature has provided a convenient content for our formal assignments. And if one of our major goals in teaching literature has been to familiarize students with the close, objective analysis of texts, then our students' writing has provided at least one measure of their critical skill. The marriage has worked not only because of its convenience, but also because the assumptions that anchor our teaching of writing and literature have been similar: both have been grounded in the belief that guided practice in formal, objective modes of analysis is the approach best suited to our students' future needs.

But the long-standing relationship between writing and literature has recently shown signs of strain. On the one hand, research in the writing process and writing instruction has introduced a promising range of alternative approaches to teaching writing — approaches that emphasize variety in form and audience and that stress the value of students' personal knowledge as a base for writing. On the other hand, recent work in reading and literary theory has questioned the validity of objective approaches to literature, stressing the powerful role that readers play in the construction of literary meaning. Even the allocation of classroom time has become problematic: as more efforts are made to work with students' writing, less time may be available to address the literature that, for many teachers, remains a primary interest.

If some of the assumptions that inform our teaching are beginning to shift, it may be time to reexamine the traditional curricular relationship between writing and literature. The marriage may be saved, but only by understanding and perhaps rethinking its dynamics. In this chapter, I hope to contribute to that effort by exploring how the conventions of classroom discourse, both oral and written, helped shape students' responses to literature in one teacher's English classes. I will be drawing throughout on data gathered during a five-month study of instruction in an eleventh-grade, college preparatory English course offered at a middle-class high school in the San Francisco Bay Area. Following an analysis of how students talked and wrote about literature in one class, I will offer an alternative framework for relating writing and literature in school.

Talking about Literature

Students often talk about literature before they write about it; in fact, writing assignments are often built upon issues raised in class discussion. Any consideration of writing about literature, then, should probably include an appraisal of the talk that surrounds it. But how does that talk proceed? What conventions does it follow? Let us look at one relatively brief example.

The students here were nearing the end of an instructional unit on Hemingway. They had read *The Sun Also Rises* and were to have completed "The Undefeated" for homework. After taking roll, the teacher asked students for their attention and began:

> *Teacher:* OK, I'd like to start talking about "The Undefeated" in general and then relate it back to what critics call Hemingway's code hero and then bring in *The Sun Also Rises*. What is this story about?
>
> *Student 1:* A bullfighter.
>
> *Teacher:* Who?
>
> *Student 2:* Fights bulls.
>
> *Teacher:* Who?
>
> *Student 3:* Isn't very good.
>
> *Teacher:* What does Manuel [the main character] think about bullfighting?
>
> *Student 1:* He has to do it.
>
> *Teacher:* He has to do it? So he admits to himself that he has to do it and yet he can't? Let's look at the beginning of the story [reads]. I think it's a pretty morbid way to begin a story. Above the man's head is the head of the bull that killed his brother. Even when Manuel first comes in, the traditions and the dangers of bullfighting are put clearly before him.

This exchange lasted only a few moments and, from one perspective, seems fairly unremarkable. The teacher's purpose is to set the agenda for the discussion, and she does so by announcing her plans (first the story, then the code hero, then *The Sun Also Rises*). She then focuses on Manuel's centrally important attitude toward bullfighting ("So he admits to himself that he has to do it, but can't"). She directs her students to a specific portion of text, confesses her distaste for the bull on the wall, but goes on to note its significance ("Even when Manuel first comes in, the traditions and dangers of bullfighting are put clearly before him"). Briefly and efficiently, the teacher has introduced her students to several issues that a critical reading of the story might address.

If we look at this episode from another angle — that of the students — a somewhat different picture emerges. The students' contributions to the discussion are minimal, consisting of four brief answers (one of them playful) to relatively straightforward questions. In many ways, even those contributions are unnecessary. Given the announced agenda, the students can do little except follow the teacher toward an interpretation of the story that is already beginning to take shape. They have few considered opinions about the story — they have read it only once — and thus their wisest course might be to listen as their teacher tells them what the story means. But the teacher's reading of the story depends critically on Hemingway's attitude toward bullfighting, and bullfighting is an issue about which students do have opinions. When those opinions emerge, the discussion becomes livelier.

> *Teacher:* Would you call bullfighting a sport?
>
> *Student 4:* They just do it to be famous.
>
> *Student 5:* It's a heck of a sport.
>
> *Student 6:* Except when they had these bullfights, people didn't have an SPCA and stuff. They didn't think it was so bad. It was like killing whales in *Moby Dick*.
>
> *Teacher:* Bullfighters are considered by Hemingway to be sportsmen. You can tell the difference between a good and a bad bullfighter. For example, why doesn't the crowd respond to Manuel?
>
> [Silence]
>
> *Student 7:* I have a hard time admiring any bullfighters.
>
> *Teacher:* What about what he did though? Do you admire the fact that he died for something he wanted to do?
>
> *Student 7:* He kind of wanted to be killed. And I still don't like bullfighters.
>
> *Teacher:* Let's look at page 86. It talks about how Manuel is a

bullfighter and thinks in bullfighting terms [reads]. This all relates
to skill and emotion. We admire him at the end. Hemingway
believed that real men don't give up. Manuel didn't give up. He
was hurt, but still he goes out and finishes the fight. He doesn't
give up.

We should note from the start that the conflict here is not between
competing interpretations of the story: the students are not yet ready
to offer any. The conflict, rather, is between competing values that
might inform such interpretations. If the teacher is right when she
speaks for the author ("Bullfighters are considered by Hemingway to
be sportsmen"), then it probably follows that Hemingway's intention
was for us to admire Manuel. If we share Hemingway's values, or are
willing to suspend our own long enough to see the world from his
perspective, then we can probably arrive at that admiration. But the
students here, at least the vocal ones, do not admire Manuel for at
least two reasons. First, they do not know, until their teacher tells
them, that Hemingway admired bullfighters. Second, even after they
are given this piece of biographical information, they do not seem to
care. Right or wrong, their allegiance to their own values interferes
with the response to Manuel that their teacher hoped they would
have. Near the close of the discussion, when the teacher declares that
"we admire him," it is difficult to determine who the "we" might be.

The teacher is of course right about the story, or at least more right
than her students. There is a rich tradition of Hemingway criticism
dealing directly with the author's conception of heroes, and Manuel
is one exemplar of the type. To suggest a reading of the story based
on a personal distaste for the violence of bullfighting would itself do
violence to what we know about Hemingway. But if the teacher is
right about the story, the students are right about their experience of
the story, and the conflict that emerged here raises questions about
the purposes such discussions serve.

On the one hand, discussions are meant as opportunities for a
community of readers to share their observations and opinions about
a piece of literature. In asking her opening question here ("Would you
consider bullfighting a sport?"), the teacher may have hoped to prompt
that kind of sharing. On the other hand, though, discussions are also
meant to arrive somewhere, usually at an interpretation that the
teacher has had in mind all along. The two purposes do not always
conflict (participants may share knowledge, assumptions, and strategies
and thus arrive at similar conclusions), but they can cross, especially
when the teacher's reading of the story draws upon prior knowledge
to which students have little access. When this occurs, as it did in the

exchange just examined, students can only draw the conclusion that the responses they have been asked to make are somehow "wrong." However they may feel privately about bullfighting or Manuel (and when we speak of admiration, we are speaking of feelings), they have learned in this exchange what it is appropriate to *say* one feels when discussing Hemingway in school. And knowing what to say plays an important role when students come to write about the literature they have discussed. We will look now at some of the issues involved in that writing.

Writing about Literature

If students' oral responses to literature are constrained by the purposes of classroom discussion, their written responses may be even more so. Writing, after all, is frequently graded, while oral responses are usually not. Writing about literature in school, moreover, often requires students to adhere to some fairly stringent, formal guidelines. Let us consider one assignment given soon after the discussion we have just examined.

Students had been told three days before that they would be writing an in-class essay on Hemingway. On the day of the assignment, the teacher handed out a list of topics; the students were told to select one. The list included the following choices:

1. Compare and contrast Jake's friendship with Cohn with Jake's friendship with Bill.
2. Compare and contrast Francis Macomber, Manuel Manola, and Jake as examples of Hemingway's code hero.
3. Analyze the men of *The Sun Also Rises* (Cohn, Mike Campbell, Jake Barnes, Pedro Romero) in terms of the code hero.
4. Do a character analysis of Brett in terms of the different men with whom she involves herself.
5. Using specific scenes from the novels and short stories, show how Hemingway's sense of the roaring twenties compares to Fitzgerald's.
6. Choose one important symbol from each work by Hemingway that we have read and trace its development.
7. Show the significance of the title *The Sun Also Rises* to the novel as a whole.

The students have a choice of topics here, but little choice of approach. With few exceptions, the topics ask students to address

themselves to a specific interpretive issue in a specific work. Although
the topics range in difficulty (compare, for example, numbers two and
three with number six), the center of each is text-based and text-
supported formal analysis. The teacher made this clear early in the
semester when a student new to the class asked how essays were
graded:

> Does it have a clearly stated thesis? Did you support your thesis
> with examples? Do you have a conclusion? Mechanics will be
> important. Organization will be important. What I'll be looking
> for is whether you've supported your ideas. That's why it's so
> important for you to have a clear thesis.

The in-class essay was to be written during a block period lasting
ninety minutes. In that time, the students were to select a topic,
generate a thesis, organize their thoughts, and write an essay free of
mechanical problems. In spite of the constraints under which they
worked, however, most of the students in the class were able to deliver
the kind of product the teacher expected. Brian, one of those students,
told me how it was done:

> You get a sheet of paper and it has five or six subjects and there's
> usually one really easy one that the whole class is going to do.
> If you write on that you've got to do it well because nineteen
> other people are going to do it. And then there's a couple that
> are in-between, and if you like one of those you're better off
> writing on that because it's easier to get an A. And then there's
> one that's the teacher's favorite and if you can do a decent job
> on that you can get a good grade, but it's usually not too much
> fun because it's usually pretty hard to understand.

What processes does Brian employ?

> The first thing I do is I just write an outline of what I'm going to
> do. I pick a subject and then I write an outline and it's always
> the same. For a five-paragraph essay the first thing I do is write
> down Roman numeral I and I write "intro" and then I pick a, b,
> c, which will give me my three middle paragraphs. For an in-
> class essay, you don't have much time to do a rough draft and a
> final, but I find it works better if you actually write a rough draft
> of your first paragraph, cause your thoughts are changing and it
> looks terrible if you scratch out. And the rest of it just kind of
> comes. The conclusion, you just restate the thesis.

Brian consistently received high marks on his essays and, given the
clarity of his system for writing, we can see at least part of the reason
for his success.

Not all of the students could handle the assignments successfully,
however. Rosemary, for example, told me what gave her problems:

> I hate those in-class essays. Because, when I read a book, I always think of some great things I can write an essay about, and they just never seem to be the same things that she lists as topics. I pick out the topic that has the most room for writing. Like whether Moby Dick is evil — you can just talk about anything really. But comparing two characters, you have to be very specific and limited in what you say.

Rosemary was less clear than Brian in describing the processes she employed in writing, but she did know what the final draft was supposed to look like:

> In a limited essay, it's already written. I mean there's an opening paragraph where you tell what it is about. This is always very technical. Automatic. The first sentence is always "In blank's novel or biographical sketch," and then there's the title. It's all by formula, it's just to what degree. And then you have an example for one character and then an example for another and then you compare the two people and then you conclude — and that's it. It's totally set.

Brian's and Rosemary's reports are not that different from one another. Both are aware of the form their writing should take, and both reveal a somewhat practical approach to the process. What distinguishes them is their ability or willingness to key into the questions they are asked. Rosemary cannot often do this ("I always think of some great things . . . but [they] never seem to be the same things she lists"), while Brian prides himself on his knowledge of the system. Discussing his essay on Fitzgerald's attitude toward the rich, for example, Brian told me:

> That went all right. I did a five-paragraph essay. The rich were reckless, irresponsible, and out of touch with reality. And then I did an introduction and a conclusion. You see I knew that [the teacher] wanted us to see that about the novel. You really got that from class. And then "out of touch with reality" seemed to describe Daisy sometimes. It should get me an A. It was kind of a report on what I already knew. Now, if anyone ever asks me what Fitzgerald's attitude toward the rich was I won't have to think about it. I'll just say they were reckless, irresponsible, and out of touch with reality.

By knowing what the teacher wanted, Brian was able to avoid at least some of the thinking that the essay might have encouraged. His honest assessment — that the essay was a "report" on what he already knew — suggests that writing about literature, at least for Brian, is not so much a process of discovery and analysis as it is a chance to show that he has been listening in class.

Brian's and Rosemary's reports on their writing, like the example of classroom discussion examined earlier, suggest that students' responses to literature were constrained by the conventions governing their expression. What they could say about literature was shaped by what they were expected (and instructed) to say and by the way they were expected to say it. One of the clearest indications of this process may be the writing that students completed for the Hemingway assignment. Brian's observation that most students wrote on one topic — the easiest one — was borne out when students' choices were tallied. From the list of topics, fully half of the students chose to write on Hemingway's code hero, the topic that had been discussed most extensively in class. Only two students chose to trace the symbolism in Hemingway's work, and only three chose to write about Brett. Evidently, students were taking the line of least resistance in completing the assignment: like Brian, they were trying to "report" on what they already knew rather than break new ground or share their own observations about Hemingway.

Even within the code hero topic, however, there were similarities in approach that made individual paragraphs almost interchangeable. Following are the first paragraphs from three essays chosen literally at random from those that addressed the topic:

> Ernest Hemingway, author of *The Sun Also Rises*, had very definite ideas as to what a man should be. The name given to this ideal man is "code hero." A code hero is brave, courageous, and independent. Many of Hemingway's novels and stories contain a code hero. In *The Sun Also Rises*, Hemingway gives profiles of many men, four of which are Robert Cohn, Mike Campbell, Jacob Barnes, and Pedro Romero. — *Andy*

> In Ernest Hemingway's *The Sun Also Rises*, the men of the book have several different personalities. Hemingway's novels sometimes share a type of man called the code hero who is Hemingway's idea of a true man. The code hero can drink without getting drunk, can have any woman he wants, and most of all is brave. Robert Cohn, Mike Campbell, Jake Barnes, and Pedro Romero share some of the qualities that determine a "code hero." — *Chris*

> In the novel *The Sun Also Rises*, Hemingway introduces a type of person called the code hero. This hero has certain qualities that distinguish him from non-code heroes. A code hero performs difficult tasks in a carefree way, and attempts not to show his emotions in most all cases. In *The Sun Also Rises*, Hemingway uses Pedro Romero, a brave bull fighter and Jake Barnes, an unfortunate man, to dramatize the part of a code hero. — *Eric*

In each of these excerpts we see exemplified Rosemary's observation about the formulaic nature of introductions. Each begins by identifying the author and the work, goes on to define the code hero (the definitions are taken directly from class discussion), and closes with a list of characters to be discussed — a form of thesis. The essays go on to examine each of the characters mentioned in the thesis, showing how they were or were not code heroes, and each concludes with a paragraph very much like Chris's:

> *The Sun Also Rises* is a novel with many kinds of men, but only a few code heroes. Jake, Mike, and Cohn each lack a few qualities that would make them code heroes.

On one level, these students have clearly learned what they have been taught. They have gained some control over the conventions of academic discourse, and through class discussion they have become familiar with conventional approaches to the work of Hemingway. To the extent that this learning will enable them to succeed in other academic contexts, the instruction they have received is both valuable and necessary. Having said that, however, we may need to ask whether this is what we wanted students to learn in the first place or, more softly, whether something may be missing from these responses. That something is of course the students' own perspective on the literature they are asked to read in school. Let us consider one of those perspectives.

Responding to Literature

We have seen that, in both their oral and written work, these students were seldom encouraged to make or elaborate upon their personal reactions to literature. To a large extent, the process of learning about literature was a process of learning what to say about literature — and then saying it in the appropriate form. Still, students do have personal reactions and, although their expression is only rarely supported in class, such reactions play an important role in shaping what students may finally learn about literature and literary response. Vince, for example, had this to say about the academic approach to literature in which he had been schooled:

> In English class they always give you that line about how they're preparing you for college. Whenever you ask teachers why you're doing what you're doing, that's the definitive answer, that we're preparing you for something. . . . The books we read, I don't know, no book is going to be fun for everyone. The teacher picks out books that are on the list of classics. But I don't know what makes

> a great work of art. I guess it has to be abstruse and have a lot
> of hidden meanings and symbolism. They want you to appreciate
> and like great classic literature. They're really not going to give
> you a great range of books. They're just setting these books in
> front of you and saying "like them." If you don't you're a
> deviant. . . . They want me to read differently for class. They want
> me to read more critically and analytically. They want me to go
> through the book chapter by chapter and page by page and
> analyze it. You're not allowed to read it for pleasure. You have
> to think about the symbols. What does the fish mean? What does
> the merry-go-round mean? It doesn't mean anything to me.

What seems lacking, from Vince's perspective, is the opportunity
for him to take ownership for the reading and writing activities in
which he is asked to engage. Even when he is giving his opinion,
Vince is frustrated:

> Like on this essay she circles "I" and says "no first person." But
> *I'm* writing the essay. I mean it's like they always say you have
> to assume that the reader hasn't read the book. But the reader
> *has* read the book, so why do I have to assume that she hasn't.
> Why can't I write in the first person? It's just a lot of stupid rules.

Whatever the accuracy of Vince's assessment, the questions he raises
are important. He would like to share his ideas about literature in a
natural form with an audience that is real: these options are not
allowed him. Instead, he must assume that his teacher has not read
the book and that he is not the author of his own opinions. In the
end, there is often a distance between what Vince writes and what
he thinks:

> What teachers want is an opinion, and they have an opinion also,
> and they grade you against their opinion. And it really gets hard
> to write to please the teacher instead of writing what you're
> thinking. . . . Sometimes I know what they want and I give it to
> them. Sometimes I know what they want and I refuse to give it
> to them because it's so absurd. And sometimes I have no idea
> what they want.

It would be unwise, of course, to generalize too freely from Vince's
remarks. Several of his classmates appreciated the academic constraints
in which they worked, and many were glad that someone was
"preparing them for college." What Vince's out-of-school perspective
allows, however, is another angle of vision on the process of learning
about literature. He reminds us that the discussions that take place in
class and the essays that get written and graded do not represent all
that is learned about literature in school. He asks with some urgency
whether there might be alternative approaches to literature, approaches

that may accommodate his developing view of literature and literary response. In the section that follows, I will offer one framework for designing such alternatives.

Writing and Learning about Literature

We began this chapter by considering the long-standing relationship between writing and literature in the English curriculum. That relationship has served us well, for it has allowed us to marry two of our most important responsibilities: to teach writing and to teach literature. But as the assumptions that inform our teaching begin to change — as we learn more about the process of writing and the process of reading — our teaching practices may need to undergo a corresponding transformation.

The key word here is *process*. The last twenty years have taught us a good deal about the recursive stages through which writers move before they arrive at a finished product, and our best teaching has found the means to accommodate and support the process. In teacher-student writing conferences, peer responses, and multiple drafts, we have begun to locate strategies that may enable students to learn what they have to say before they are asked to present it for evaluation. We have also learned that students' writing may become richer and more powerful to the extent that it belongs to them, reflecting their own knowledge and purposes.

I would like to suggest that coming to terms with a literary text is also a process, one that may move from tentative, incomplete, and perhaps mistaken readings to those that are fuller, more detailed, and more thoroughly reasoned. First readings, like initial drafts, are likely to be personal, unready for public evaluation. Yet like first drafts, first readings are the place where the process begins, the necessary if insufficient first step in discovering what one thinks, even when these early discoveries are later abandoned.

If we have made room for first drafts in our writing instruction, perhaps we can also find room for the articulation of first readings. Consider, for example, the last paragraph of a personal essay that Steve wrote in response to the J. D. Salinger story "Pretty Mouth and Green My Eyes." In the assignment, Steve was asked to explain how he personally felt about the relationship among the story's three characters:

> Looking at the three-way relationship as a whole, I am convinced that something foul is going on. I haven't yet determined exactly

what is going on, but I feel it is safe to conclude that Arthur is
the victim of a conspiracy in this awkward three-way relationship.
Perhaps the girl is Joanie and Arthur is lying about Joanie's
returning home. Still, I can't decide whether Arthur is telling Lee
of Joanie's return to taunt Lee by insinuating that Arthur knows
what's going on, or whether Arthur is just saying that because
he realized that he could never leave Joanie, and since he said
that he was going to leave after the incident, he has to make up
a story to make it look like it was all a big mistake. This idea
might explain Lee's guilt and his sorrow for the cruelty and abuse
of his friend.

Here Steve admits his uncertainty and seems to be using his writing
to explore the implications of various readings of the story. He is not
"reporting" on what the story means (as we saw Brian and his
classmates doing earlier). Rather, he is trying to discover what the
story means, and his writing is a way to reach that end. He has not
yet come to a reading he can defend, but he has located some of the
issues such a reading might address. We can contrast his approach
here to his approach in a more formal effort, where he was to write
a "well argued essay" on Salinger's "The Laughing Man":

In conclusion, it is evident that the tale followed closely the mood
of the Chief throughout the story. Using the method of incorporating a tale within a tale, Salinger was able to portray loyalty to
friends in his short story "The Laughing Man."

In this excerpt, Steve is much more concerned with showing what
he knows, both about the story and about the routines of formal
writing. The beginning of the paragraph is marked formulaically for
what it is (a conclusion), while the second sentence formulaically
summarizes the gist of the argument that has gone before. Both in
the excerpt and in the essay as a whole, Steve has not taken risks,
has not expressed uncertainty. His purpose is to answer questions, not
ask them, and the formal conventions of "well argued essays" seldom
allow students the scope to be intelligently unsure of their answers.

But students' initial readings of texts — especially texts that are
difficult — are bound to be tentative, are bound to raise more questions
than the students can confidently answer. Recognizing this fact, we
have two options. We can give students the answers (*this* is what the
story means) and then ask for formal written reports on what we have
told them. Or we can initiate and support their own process of discovery
through writing, knowing that they may arrive at readings different
from and perhaps less informed than our own. To follow the latter
course would involve relinquishing some of the authority we have
traditionally held over the meaning of literary texts. It would also

mean that questions concerning the nature of evidence and argument and response would remain essentially open. It would mean finally that we would often use writing not to test our students' understanding, but to provide them with a means of achieving it. Formal arguments addressed to more public audiences may well follow students' initial, exploratory efforts. But those arguments will achieve authority and richness only to the extent that they remain anchored in the students' own reasoned interpretation of the text.

There is of course nothing especially new about such a proposal. The way we go about teaching literature is full of arguments for the increased use of writing across the curriculum, and increasing research evidence suggests that writing is indeed a powerful tool for learning. But although we have sometimes been successful in persuading our colleagues in other disciplines that writing is valuable, our own house may need attention as well. The evidence we have examined here is perhaps suggestive of patterns that often obtain in our classrooms. We have frequently asked students to write about literature, but our purposes for that writing have been largely evaluative. Our writing tasks have followed discussion, and our students' written products have formally reported on that discussion. But the structural demands of formal writing — its reliance on top-down logic, textual evidence, and proof — may serve to close down inquiry into a text if those demands are imposed before students have come to some possession of the text's possibilities.

My argument here is that writing should serve also to initiate such inquiry, that it become a means of opening and sustaining the discussions in which we engage. If the mutually supportive relationship between writing and literature is to be preserved in our teaching, we may need to give writing a larger, more flexible, and finally a more powerful role.

5 Readers and Texts in a Fifth-Grade Classroom

Dorothy J. Watson
University of Missouri

Suzanne C. Davis
Robert E. Lee Elementary School
Columbia, Missouri

The first morning of the new school year was typically hot and humid. Little wonder that Suzanne Davis's fifth graders were incapable of much enthusiasm when their teacher began talking about a new reading program. Showing no signs of hearing the word *new*, the children politely settled down, fully expecting to hear the familiar. Most of them, after all, had been in Davis's classroom the year before and knew that reading meant basals, workbooks, and endless skill sheets. There was also no doubt about what was expected of them as readers: they were already categorized as poor, average, or good and assigned to ability groups according to the end-of-level basal reader test given the previous year. Their reading performance had always seemed to reflect and confirm their poor, average, or good labels. Why should it be any different this year?

Davis's students were in for a surprise: the familiar was not forthcoming. Their teacher held up four paperback books, *Where the Red Fern Grows, Island of the Blue Dolphins, Ralph S. Mouse,* and *Nothing's Fair in Fifth Grade.* She proceeded to tell a bit about each book and then asked each student to select one book to read. She explained that there would be no low or high groups, no work sheets to fill out, no vocabulary words to find in the dictionary before reading, and no questions to answer at the end of two or three pages. The children would, however, be expected to read silently a great deal, to think

Authors' note: The authors are indebted to Ralph Peterson, Arizona State University, whose conceptualization of the use of literature in classrooms has been the basis of this project; and to Debra Crouse, University of Missouri, whose research field notes are quoted here.

about their books and their reading, to talk with others who were reading the same book, and to write about their books and their reading.

Davis and her students embarked on a year of extensive and intensive reading. They read a lot of quality literature, and they reflected and responded to the literature by making connections between it and their own lives and between the books they currently were reading and the literature they had read in the past. In Davis's words, it was a year neither she nor the students would forget.

Reasons for the Literature Project

Davis felt that something was missing in her traditional basal reading program. The children were learning to read, but in the case of some it seemed as if they were learning despite the program. Furthermore, her program had inspired little if any enthusiasm or love of reading. Writing, other than fill-in-the-blank or an occasional story starter, did not exist in the program.

Aware of her students' lack of interest and at the same time intrigued by the new research in reading and writing, she was eager to test a model of literacy instruction which insists that language presented to children must be as alive and whole as the children using and learning that language. Davis made a decision: she would no longer expect children to become proficient and eager readers by presenting them with small units of language in regulated and controlled pieces (pre-selected paragraphs and stories with stilted syntax and controlled vocabulary). That approach would be replaced by increased reading of trade books, talking in small groups with others reading the same books, and bringing the reading process to a conscious awareness by talking about what readers do to become more proficient. Another major change in the reading instruction involved having the children and the teacher write about what they read, about their reading (the process), and about things important to them.

Literature Study Groups

The topic of this section, literature study groups (LSG), states exactly what the activity involves: real literature for children, high level thinking about the literature, and readers meeting together in small groups to talk and think about what they are reading. In most upper elementary LSG programs, there are three or four groups in the classroom. Members of a group, those seven or eight students who choose the same book to read, meet with their teacher for thirty or forty minutes twice a week.

Literature study groups provide a curricular framework in which students can read extensively. In Davis's class, each student read approximately sixteen books throughout the year for his or her study group. On average, the LSG program also promoted the reading of approximately twenty-two non-LSG books, which were borrowed from the library, brought from home, or ordered through book clubs.

Books chosen for the study groups are selected on the basis of children's interest, quality of the text, and availability. (Although availability is a factor, no book is selected just because it is accessible.) The teacher introduces five or six books to the students by briefly discussing the title, author, plot, and so forth. During this introduction, the teacher challenges students to explore new genres and subjects — to extend their ability to make meaning in unexplored territories. Students bring their background of life and literature to this discussion and select a title for personal or social reasons. On the basis of their first or second choice, the children are assigned to groups. The most proficient and the least proficient readers sometimes select the same title and are therefore in the same group. Groups are never formed on the basis of reading ability or test scores.

Response to Literature

Students are expected to read, read, read — a great many books. But just as important as *extensive* reading is *intensive* reading. The LSG program does more than add another title to a list of books read or another segment to the bookworm elongating itself around the room. Children are asked to slow down, move back and forth between their lives and the text life, to consider meaning embedded in characterization, mood, pattern, ordering of time, circumstance of setting, even conventions of print. In other words, they are encouraged to participate in higher order thinking — anything that helps them live through the literature experience, learn from it, and value it.

When students and teacher come together in a small group, the emphasis is on sharing impressions, ideas, and problems encountered in constructing meaning from the text. At this point it becomes evident that readers are as important as authors. When a topic surfaces that holds a common interest and has the potential for deepening perceptions, the teacher's help shifts from sharing to dialogue. Through dialogue (a shared experience that encompasses critical thought) the group discloses and constructs meaning. Through group power, meanings of the text held by individuals are expanded. In a cooperative undertaking, readers reflect on the importance of events, both within and outside the text, that move the story and themselves forward.

Before the group discussion, students are invited to respond personally in their literature logs, which they receive the day they select their first LSG book. It is made clear to the children from the outset that they are free to write as personally, specifically, or generally as they care to in their logs. They are encouraged but not required to write and to share their writing with the study group. In Davis's class, some children were comfortable with the writing and sharing, while others cared only to write and not share their thoughts. Occasionally, when there was little or no time for learning log entries, a few minutes either before or after the discussion group were devoted to writing. Toward the middle of the year, many students wanted to read the entire book before they responded in their log.

Davis never asked students to do anything she was not willing to do herself. As an authentic member of the group, she read all of the books and responded in her own log. The necessity of the teacher participating in this way became apparent early in the year. The dialogue could never have been as intense and as important if any members, including the teacher, had failed to read the literature. Davis's sharing was always an invitational demonstration. It was never presented as *the* model towards which the students must strive. Rather, sharing was simply her honest response to the literature. She wrote in her log and shared it as a way of making her own connections with the literature, contributing to the group, and modeling and inviting the students to write. Following are two entries from the teacher's learning log:

September 25

I began reading *Island of the Blue Dolphins* today. When I first began reading this book, I didn't think I was going to like it very well. Some of the names were unfamiliar, and I wasn't sure how I was supposed to pronounce them. I decided to settle on one way to pronounce each name and continue reading. Once I quit worrying about how to pronounce each name, I began to become more interested in the story.

I thought it was interesting that the people on the island had a real name, or a secret name which is seldom used, and a common name that is used most. It might be fun to have a secret name that had a certain magic to it when used!

I stopped reading today at the point where the leader of the island left the island in search of a country he knew as a boy. He's going there to make a place for his island people. I have a feeling he may not return.

April 1

When I began reading *The Book of Three* I wrote in my log that it was difficult to pronounce the names and to keep the characters straight. It seems odd to me now that I could have gotten the characters confused. The characters were easier to keep straight along about the 4th or 5th chapter. Once I figured out my own strategy for pronouncing unusual names, then I could get on with the business of reading and getting to know the characters. I think only Lloyd Alexander himself knows how to pronounce them all correctly anyway!

I said earlier in my log that when I started this book I didn't know if I like C. S. Lewis or Lloyd Alexander's books better. I've now decided that's like trying to choose between rocky road and burgundy cherry ice cream — impossible! I like them both!

I must confess. I've always been afraid of reading high fantasy or science fiction. I was always afraid I would never really understand it and people would think I was dense. I enjoy this high fantasy of Lloyd Alexander's and I can't wait to read the next one. He is a creative author and uses such good description and imagery that I was drawn into the book and felt I was right there with the characters.

Alexander has a subtle way of getting you to think about something that could be a rule to live by. For example, when Gwydian discusses what brought the fall of the Horned King (on page 216), he says, "Once you have courage to look upon evil, seeing it for what it is and naming it by its true name, it is powerless against you, and you can destroy it." Somehow, that really struck me and I think there's a powerful message there.

Not only does Davis write about the content of the story and how it makes meaning for her, but she writes about the reading process itself and the strategies she uses to help her make sense of and through the story. The impact of a teacher's sharing such information is powerful. Imagine the surprise and relief of an unsuccessful reader on learning that teachers also have problems when reading. As Brice's entries indicate, he learned from his teacher's example and accepted the invitation to write in his log (children's nonstandard spellings and sentence structures are not corrected in their logs):

December 19

I just finished *The Witch of Blackbird Pond*. It was a terrific book. I would recommend this exciting book. The author did a terrific job of portraying characters. The author always kept secrets from the reader. This book is for all ages, well thats what I think. Now

I know why it got the Newberry Medal. My two favorite characters are Nat and Matthew Wood. I liked how Nat became the captain of a ship that he called "The Witch." That was a neat name to me. Now I'll tell you why I said Matthew Wood. I like how Matthew changed. For instance, he stood up for Kit 3 times at the end. I think that he just got more used to Kit. — *Brice*

April 1

I finished *The Book of Three* last Friday. It was the best book I've ever read! Except for *Where the Red Fern Grows!* I think Lloyd Alexander is one of the best authors that I know of. He is a very adventurous writer. I think that Eilonwy is selfish. I wouldn't be surprised is she wanted to be *queen of Prydain!* Flewdur Flam is a pretty nice sort of character. He sounds like a nice sort of guy. Gurgi is kind of a wierd sort of thing. He runs up trees like we run on the ground. Taran was sort of a coward at the beginning but in the end he was very courageous. I think that Lloyd Alexander made a terrific ending when Gwidion came to Taran's room and Lloyd kept Gwydion alive. I'm thinking of writing a story similar to this one. — *Brice*

What Was Learned

In the past year we have seen children become proficient and avid readers by having the opportunity to read real literature and to respond to it through discussion and writing. The children and the literature have taught us a great deal.

1. We have a sharper definition of *extensive reading*. Students are placed in a context where they are surrounded by literature. They see other students and their teacher spending a great deal of time with their noses in books, not only books from the literature study groups, but from the library and other sources as well. Children are encouraged to live through different kinds of literature and to make connections among plots, themes, characters, illustrations, and authors.

2. We have a sharper definition of *intensive reading*. It is not enough to read many books; the reading must be personalized in a way that taps children's world views in order to construct meaning and ownership through reading. In intensive reading, children return to the text to explore relationships, find links with their past experiences, build on previous readings, and explore what it is that makes the story.

3. The literature that students are asked to read must be of value. It can be professionally authored or written by classmates or the teacher, but it must have integrity. Trivialized text does not lead to

future readings or to reading in depth. When children are invited to reflect on what they have read, something must be there to reflect on, to mull over, to savor. The issue of basal readers cannot be ignored. On the basis of a miscue analysis of the fifth graders in Davis's class, we have learned that in no way do the basals meet the cognitive-linguistic needs of these readers.

4. Reading is both a personal and a social activity. Children must have time to read silently, personally. They must also have the opportunity to talk with others about books. From social interaction, children find that others have similar and different interpretations and opinions. Through confrontations with ideas, formation, and perspectives other than their own, members of the group are challenged and grow.

5. Reading groups to which children are assigned on the basis of traditional reading test scores are harmful to their linguistic and social health. Literature study groups provide a safe harbor for all readers to take risks, contribute, and become more proficient and more avid readers. Esteem for self and others is kept intact.

6. Many times it is useful for the student to bring the processes of reading and writing to a conscious level of awareness. One group discussed the use of parentheses, while two other students saw the need to bring in resource books to find out more about tarantulas, the topic of their LSG book. The students often talked about what they did when they came to something unfamiliar in a story, how they handled unknown concepts and unpronounceable words. They discussed the roles of writers and readers. All of these discussions occurred in the context of "the teachable moment."

7. The role of teacher is crucial. Literature study groups do not have much of a chance if the teacher fails to accept his or her primary role as a contributing member of the group, understanding that no member has the right to dominate. However, the teacher is the teacher, and there is no better, more natural place to gather information about students and their learning than in the LSG. The teacher can teach. For example, it may be appropriate, even crucial to the thinking process of some students, for the teacher to spend five or ten minutes with a single group or with the entire class, talking about how readers can look at the relationship of characters in a story, or discussing the framework of a good detective story, or illustrating by using excerpts how understanding the setting of stories may help readers understand the motivation and behavior of characters.

8. Reading and writing are mutually supportive. Writing helped the

students focus and extend their understanding of the text. Reading gave them background, motivation, pattern, and convention for their own writing.

9. Teachers must be actively involved in the literature study group: they must read the books and respond to the literature in both discussion and writing. Davis usually read the books before she introduced them to the students, but the children enjoyed it when she read along as they were reading. Authentic participation can happen only when teachers do what they ask their students to do — read and write.

10. Involvement of group members in real dialogue takes time, patience, knowledge, and experience. Most students and teachers expect any "discussion" to be teacher directed, teacher controlled, and even teacher centered. In literature study groups this cannot be the case if intensive reading is a real goal. For Davis, initial sessions were sometimes discouraging when the discussion seemed to be going nowhere or had nothing to do with the book. Discussions must be more than question-and-answer periods, bull sessions, or chitchat. Ways of involving children in dialogue, promoting real questions, and making appropriate comments continue to be basic concerns.

11. Making writing a part of the literature study program requires time, patience, knowledge, and experience. For some children, inviting them to write about their reading and then giving them time and facilities for the activity is enough incentive to set them immediately to the task. For most, it is not enough, however. Teachers and children must help each other learn to read intensively through writing. The literature log provided Davis's students with the means for writing; she made sure they had time to write daily, and she gave an invitational demonstration by sharing her own writing with group members. Ways of involving children in response to their books through writing continue to be a basic concern.

This year-with-real-kids-and-real-literature has been a rejuvenating experience for everyone involved, including children, researchers, parents, and other teachers. It has been a time of learning for all. But for the teacher who had the most to gain or lose from the experience, it was also a time for taking risks. Suzanne Davis did just that. In the process she gained a confirmation of her practical theory of literacy and lost her hesitancy in speaking out for a curriculum that intrigues, enlightens, and empowers students.

We strongly recommend that teachers (because they know their students) choose the books to invite their children to read. Although

Davis will change her list each year, the following were her first-year LSG books:

Louisa May Alcott: *Little Women*

Lloyd Alexander: *The Black Cauldron; The High King; Taran Wanderer*

Clyde Robert Bulla: *Shoeshine Girl*

Betsy C. Byers: *The Summer of the Swans; The Cybil War*

Beverly Cleary: *Ralph S. Mouse*

Vera and Bill Cleaver: *Where the Lilies Bloom*

James Lincoln Collier: *My Brother Sam Is Dead*

Margaret Davidson: *Helen Keller's Teacher*

Marguerite de Angel: *The Door in the Wall*

Barthe DeClements: *Nothing's Fair in Fifth Grade*

Jeannette Eyerley: *Jeannette. The Seeing Summer*

Paula Fox: *The One-Eyed Cat*

Kenneth Grahame: *The Wind in the Willows*

Madeleine L'Engle: *A Wrinkle in Time*

C. S. Lewis: *The Lion, the Witch, and the Wardrobe; Prince Caspian*

Jack London: *The Call of the Wild*

Jane O'Connor: *Yours Till Niagara Falls, Abby*

Scott O'Dell: *Island of the Blue Dolphins*

Katherine Paterson: *Bridge to Terabithia; The Great Gilly Hopkins; Jacob Have I Loved*

Wilson Rawls: *Where the Red Fern Grows*

Willo Davis Roberts: *The Girl with the Silver Eyes*

Marilyn Singer: *Tarantulas on the Brain*

Doris Buchanan Smith: *The Taste of Blackberries*

Elizabeth G. Speare: *The Witch of Blackbird Pond*

J. R. R. Tolkien: *The Hobbit*

Jules Verne: *Around the World in Eighty Days*

Bibliography

Kinder, S. 1987. *Assessment of Reading Development of Students in a Fifth-Grade Literature Study Program.* Dissertation in progress, University of Missouri.

6 First Graders' Responses to a Literature-Based Literacy Strategy

Nancy Knipping
University of Missouri

Marilyn Andre
Lee Elementary School
Columbia, Missouri

As a small group of Marilyn Andre's first graders settled down with their teacher at the reading table, she handed each child a copy of Paul Galdone's *The Three Little Pigs* and asked, "What do you know about this story?" After the children discussed versions that they had already heard, the teacher began to read the Paul Galdone version, inviting the children to join her. As the group chorally read that the wolf ate the first little pig, Henry's mouth dropped open and his eyes widened. "Poor little pigs got eaten," he said. Mandy commented, "Actually, the third little pig ate his brothers because he ate the wolf. That's not nice." Henry's reply was quick: "I would have hurting feelings if that happened to my sister." Later, when the children returned from recess, Chuck walked in from the playground chanting, "Little pig, little pig, let me come in."

During the 1985–86 school year as the literature study group strategy developed in Suzanne Davis's fifth-grade classroom (see chapter 5), Marilyn Andre's first graders one floor below were demonstrating that they could do it, too. As an observer, I worked collaboratively with Andre to develop a literature-based strategy that enabled children to become active, involved readers. Concurrently, we documented the evolution of the strategy and the children's responses to it. Later we analyzed the strategy.

For years Andre had enthusiastically read a wealth of children's literature to her young students and had encouraged them to read to themselves and to each other. Watching the children's excitement as they enjoyed literature, she was eager to explore alternatives or supplements to a basal reading program. Also intrigued with the potential of a literature-based literacy strategy, the observer was pleased to spend two mornings a week throughout the year in the classroom, recording the study group discussions in field notes and periodically on audiotape (approximately 20 percent of the total number of discussions).

The children's responses to the strategy delighted us. We have learned that, when young children read and share valued pieces of literature with their teacher and a small group of peers, their responses reveal careful thought, spontaneous emotion, and surprising depth.

Organization of the Strategy

School district policy required that Andre use basal reading materials and traditional ability grouping three mornings a week. Encouraged to use the literature study groups (LSG) as a complementary program, however, she chose to have the groups meet on Tuesday and Thursday mornings. Each Monday afternoon she invited the children to browse through the four LSG selections for the week and to indicate their first and second choices. Three of the four titles each week had been offered previously, and one was a new book. Making every effort to honor first choices, the teacher assigned the children to study groups of no more than eight.

On Tuesday mornings after helping her students settle into independent writing, Andre called the first study group to the reading table. They each received a copy of the selection and began leafing through it. Before reading, group members discussed their expectations for the book, their reasons for choosing it, and prior experiences with the book or other versions of the story. The teacher then invited the children to read the book chorally with her, allowing her voice to fade whenever possible. They preferred to read the entire text the first time with few interruptions. Although the children enjoyed short, spontaneous comments that either the teacher or a child made in response to the literature, long discussions were often interrupted with, "Let's get back to the reading." After the choral reading, group members shared their favorite parts, compared characters in the book with people they knew, raised questions they wanted to ask the author or other group members about the text, and compared their current LSG selection with other books they had read.

As a way of helping them return to the text to consider it from a different perspective, Andre asked the children to complete literature projects. Before leaving the reading table on Tuesday, the children would choose a project that involved reading the book again. Popular choices included writing a child's own version of the book, doing an audiotape for the listening center, making a poster or bookmark to advertise the book, and preparing to read the book to another class. While members of the first group worked on their project during independent study time, Andre called the next group. On Thursday mornings the groups shared projects, reread favorite parts of the selection, and discussed topics of interest.

The Teacher's Role

As the strategy developed over the course of the school year, Andre gained skill in helping the children communicate their responses to the literature. In September, although she realized that her role was to be a catalyst, she was frustrated to find herself taking a directive stance. For example, she would set the purpose for reading ("Read the page that tells . . ."), ask detailed, factual questions ("From the title, what kind of a seed is it?"), and assign projects ("Write about what you would do with an enormous carrot"). The so-called discussions were very similar to directed reading lessons.

During the first few months she learned that her own honest comments about the literature stimulated the children's comments. She also learned to encourage dialogue with open questions: "Why did you choose this book?" "Does this book remind you of anyone you know?" "Would you like to share something with us?" Although she was prepared with discussion ideas, she often waited for other group members to begin. By midyear a child often initiated group conversation.

Children's Concepts of Themselves as Readers

The children's responses to the LSG selections were enthusiastic throughout the year. In September a child remarked, "I love this book; I can read it." In May another child echoed the same sentiment, while a third child commented from a more sophisticated perspective, "This is good writing."

The children's confidence in themselves as readers was also evident throughout the year. On the first day of the strategy, Mark asked the teacher, "How many times can I read this book?" He smiled broadly when she answered, "As many times as you want." A month later as his group discussed *The Teeny Tiny Woman,* Mark commented, "Don't you think I'm a good reader? Here, I'll show you."

Predictable language patterns helped to support the young readers. In October Jan explained that she loved *It Didn't Frighten Me* because she could read it. A week later John explained why he chose to read the book again: "It has easy words like 'One pitch black very dark night.' Those are easy words." Many children continued to appreciate predictable texts throughout the year. In early May Lisa remarked about *The Gingerbread Man,* "This is easy, like a rhyme book; there's a pattern."

Reading is both a personal and a social experience; the children valued the support that reading with a friend offered. In early June Lisa commented about *Miss Nelson Is Missing,* "I've been reading with Ellen and I'm getting to know how to read this book as I get farther along in it." Carrie countered, "Well, I'm not." Lisa reassured her, "Get Ellen to read with you and just keep practicing. Don't pout about it. I've pouted before and it doesn't help. Get Ellen and just keep reading. You'll get it."

Demonstrations of Engagement

A primary reason for developing this strategy is to find ways to help children become engaged with literature or to have, in Louise Rosenblatt's terms, a "lived through experience" and then to share the ways that the literature touched them. As we looked at the children's responses throughout the year, they fell into seven categories.

Noticing Illustrations

The children carefully observed the illustrations in the books they read. They noted details and sometimes took issue with an illustrator. On the first day of the LSG strategy, several children examined the illustrations in *I Know an Old Lady.* Andre asked them what made the lady look old, and they answered that it was the lines in her face. The children also noticed that, as the lady in the story ate various animals, her face and body became rounder and the lines in her face disappeared. Bryce commented about the change, "Hey, she looks younger and younger and younger."

In October Mark disagreed with the illustrator of *The Carrot Seed* about the drawing of a very large carrot top. He said, "That carrot wouldn't really grow so fast. It's gigantic. It would really only be a little rumbling. It wouldn't come up so fast."

In January several children noticed various characteristics of the illustrations in *The Very Hungry Caterpillar.* Mark asked why the caterpillar ate the book. Mandy replied with a smile, "Because he's a bookworm." The teacher then asked why they thought Eric Carle chose to make the pictures with a hole in the fruit. Jan answered, "I don't know, but I think it's good picturing." Lisa added, "And they make a pattern — one orange, two pears, three plums, four strawberries, five oranges." Mark chose the book again the following week and noticed that the hole in the lollipop went right through the stick.

Several children commented repeatedly that they liked the illustrations to match the text. In late April when Mandy received a copy of *Make Way for Ducklings,* she commented, "I'm going to flip through this book because I haven't read it and see if the illustrations fit. Oh, here's the best illustration. It has the most details." Patrick offered his critique of *The Tortoise and the Hare:* "I like the illustrations better than the words. This would make a good wordless book."

Making Connections between Books

By early winter the children regularly linked the book they were reading with others they knew. While reading *No Baths for Tabitha,* Carrie said, "I saw this dog in *My Icky Picky Sister.*" This comment precipitated a comparison of the illustrations and a search for the illustrator's name. They were pleased to validate their hypothesis: Don Robison was listed as the illustrator on the front cover of both books.

The children were also able to observe more abstract similarities among books. During that same discussion period, Ellen noticed another similarity between *My Icky Picky Sister* and *No Baths for Tabitha,* this time involving the plot structure. The teacher reminded the children that, before they read *No Baths for Tabitha,* they predicted that Tabitha would not take a bath. After they finished the book, she asked them if they were right. Laura replied, "Not exactly; she did at the end." Ellen explained that *No Baths for Tabitha* was like *My Icky Picky Sister* because the girl in each book had changed by the end.

In February Mandy compared the type of characters in two books. *The Little Red Hen* reminded her of a book she had at home, *A Treeful of Pigs,* because both books contained lazy characters. When Andre introduced *Henny Penny* in the spring, she mentioned that the book was written by Paul Galdone, the author of several other books the children had read. Jan quickly added, "Yes, *The Three Little Pigs, The Little Red Hen,* and *The Three Bears.*"

Using References

For the literature projects, the children frequently had to consult reference materials for additional information. When Laura wanted more information about dogs for a book she was writing that was patterned after *All Kinds of Cats,* she knew to look in the encyclopedia. She also remembered that *Animal Babies,* which she had read more than two months earlier, contained information about dogs. Other children who were looking up information about cats decided to consult Tomie de Paola's *The Kid's Cat Book,* which the teacher had read to them earlier in the week.

Connecting Life Experiences with Literature

Links between the children's lives and the literature they read were numerous. When asked to write about something that *Ten Little Bears* called to mind, Ellen chose the picture of the bear flying in an airplane. It reminded her of a sad parting with her aunt when Ellen's family left Africa to come to the United States.

T.J. chose *Kangaroo Stew* three times in January. He said that he liked the part where the kangaroo went "poof" and jumped out of the container. It reminded him of the time his mother's cake went "poof" and set off the fire alarm.

For their science program, the children observed various animals in the classroom, among them cabbage moths, leopard frogs, and box turtles. They compared the moths with the butterfly in *The Very Hungry Caterpillar,* the leopard frogs with the frog in *Frog Went A-Courting,* and the box turtles with the tortoise in *The Tortoise and the Hare.*

Noticing Patterns

The children began to notice various patterns in the literature on the first day of the strategy. They commented that the lady in *I Know an Old Lady* ate larger and larger animals. As the year progressed, they continued to demonstrate their ability to identify patterns. Mark commented that the illustrations in *Goodnight, Moon* alternated between black and white and full color.

Several children noticed that on each page of *The Bus Ride* an additional character boarded the bus. Mandy noticed the inverse of that pattern in *Ten Little Bears*. As the number of bears remaining at home diminished, she commented, "They keep subtracting bears."

Ellen noted that the soldier in *Stone Soup* kept sending the woman to find more ingredients. When the teacher commented that Ellen had noticed a pattern, the child quickly replied, "Yes, and I know two more. They keep repeating all the food and the woman keeps saying, 'Fancy that!' "

Noticing Print Conventions

Early in the year the children began attending to the conventions of print in the literature. Mark asked why there were three marks on the last page of *My Icky Picky Sister* where the text says, "She liked it!!!" When the teacher asked him what he thought, he suggested that it was a mistake. She then told him about the careful editing process through which books go before they are published. Laura explained that the marks meant the author was saying something unusual, and Andre introduced the term *exclamation point* in a meaningful context.

The last two examples demonstrate the children's thought processes in connection with print conventions. Henry asked why the title of the book was *The Lion's Tail* when the story had only one lion. Later he asked why the title of another book was *The Tale of Peter Rabbit* when the story was not about Peter's tail.

Making Inferences

The children revealed their abilities to notice discrepant details, hypotheses, and make inferences at several levels of sophistication. Noticing the illustration of the dog dreaming of a bone in *The Little Red Hen*, Mark asked why a dog would dream of a bone with a flea on it. That same week in March Mandy noticed that in *Corduroy* the order of the toys on the shelf varies from page to page. The children suggested that maybe the saleslady had rearranged them.

A month later Gina asked Mandy which duck was the mother in *Make Way for Ducklings*. When Mandy pointed to one, Gina asked her how she knew. Mandy replied, "Look at her in this illustration where it says it's the mother. This illustration looks the same, so it's the mother." The last week in May Mark explained that he liked the illustration of the spitballs on the ceiling in *Miss Nelson Is Missing* because it showed how bad the kids were.

Other inferences were drawn from the text. After the group read the sentence "Who's been here while I've been gone?" in *Frog Went A-Courting*, Patrick commented, "He sounds bossy, doesn't he?" When the children discussed *The Gingerbread Man,* Carrie commented, "I wouldn't want to eat that gingerbread boy. His feet would be dirty from all that running."

The Importance of Choice

The children's joy in choosing the books they read and their ease in explaining the reasons for their choices continually confirmed our belief in the importance of choice. We often heard them say, "Oh, good. I got my first choice." In March and in May the children were asked to choose three books that should be included as LSG selections the following year and to explain the reasons for their choices. In the books they chose, the children enjoyed the following elements:

1. The illustrations such as the bowls on the Christmas tree in *Chicken Soup with Rice,* the real holes in *The Very Hungry Caterpillar,* the animals in Henny Penny
2. The patterned language such as the phrases in *My Icky Picky Sister,* the song in *Frog Went A-Courting,* "Goodnight" in every sentence of *Goodnight, Moon*
3. The rhyme in *"I Can't," Said the Ant, Over in the Meadow,* and *The Three Billy Goats Gruff*
4. The humor in *Caps for Sale, No Baths for Tabitha,* and *What Do You Do with a Kangaroo?*
5. The plot, for example, the way the little pig outsmarted the wolf in *The Three Little Pigs* and the way the boy was not frightened by imaginary animals in *It Didn't Frighten Me* but was afraid of the real owl at the end of the book
6. The learning opportunities provided by such concept books as *Animal Babies* and *All Kinds of Cats*
7. The familiarity of books that had previously been read at home or at school. Every child chose at least one book for a second time as an LSG book.

By spring the children were choosing books for three additional reasons: recommendations from other children, books by a known author, and alternative versions of a familiar story.

Conclusions

We have learned that young children can indeed respond critically to literature. Their responses indicated greater intensity of emotion and depth of thought than we had anticipàted. First graders were able to express their opinions and to have them accepted; they often took issue with an author, a publisher, or a member of the group. They compared plots, linked story themes and characters to their lives, noted details and patterns, offered hypotheses, and made inferences. Their responses, which grew more explicit and varied over the course of the year, indicated that they were internalizing the literature in a myriad of ways.

Our work with literature study groups continues, for the strategy is ever evolving; it is meant to vary each year with each teacher and each group of children. A teacher who plans to use literature study groups must choose books based on the interests and needs of the particular children involved. The following favorites of Andre's children are therefore only suggestions:

> Henry Allard and James Marshall: *Miss Nelson Is Back; Miss Nelson Is Missing!*
>
> Nina Barbaresi: *Frog Went A-Courting*
>
> Norman Bridwell: *Kangaroo Stew*
>
> Margaret Wise Brown: *Goodnight, Moon*
>
> Polly Cameron: *"I Can't," Said the Ant*
>
> Eric Carle: *The Very Hungry Caterpillar*
>
> Don Freeman: *Corduroy*
>
> Paul Galdone: *The Little Red Hen; The Three Little Pigs*
>
> Janet L. Goss and Jerome C. Harste: *It Didn't Frighten Me*
>
> Beth Hazel and Jerome Harste: *My Icky Picky Sister*
>
> Maurice Sendak: *Chicken Soup with Rice*
>
> Sharon K. Thomas and Marjorie Siegel: *No Baths for Tabitha*
>
> Margot Zemach: *The Teeny Tiny Woman*

References

Allard, Henry, and James Marshall. 1982. *Miss Nelson Is Back.* Boston: Houghton Mifflin.

———. 1977. *Miss Nelson Is Missing!* Boston: Houghton Mifflin.

Barbaresi, Nina. 1985. *Frog Went A-Courting.* New York: Scholastic.

Blair, Susan. 1963. *The Three Billy Goats Gruff.* New York: Scholastic. (Currently out of print, but other versions are available.)

Bonne, Rose. 1961. *I Know an Old Lady.* New York: Scholastic. (Currently out of print, but other versions are available.)

Bridwell, Norman. 1979. *Kangaroo Stew.* New York: Scholastic.

Brown, Margaret. 1977. *Goodnight, Moon.* New York: Harper Junior Books.

Burke, Carolyn L., and Jerome C. Harste. 1983. *All Kinds of Cats.* Worthington, Ohio: School Book Fairs. (Currently out of print.)

The Bus Ride. 1976. Illus. Justin Wager. In *Reading Unlimited* (basal reader). Scott, Foresman Systems Revised Level 2. Glenview, Ill.: Scott, Foresman.

Cameron, Polly. 1961. *"I Can't," Said the Ant.* New York: Scholastic. (Currently out of print.)

Carle, Eric. *The Very Hungry Caterpillar.* 1981. New York: Putnam Publishing Group.

de Paola, Tomie. 1984. *The Kid's Cat Book.* New York: Holiday House.

Freeman, Don. 1968. *Corduroy.* New York: Viking.

Galdone, Paul. 1968. *Henny Penny.* New York: Clarion Books.

———. 1973. *The Little Red Hen.* New York: Clarion Books.

———. 1973. *The Three Bears.* New York: Scholastic.

———. 1984. *The Three Little Pigs.* New York: Clarion Books.

Goss, Janet L., and Jerome C. Harste. 1985. *It Didn't Frighten Me.* Illus. Steve Rommey. Worthington, Ohio: Willowisp Press.

Harste, Jerome C., and Carolyn L. Burke. 1982. *Animal Babies.* Worthington, Ohio: School Book Fairs. (Currently out of print.)

Hazel, Beth, and Jerome C. Harste. 1982. *My Icky Picky Sister.* Illus. Don Robison. Worthington, Ohio: Willowisp Press. (Currently out of print.)

Krauss, Ruth. 1945. *The Carrot Seed.* Illus. Crockett Johnson. New York: Harper Junior Books.

The Lion's Tail. 1976. Illus. Joe Szeghy. In *Reading Unlimited* (basal reader). Scott, Foresman Systems Revised Level 2. Glenview, Ill.: Scott Foresman.

Lobel, Arnold. 1979. *A Treeful of Pigs.* New York: Greenwillow Books.

Mayer, Mercer. 1975. *What Do You Do with a Kangaroo?* New York: Scholastic.

McCloskey, Robert. 1976. *Make Way for Ducklings.* New York: Puffin (imprint of Penguin Books).

McGovern, Ann. 1986. *Stone Soup.* Illus. Winslow P. Pels. New York: Scholastic.

Potter, Beatrix. 1986. *The Tale of Peter Rabbit.* Illus. David McPhail. New York: Scholastic.

Ruwe, Mike. 1976. *Ten Little Bears.* Illus. Dezso Csanady. In *Reading Unlimited* (basal reader). Scott, Foresman Systems Revised Level 2. Glenview, Ill.: Scott, Foresman.

Schmidt, Karen. 1985. *The Gingerbread Man.* New York: Scholastic.

Sendak, Maurice. 1986. *Chicken Soup with Rice.* New York: Scholastic.

Slobodkina, Esphyr. 1984. *Caps for Sale.* New York: Blue Ribbon (imprint of Scholastic).

Stevens, Janet. 1984. *The Tortoise and the Hare: An Aesop Fable.* New York: Holiday House.

Thomas, Sharon K., and Marjorie Siegel. 1985. *No Baths for Tabitha.* Illus. Don Robison. Worthington, Ohio: Willowisp Press.

Wadsworth, Olive A. 1985. *Over in the Meadow.* Illus. Ezra J. Kents. New York: Scholastic.

Zemach, Margot. 1965. *The Teeny Tiny Woman.* New York: Scholastic. (Currently out of print, but other versions are available.)

II Texts:
Interpretive Approaches
to Literature

7 "My Kinsman, Major Molineux": Some Interpretive and Critical Probes

Eugene K. Garber
State University of New York at Albany

We teachers of literature at every level, kindergarten through college, are working in an exciting time. Our discipline is experiencing a wonderfully yeasty period of theoretical debate and pedagogical experimentation. To be sure, our teaching will always derive primarily from intuition and experience as manifested in the rich lore of the staff room and the wider community of teachers of literature. That's because we are a pragmatic lot. Anything that does not help us teach the students who appear in our classrooms is consigned to the airy fabrications of the hermeneut's imagination. It follows that we do not think of ourselves as theoreticians, exegetes, or critics. But in fact current theory and research are challenging the old notions of how we read, how we interpret, and how we evaluate literature. A number of teachers have put current scholarship to work to achieve rich and rewarding innovations in their teaching of literature. So now, as at no time since the insurgence of the New Critics in the 1940s, theory and research and pedagogy are engaged in a dynamic dialogue that is creating new opportunities for us and our students.

The essay that follows is not primarily about the teaching of literature. It is a modest demonstration of some ways to apply interpretation and criticism and is meant to serve as a prologue to more specific discussions of pedagogy. Among the first questions our students ask are these: What does the story mean? What is its significance and value for me? I suspect that it is a rare teacher who embarks on the teaching of a work without having in mind some array of interpretive and evaluative possibilities, however fractional and tentative. So here is an essay about Hawthorne's "My Kinsman, Major Molineux." It is not, let me hasten to note, a pedagogical paradigm, a set of analytical strategies, all of which must be explored in the successful teaching of a text. Many of the probes here may be unconvincing to some readers. In any case, as we teachers know all too well, we always select literary texts for the particular students we have. Our teaching can never be exhaustive. I discuss this matter a bit more fully later in the essay, but for now let us put aside the difficulties that inevitably attend our teaching and plunge into Hawthorne's wondrously rich and imaginative story.

Summary of the Story

In case you do not have the outline of "My Kinsman, Major Molineux" firmly in memory, let me rehearse it here. Some time about 1730, Robin, a New England lad of almost eighteen, travels several days from his country home to Boston, where he hopes to find employment and good fortune under the auspices of a well-placed relative, Major Molineux, who is a second cousin on his father's side. Arriving just at nightfall, Robin takes a ferry across the river to the city. Here he inquires unsuccessfully about his kinsman's whereabouts. First, a well-dressed elderly gentleman not only refuses Robin the information, but threatens him with the stocks. In a tavern his inquiry is again rebuffed, this time by the innkeeper, who accuses him of being a runaway indentured servant. Presently Robin wanders into a dubious district where a young woman in a red petticoat invites him into a house that she claims is the Major's dwelling. The intervention of a nightwatchman and Robin's sometimes wavering conscience enable him to resist this temptation.

Back on a more favorable street, Robin demands of a muffled stranger information about his kinsman's whereabouts, only to discover that the stranger has the shaggy brows and fiery eyes of a figure he had encountered at the inn. The stranger tells Robin to stay where he is and the Major will come by within the hour. To pass the time Robin surveys the facade of an impressive house, looks in a church window, and imagines his family at evening prayer. At this point a well-favored stranger pauses, listens in friendly fashion to Robin's story, and offers to await with Robin the coming of his kinsman.

Not long after, a wild parade of rebellious colonials passes. The figure with shaggy brows and fiery eyes is on a horse, and the Major, tarred and feathered, is drawn in an open cart. Seized at first by pity and terror, Robin quickly experiences a strange excitement that leads him to burst forth with a shout of laughter. When the parade has passed, Robin asks the kindly stranger for directions back to the ferry, but the stranger urges him to stay in town and see if he cannot make his way without the aid of his kinsman.

This is of course merely the bare bones of the plot. The story is brilliantly detailed, complex in tone, and suffused with an almost hypnotic ambience of mystery and ambiguity. We will try to bring out this richness in substance and texture in the explorations that follow.

Structure

Perhaps the most useful first step is to identify the basic building blocks that undergird the plot and reveal patterns beneath the familiar narrative of quest with its series of frustrations followed by fulfillment, though the fulfillment in this case is surprising and uncertain. One way to do this is to identify the oppositional pairs that structuralists have found so useful in clarifying the meanings of literature. Here are some pairs that impress themselves forcibly on the reader:

The repressive rule of the King of England versus the colonists' desire for freedom

Country piety versus city worldliness

The quiet sanctity of the church versus the riotous throng of colonists

The romantic illumination of the moon versus the blinding garishness or inadequacy of various artificial lamps and flambeaux

The fine streets and resplendent mansions of the city versus its crooked ways and dubious houses

Robin's simple rural clothing and crude country cudgel versus the wigs, finery, and swords and canes of the city folk

The divided face, red side versus black side, of the leader of the mob

Robin's alleged shrewdness versus his naivete

The constant use of Robin's country name versus the Frenchified and highfalutin name of Molineux

Robin's respectful eagerness to find his eminent kinsman versus his irrepressible pleasure at finding him in utter disgrace

There are other polarities as well, but these will suffice to illustrate that the story is built on a series of sharp conflicts that can almost be summed up as innocence versus experience, or simplicity versus ambiguity.

Robin is at first identified with the first set of terms, innocence and simplicity. His adventures in the city constitute a series of sharp encounters with the second set of terms, experience and ambiguity. Such encounters are a frequent theme in Hawthorne. The question is, put simply, whether the protagonist will recoil from the encounter with ambiguity, become obsessed with it, or find a middle way. Giovanni in "Rappaccini's Daughter" never successfully confronts evil or ambiguity, and young Goodman Brown is obsessed with the dark doings, real or imaginary, that he encounters in the midnight forest. Robin, on the other hand, seems to be one of those fortunate characters who discovers the middle way between regressing childishly (by fleeing back home after witnessing the disgrace of his kinsman) and abandoning himself to the dark and demonic (by joining the riotous persecutors of his would-be benefactor).

If Robin does find the middle way between sets of opposites, how does he do so? We must partly credit some inherent balance among the dichotomous elements themselves. Those who rebuff Robin's efforts to find his kinsman have sufficient forbearance not to subject him to extreme ridicule or persecution; the tavern contains bucolic reminders as well as "Nicotian" and spirituous influences; the temptress and the watchman appear in tandem; and so forth.

Similarly, the discovery of the middle ground must be credited in part to Robin's own balance of mind. Though his equanimity is certainly threatened and though he is constantly mystified and tugged this way and that, he possesses a genuine element of New England shrewdness and prudence that prevents him from lurching in one direction or the other. And then, of course, the kindly stranger's moderating aloofness and good counsel virtually personify the wisdom of the middle way. In structuralist terms we may interpret the story as the mediation of polarities. But to do so exhaustively would involve us in an array of contrarieties whose complexity I have only suggested.

History

Let us turn now to matters of historical context and historical encoding. The opening paragraph of the story sets forth the prerevolutionary setting and suggests that the story will deal with an "inflammation of the popular mind." Thus we understand that Major Molineux is brutalized because people are dissatisfied with the king's interference in colonial matters and that their acts presage the Revolutionary War. That much seems relatively simple. The matter of historical perspective complicates things, however. We can identify three sets of attitudes: those of the colonists in about 1730, as Hawthorne reports them to us; those of Hawthorne himself, the nineteenth century American Romantic who held to a curious mixture of political liberalism and psychological conservatism; and those of the contemporary reader — in my case a rather traditional American who tends to view the American Revolution as a more or less heroic act of conscience and of self-liberation. The intermingled presences of these several "horizons," to use a term in currency with a number of theorists, help explain the unsettling portrayal of the prerevolutionary throng and also the complex tone the narrator uses to describe its acts.

Obviously we do not have here simply an admirable band of self-disciplined and purposeful patriots initiating a process of self-liberation. If our sympathies lie with the colonists, it probably is in spite of certain aspects of their behavior and because we disapprove of colonialism and foreign rule and also, quite frankly, because we are American readers who have accepted a favorable interpretation of the Revolution. But Hawthorne insists that we confront the unruly mob, as well as its barbarous cruelty. Three times we encounter the ferocity and the demonism of its leader, and by the end of the story we are aware that the tarring and feathering of Major Molineux is the fruition of a carefully conceived and guarded conspiracy.

Well, some will say, revolutions do not get their business done politely, for only violence will dislodge tyrants and their agents. Historical accounts of revolutionary times certainly describe all too vividly not only campaigns against the British, but also the treatment of American Tories who favored loyalty to the crown. Still, it seems unlikely that Hawthorne intended to present here a revisionist interpretation of the American Revolution along arch-conservative lines. Some kinds of liberalism he found naive and fatuous. But he was no reactionary. What he does in writing this story, at least in my case, is to complicate my view of the rebellious colonists and the acts they perpetrated on their own countrymen. We may surmise that the conspirators considered their acts entirely justified. We may further suspect that the citizenry who were not in on the conspiracy, and who were therefore awakened in alarm by the parade of rebels, came to share this conviction, though the story does not say so. What we are hardly free to do is entertain a vision of simple revolutionary heroism. The necessary mingling of colonial perspectives, Hawthorne's perspective, and our own contemporary horizons militates against any simple historical view.

We see, then, that the relationship between literature and history is a complex one. Sometimes we tend to think of literature as merely incorporating historical materials or merely reflecting, as a mirror reflects, its historical contexts. But literature is much more active than that. With or without conscious ideological intent, it inevitably interprets history, providing perspectives that challenge our own contemporary horizons. If the study of the literature of the past truly liberates, it does so less by showing us where we came from than by inviting us to interpret and reinterpret our origins.

Myth

Many readers will remark immediately that this is a very old archetypal story — the story of the young hero whose quest for personal, religious, or cultural identity necessarily leads him down into the underworld. There, depending on the version of the myth, the hero will encounter threatening monsters and demons on the one hand and, on the other, helpful guides and tutelary figures who may include ancestors. Why must the young hero descend to the underworld? Dangerous as it is to rationalize myth, we can speculate that the hero must encounter the darkness in the world, which is in the very nature of things, and also the darkness in his own psyche. Robin's entry into the underworld across a dark river by ferry will be familiar to readers of classical epic — *The Odyssey* and *The Aeneid* — as well as Dante's *Divine Comedy*. Mythical examples could be multiplied: Orpheus, Isis.

Equally familiar will be the demonic figure that Robin encounters and by whom he is so fascinated and compelled — the cloaked and muffled personage whose forehead bulges into a double prominence (like the incipient horns of a devil or a satyr), whose eyes burn with fire, whose nose is hooked, and whose face is divided between red and black "as if two individual devils, a fiend of fire and a fiend of darkness, had united themselves to form this infernal visage." This demonic figure and his co-conspirators are consistently interposed between Robin and his mission of finding his kinsman Major Molineux.

Nor does Robin have any talismanic object with which to counter these threatening and frustrating figures. Virtually all of his meagre patrimony ("a little province bill of five shillings" and "a sexangular piece of parchment, valued at three pence") is expended in paying the ferryman. His crude country cudgel proves no match for the polished cane of the old gentleman who first rebuffs him, or for the watchman's pike, or for the drawn sword of the leader of the rebellious throng. Where, then, or with whom will Robin find aid and guidance for his perilous quest in the underworld? The kindly stranger, though late-appearing, serves as the mentor, the tutelary figure who helps

Robin persevere in confronting the problematic events of the nighttime city. It is he who urges Robin not to turn aside from his mission, not to return home in defeat.

In mythical terms, what is the treasure or boon that Robin seeks and must acquire to succeed? Obviously Robin seeks an ancestral figure, his kinsman Major Molineux, who possesses — or so Robin and his family think — influence and power. But of course when Robin finally meets him, the Major is not only dispossessed of his powers, but is the subject of disgrace and ridicule. What, then, could be the bequest of the ancestral figure? Beware sycophancy to alien rulers? Or, conversely, beware the excesses of rebelliousness? Both perhaps, paradoxically. If we are to judge by Robin's lusty laughter, followed by his statement that his kinsman will scarcely want to see him again, we can with reason surmise that Robin has experienced, if not entirely understood, the ambiguity of the ancestral message. Unlike Aeneas, he will not ascend from the underworld to found the mother city of a great empire, but he probably will stay in town and "rise in the world," just as the kindly stranger suggests.

But perhaps we ought to focus less on the boon of public or political understanding and more on the personal gains that Robin is making when we last see him. He is learning that society is a complex entity sometimes divided against itself. He is learning that his own psyche is also a complex entity sometimes divided against itself. He is taking leave of his childhood, perhaps already prolonged by the close and pious nature of his family. He is entering manhood. There is fair prospect that he will mature into self-reliance, that cardinal virtue traditionally identified with our national character.

The Unconscious

Since we have been thinking about Robin's psychic growth, let us continue along that line for a while, but in different terms. Few readers will be surprised by the suggestion that Robin is at best only dimly aware of unconscious forces, motives we might even call them, at work in his psyche. *Shrewd* is Robin's constant epithet, but a shrewd and cunning youth in search of a prominent kinsman should not forget to ask the ferryman his cousin's whereabouts. Nor should a shrewd youth look for his eminent kinsman's domicile down crooked streets in dark and dubious districts of the city. We could point out again that a conspiracy is afoot and that Robin is not in on it, and we could claim that this is what defeats his shrewdness as he searches for his cousin. But we should consider here the possibility that there is a conspiracy, so to speak, in Robin's head. Consciously he is a dutiful son wearing his father's hat, seeking his father's surrogate in the city. Unconsciously he is rebelling against his father, seeking the illicit pleasures of the city among taverners and prostitutes. This possibility of Robin's divided mind will help explain his partly self-deceptive dealings with the young woman in the red petticoat and his antipathy toward the nightwatchman, a personification of law and order (though this identification proves somewhat illusory when the watchman appears near the end of the story, joining in the merriment of the riotous throng).

The conflict between the conscious and the unconscious can also help explain why Robin is more fascinated than repelled by the demonic figure he encounters three times. It can illuminate the repetitious appearance of Robin's cudgel, which we now see not only as an index of his rural origins, but also as an instrument of potential aggression against those who would hobble his freedom and as an emblem of sexual exploration. In this light, the polished cane of the virtually ubiquitous old gentleman and the watchman's pike are contrary agencies of adult authority and experience. The silver-hilted swords of the gallant young gentlemen trodding jauntily along the fashionable street represent a worldliness and sophistication that are quite beyond Robin at this stage of his development.

Postulating antagonistic forces within Robin's psyche will also illuminate two key incidents in the story. In one, Robin returns in fantasy to his home, where his father performs the office of domestic worship under the huge tree. By means of this fantasy, Robin rejects his rebelliousness and returns, prodigal son, to the bosom of his family. But something interposes itself between this motion toward return and its effect, something more than the literal fact of physical distance. In his fantasy Robin does not appear among his family. Indeed, his absence is a matter of central concern, grieved by mother, father, and siblings. When Robin might, by a strenuous act of imagination, have projected himself back among them, he sees instead the family going in at the door, hears the latch fall in place behind them, and understands the "he was excluded from his home." For better or worse, Robin's rebelliousness has removed him forever from his family. You can't go home again. That is part of the kindly stranger's message, which leads us to consider again the story's final scene.

The visionary parade of rebels comes down the street "as if a dream had broken forth from some feverish brain. . . ." And there is the Major, tarred and feathered. His eyes meet Robin's. The two kinsmen recognize each other instantly. Robin experiences Aristotle's pity and terror, but not the catharsis and return to equanimity that Aristotle postulated for the audiences of classical tragedy. On the contrary, after pity and terror Robin experiences "a sort of mental inebriety," followed shortly by the contagious influence of the mob and eventuating in his loud shout of laughter. During this rapid chain of external and psychological events, rebelliousness has clearly triumphed over the dutiful intentions of the shrewd youth. Moments later he is chastised by what he takes to be a perpetual separation from his kinsman. But there is no turning back, counsels the kindly stranger. The Oedipal conflict is inevitable if the young man is to assert his own identity, sexual and otherwise, against those who would have him remain a child.

A Consummate Text?

Although some of our interpretive probes so far may be more convincing than others, readers will probably agree that all of these explorations have been interpretive rather than critical. That is, they have focused on explicating the meaning in the story rather than on evaluating its significance. And they have not, at least in any obvious way, been contradictory. Seeing the story as a structure of contrarieties among which Robin seeks a set of median terms is consonant with seeing the story as historically contextualized and as encoding a set of conflicting or ambiguous historical attitudes and evaluations. Nor does either interpretation disturb in any essential way the view of the story as a retelling of the ancient and familiar myth of the hero's descent into the underworld. And finally, the psychological view of the story as a contest between certain conscious and unconscious motivations can also be harmonized.

At the center of all of these interpretations is postulated a similar conflict that Robin must experience and try to resolve: innocence and simplicity versus experience and ambiguity, political freedom versus the sometimes devious means and cruel excesses of revolution, the heroic quest for knowledge and identity versus the opposition of demonic and infernal agents, and the struggles of reason and ego to assert themselves against the oppression of the father and the undisciplined propensities of aggression and sex.

We can go on to claim that the *meaning* of the story is really the same in each of these readings. Only the terms of the interpretations have changed. Such a claim posits that this text (and by extension all successful literary texts) has a purpose, an organic wholeness, and a fixed center of meaning which it is the business of interpretation of any kind to locate and illuminate. Such a view of the integrity of literary texts is reassuring and perhaps even noble, but it is limiting. Consequently, like Robin we must question our own endeavors. We must confront the conflict between the concept of the text as consummate and knowable and the concept of the text as open and even self-conflicted.

Economics

We might, then, begin our interrogation by way of ideology. We could say that what the story acknowledges itself to be about is scarcely more important than the unconscious assumptions it makes. And if it be objected that Hawthorne was an eminently self-conscious and shrewd writer who knew exactly what he was doing, we will rejoin that ideology is by its very nature largely unconscious. In fact, the business of ideology is to make its tenets seem natural and inevitable rather than stipulated or arbitrary. In any case, let us turn our attention to the economics of the story, setting aside the question of how conscious Hawthorne was of this stratum of potential meaning.

We begin by noting that Robin must pay extra to cross the river at night. The ferryman charges what the traffic will bear and discounts Robin's provincial currency at that, leaving him without enough money to buy himself a meal at the inn. What Robin hopes to trade on in general is the Major's name and influence. Let us focus for a moment on the scene at the inn. Here we encounter mariners, craftsmen, and shepherds, each in the process of exchanging the fruits of his labor for food, spirits, or tobacco. The rudiments of international trade (rum comes from the West Indies) and of a market economy are found here, crude as they may be. In such an economy virtually everything is a commodity — name, class, position, influence, and sex, as well as the more obvious "gorgeous display of goods in the shop-windows" on the spacious, lamp-lit street frequented by the affluent. Already in prerevolutionary Boston, we have advertising and conspicuous consumption. Remember the "embroidered garments of showy colors, enormous periwigs, gold-laced hats, and silver-hilted swords" sported by the well-traveled gallants.

What, then, are the real motives of this night's conspiracy and the incipient larger revolution of which it is a part? Ideals of political independence and individual liberty and rights? Or freedom from the economic strictures and depredations of the crown? Commentators have noted that, though historical references locate the action of the story in about 1730, the behavior and attitudes represented evoke the protests of the 1760s against the Sugar Act, the Stamp Act, and the Townshend Acts. Hawthorne has in effect telescoped several decades of colonial disturbances and in doing so has put the economic motives of the Revolution into the foreground.

Obviously we are now moving from interpretation to criticism. We are suggesting that the story contains ideological crosscurrents that are working against its manifest meanings. What might be thought of as a revolution of almost demonic proportions, a radical rearrangement of the social order, is really little more than a home-rule appropriation of political and economic power that leaves essentially intact a structure of class, wealth, and privilege. What might be seen as a story of initiation of profound if not heroic proportions turns out to be little more than a kind of insipid Horatio Alger story. Stripped of the advantages of the Major's name and position. Robin must make it on his own. After all, the capitalist myth holds that the deserving, despite minor corruptions, finally get rich. Individual readers will judge the relative truth and falsity of this myth. In any case, we may argue that the kindly stranger presides not so much over the transcendence of dualism, the history of a heroic revolution, the ancestral quest, or the profound drama of psychological conflict as he does over the ratification of the American dream of making it big in the city.

Gender

We can turn now to the matter of gender. If economic aspects of ideology account for subliminal themes that in many ways run counter to the manifest themes of the story, then the gender aspects of ideology are perhaps even more problematic and contrary. Consider. We encounter three classes of women: the seductress of the red petticoat, the good wife and mother who grieves the loss of her son to the city, and several women who run beside the riotous parade sounding "their shrill voices of mirth or terror." There is little to suggest that the experience of women is central to moral and political seriousness, to initiation, to personal or national myth, or to significant psychological conflict. Women here are ancillary or at best necessary agents in the process of male self-realization. Given the massive repetitions of certain male symbols, it is not too harsh to say that the story is phallocentric. Its treatment of woman is epitomized in the following exchange between the kindly gentleman and Robin: "May not a man have several voices, Robin, as well as two complexions?" the gentleman proposes. "Perhaps a man may; but Heaven forbid that a woman should!" Robin rejoins.

Some may counter that the story is about a young man's initiation. Women are central in other stories in which men tend to play subservient roles. Some people will find this argument convincing. But this story is in many ways too big and ambitious for such excuses to be acceptable. It gives an account of the very founding of the nation and dramatizes the creation of an origin myth. It can scarcely afford to belittle women. Never mind the accusatory terms *sexist* and *phallocentric*. Keep the objection simpler and lower keyed: the story's portrayal and therefore its appeal are narrow and clichéd.

What if some argue that Hawthorne was simply being historically accurate, that the role of women was minor? In that case, we find ourselves entangled in very complex questions indeed. Who has construed history so that it portrays the role of women as minor at the time of the Revolution? Would *disenfranchised* or merely *unrecognized* be more accurate terms? Is the role of writers of later ages merely reportorial, interpretive, or reconstructive? What were the gender issues of Hawthorne's time? Were they different from those of the mid-eighteenth century? Which position is Hawthorne reflecting in the story?

Let me point out again that we have shifted from interpretation to criticism. Ideological encodings, whatever they involve — politics, economics, gender — may run counter to more manifest meanings. Texts may be conflicted, even self-contradictory. Our earlier concept of the consummately unified text is called into question.

Deconstruction

Perhaps the textual readings that most seriously disrupt the organic and determinate work are those termed deconstructive. In deconstructive readings, the reality to which the words of the text refer is at issue. We are all aware that the story is a fiction, but we have tried to see it as a fiction representing something actual outside itself, for example, an actual historical process or a psychological struggle.

Let us complicate the matter. At important points, the text questions the status of its own representations. Seated on the steps of the church-door while waiting for the appearance of his illusory kinsman, Robin discovers that the moonlight imparts a strangeness to objects he once thought constant and familiar. "Next he endeavored to define the forms of distant objects, starting away, with almost ghostly indistinctness, just as his eye appeared to grasp them. . . ." Some minutes later he discovers that "the pillars of the balcony lengthened into the tall, bare stems of pines, dwindled down into human figures, settled again into their true shape and size, and then commenced a new succession of changes. For a single moment, when he deemed himself awake, he could have sworn that a visage — one which he seemed to remember, yet could not absolutely name as his kinsman's — was looking towards him from the Gothic window."

At this point, readers may be tempted to say, "All of this illusoriness can be explained by Robin's fatigue and by his ignorance of the plot afoot in the city. We readers, like the omniscient narrator, know what's going on, what's what." And indeed we may be somewhat wiser than the naive Robin. But any claim that we possess the settled reality of the story will ultimately prove to be unfounded. The mysteries of the tale strike deeper than the confusions of a country lad come to town. From the very first, the whole nighttime scene has had an elusive, dreamlike quality about it, just as Robin's quest has been frustrating and baffling from the moment he entered town. In the world of this unsettling story, even light itself does not illuminate. The moon romanticizes, distorts, and transforms. The torches of the rebels are "concealing, by their glare, whatever object they illuminated," forming "a veil he [Robin] could not penetrate."

What creates this profound illusoriness? Is the quest for a steady identity doomed to failure? Most of us American readers, with our insistence that we know who we are, will resist this proposition. Perhaps Robin once thought he knew who he was, but that was in the innocent days of his childhood in the bosom of his family. Now, he can no longer even imagine himself in his home. Where he would be, there among his family, is only an absence. And in fantasizing inconclusively about home, he virtually loses his presence in the city. "Am I here, or there?" he cries out; but he cannot quite ask the deeper question, *Am I at all?* What identity is he to have there in the city? The innkeeper ascribes to him the identity and ridiculous name of Hezekiah Mudge, a runaway indentured servant. The young woman of the red petticoat says that he is the very picture of the Major, but her dealings with him are merrily duplicitous.

We readers see that these identities are chimerical, but what is Robin's real identity? Perhaps if only he could find his kinsman Major Molineux, he would know who he was. But who is *Molineux* (Robin's patronymic by which he is never called)? What is in this name that suggests a mill, ever turning, never steady? The name is a trope, that is, a verbal "turning," a figure of speech that signifies something other than itself and more self-consciously than the "literal" linguistic signs that point toward something other. We are reminded that Robin encounters conspirators who use words in some language that neither he nor we can decode. We are also reminded of the speech of the reappearing old gentleman whose words are always interrupted by the nonsignifying "hem hem."

In short, there is something very problematic in this story about the way names name and words signify. Not only are they massively figurative (tropes) instead of literally true, we even suspect that they do not relate to things outside language at all but only to other words. In these terms, Robin in his quest for an identity is lost in the ultimately referenceless labyrinth of language. He thought he was the shrewd reader of the signs of his own story — as indeed we have at times considered ourselves the shrewd interpreters of Hawthorne's text. But for all of our cunning, we readers are trapped within language, from which there is no exit to the world of real objects.

We see, then, that a deconstructive reading of the story reveals the holes, the contradictions, and the reflexivity that render determinacy of meaning impossible.

Other Interrogations

Deconstruction is only a special, if very important, case of what has come to be known as post-structuralism, a term hard to define but one that embraces, at least in my mind, a fundamentally questioning attitude. Post-structuralist critics tend to question assumptions, values, and ideologies and to interrogate systems, methods, and analyses. They are skeptical. Let us take our cue from the post-structuralists and intensify the questioning attitude we began to put to work in our treatment of economics, gender, and language in the story. Let us see how our structuralist, historical, mythical, and psychological readings stand up under interrogation. In each case we will bring into the foreground only a very few details, question them, and let the process illustrate how a more complete interrogation might proceed.

Let us look again at two structural polarities: the romantic illumination of the moon versus the blinding garishness or the inadequacy of artificial light, and the quiet sanctity of the church versus the riotous throng of colonists. Artificial light in this story tends to be dim or to obfuscate rather than illuminate. But is the moon so clearly associated with a contrary romantic illumination? Often it is, as in the church, but sometimes it is associated without much contrast with artificial light, for example, the ferryman's lantern, the shop-window lamps, and the watchman's lantern. More serious questions involve the way the moonlight transforms, rather than illuminates, the familiar objects that Robin views from the church steps and the way the Man in the Moon comments that the earth is frolicsome. The suggestion that the moon is related to lunacy is more than etymological. Opposing the clarity of the moon to the murkiness of artificial light turns out to be not so neat as we first thought.

The same objection might be raised against the dichotomy between the sanctified church and the riotous throng. According to historical research, the church is very likely the Old South Church in Boston, a bastion of democratic Puritan sentiment. This means that the church does not oppose the political purposes of the throng, though it would no doubt oppose any tendency toward mobocracy. Let us stop here. The point is made. Positing structural oppositions is interpretively useful, but they must be interrogated carefully to show complex qualifications and ambiguities, if not outright contradictions.

At this point, I will not interrogate the historical reading offered above. It has already been questioned, in part by the changes in temporal perspective described and in part by our later consideration of the economic and gender aspects of the story's latent ideology. Further complications are mentioned in the bibliographic postscript below.

When we turn to the mythic reading of the story, described as essentially a rehearsal of the questing hero's descent into the underworld, we find a very interesting complication. Suppose we see the mythic substructure of the story not as quest and descent, but as a ritual sacrifice. What we have in effect is a saturnalia orgiastically celebrating the interregnum, that is, the time between the deposition or murder of the old king and the enthronement of the new. True, Major Molineux is not really the old king. (George II is safely on his throne in England.) But mythographers and anthropologists give us ample evidence of the use of surrogates (animal and human) in sacrificial rites. Major Molineux, one of the king's agents, will certainly do as a substitute for the king. Although he is not actually killed, by being tarred and feathered and ridden out of town, he is effectively stripped of all regal office and dignity. The new king of course has not yet arrived. In a manner of speaking, he is the young American republic just coming into power and is perhaps as well represented by Robin as by anyone. Such a reading can certainly be supported by many details in the story. Can we have both of our mythic readings, quest and sacrifice, or do we have to make a choice? Do contrastive readings tend to undermine all mythic interpretations? Post-structuralist interrogations of texts and interpretations tend to raise exactly these kinds of questions. Before taking the matter up in more general terms, let us briefly question again our psychological reading of the story.

Our earlier reading centered on Robin's profoundly ambivalent feelings toward the Major. In Freudian terms, the ambivalence arises from an essentially Oedipal conflict with the father and consequently with all father surrogates like the Major. We claimed that such a reading can help explain important incidents and symbols in the story and can be convincingly supported. Nevertheless, we could have introduced a different set of psychological terms. Suppose, for instance, that we take our cue from the existential psychology of R. D. Laing and replace the unconscious Oedipal conflict with a more conscious identity crisis. In developing this reading, we would see Robin encountering alien experience, losing his sense of himself and of reality in general, which results in a profound ontological insecurity. In these terms, the story traces Robin's struggle to work his way from an inherited and now useless family identity toward a true existential freedom that will enable him to base his identity soundly on his own growing sense of his integral self.

Similarly, we might work out a reading based on the provocative work of Erik Erikson. Such a reading would probably fall somewhere between Freud and Laing, perhaps more insistent than either on the historical as well as the individual or familial aspects of the psyche. Or we might work from the neo-Freudian concepts of Jacques Lacan, focusing on the ways that the language of the story, the various namings and discourses of identity, either help or hinder Robin in his search for a self and its relationship with significant others. The point is that these psychological possibilities raise the same kinds of questions that the disparate possibilities of alternate myths raised.

Interpretation, Value, and Teaching

It is time to step back, sum up what we have been saying, and speak of our special responsibilities as teachers of students in various stages of development and with a wide variety of needs. First we offered several interpretive perspectives on "My Kinsman, Major Molineux" — structural, historical, mythical, and psychological. Such perspectives, we claimed, could be harmonized to describe a richly layered story of consummate craft and unbroken integrity. But hardly had we arrived at this confident orchestration when we began to undermine it by questioning the economic and gender aspects of the story's latent ideology and by offering certain deconstructive observations of the instability, illusoriness, and self-contradictory tendencies of the text. We even circled back to show that each of our four original, more or less stable readings could be challenged by an alternate set of premises.

At this point, let me postulate two kinds of readers of this essay, each at a different end of the spectrum. One reader will be delighted with the questioning strategies of the latter part, evidence that texts are always open to new interpretations of meaning, to new criticisms, and that all responses are legitimate. The other reader will have much preferred the earlier interpretive probes, feeling that the questioning strategy leads to a lamentable relativism that leaves stories and their interpretations without substance and integrity. Still other readers will occupy various positions on the spectrum between the two extremes.

Let us explore this matter of interpretive disagreement. Why are some treatments of literary works acceptable to and even cherished by some and rejected by others? It is that literary interpretations and criticisms are, in the final analysis, rarely matters of convention internal to literature itself. Rather, they rest on beliefs and values that lie outside literature. Here are some crude yet apposite illustrations of how beliefs, even if provisional, underlie literary analysis. A structuralist reading suggests a belief in inherent structure-seeking (structure-imposing?) elements of mind and may even suggest for some readers an order intrinsic to the very nature of things. Historical readings presuppose history as a knowable process with significant, if not determinative, relationships to literary texts. Archetypal readings posit the existence in culture, mind, or cosmos of recurrent patterns that order human experience and make it meaningful. Psychoanalytic readings rest on a belief in the power of the unconscious, however sharp the disagreements about the content and processes of the unconscious. Ideological readings take as their starting point the conviction that cultures tend to impose upon themselves a paradigm of operative assumptions that are often unconsciously held and are all the more powerful precisely because they are unexamined. Deconstructive readings are based on a belief in the porousness and self-referentiality of language, even though it seems to bring to us "things" outside itself by means of its signs, its pointings. Other readings, whether referred to here or not, can virtually always be driven back to some basic tenets.

This variety, indeed this sharp conflict among interpretations and criticisms of texts, is instructive for us as teachers. It continually reminds us that we are engaging our students in questions that are preeminently value laden. Not even our innocent-seeming discussions of literary terminology, form, and historical setting are free from assumptions about value. An immediate question is therefore this: Which readings of texts and which values will be represented in our classrooms? Our answer may honestly be those we feel most committed to — on the grounds that one teaches well only what one has considerable sympathy with and on the grounds that students will get other views from other teachers. Or we can argue that we are responsible for teaching with as expansive an eclecticism as possible regardless of our own sympathies, for only then will students see how the many facets of texts can be exposed to the illuminating perspectives of various readings. Still another possibility is to put the matter essentially in the hands of our students. What are their own responses, observations, and questions about a given text? What readings do they want and need to explore? Indeed, what readings will they themselves bring to our discussions, readings that we ourselves may not have anticipated? Obviously I cannot adjudicate the matter. Individual teachers and staffs will have to decide about these conflicting values. But practical matters must be considered as well. Let us take a look at those.

Can our students really be expected to work through a virtually exhaustive set of interpretive and critical readings for every text they study? Would they not grow tired of the text in question? How would they acquire the background necessary for a sufficient understanding of the several readings? And what about developmental factors? Are some kinds of readings more accessible than others as students have more complex experiences of life and literature? In other words, is there a curricular decision here about the order of interpretive and critical instruction?

At this point I want to note the importance of reader-response criticism. Some teachers of literature may be thinking that I have placed too much emphasis on the text, that I have failed to acknowledge the important transactive and constructive role of the reader that reader-response critics such as Louise Rosenblatt and Wolfgang Iser describe. Throughout this essay I have tried to give the sense of readers construing texts and, implicitly, that there is no such thing as *the text*. There is always only a reader reading. The act of reading is the act of constructing. If I have failed to suggest the dynamics of literary response, other contributors to this volume will certainly correct me in their fine reports of teachers and students engaged in powerful dialogues with literature.

I would like to close on a paradoxical note of measure and enthusiasm. The movement from richness of theory, interpretation, and criticism to a parallel richness and effectiveness in the teaching of literature is not obvious or easy. But the dialogue between research and practice is vital and powerful. Perhaps I am only saying the obvious: opportunities are always problems and vice versa. This volume, happily, attests to the fact that we teachers of literature are eager to meet the challenge. And that is all to the good.

Bibliographic Postscript

Readers of this synthesizing essay may have wondered why I did not explicitly acknowledge my debts to many critics and commentators in the text. In saving acknowledgment for this bibliographic postscript, I had two motives: to avoid a distracting density of footnotes and to set down in a leisurely and, I hope, inviting manner resources that busy teachers might actually use.

Introductory Works

To begin, then, there are two quite accessible introductions to modern literary theory and criticism: Terry Eagleton's *Literary Theory: An Introduction* (Minneapolis: University of Minnesota Press, 1983) and Ann Jefferson's and David Robey's *Modern Literary Theory: A Comparative Introduction* (London: Batsford Academic and Educational, Ltd., 1982). Both are in paperback, and both are short but reasonably comprehensive. The Eagleton is perhaps the more readable. Witty and trenchant, it is not badly skewed by its Marxist bias. The Jefferson-Robey is more measured and a bit denser. Both provide useful bibliographies for readers who wish to go further.

Theoretical Works

At a second level are the more or less theoretical works that have been particularly useful to me in thinking about "My Kinsman, Major Molineux" and other literary works. First, there is Claude Lévi-Strauss's often anthologized essay on the Oedipus myth, "The Structural Study of Myth," in *Structural Anthropology, Vol. 1* (New York: Basic Books, 1963). It sets forth certain structuralist principles. The much discussed topic of literary history and of the relationships between literary and cultural history has been greatly illuminated for me by Hans Robert Jauss in *Toward an Aesthetic of Reception* (Minneapolis: University of

Minnesota Press, 1982). Both works are dense and complex, but in my judgment the rewards of reading them with care are worth the effort.

Two books on myth are easier going: Joseph Campbell's *The Hero with a Thousand Faces* (New York: Pantheon Books, 1949) and Rene Girard's *Violence and the Sacred* (Baltimore: The Johns Hopkins University Press, 1977). Some readers will find Campbell and Girard strange bedfellows, the former older and in the tradition of such writers as Frazer and Jung, the latter indebted to Lévi-Strauss and certain post-structuralist thinkers. I find the marriage fruitful, however.

So massive is the literature of psychological and explicitly psychoanalytic criticism that virtually any selection of texts will seem arbitrary. Best, then, in this case simply to report what has been personally useful. I always find it fruitful to revisit Freud's essay "The Dream-Work" in *Introductory Lectures on Psychoanalysis* (New York: Liveright, 1977). I also like the rather gentle literary application of Freudian concepts in Simon O. Lesser's *Fiction and the Unconscious* (Chicago: The University of Chicago Press, 1975). More systematic and probing perhaps (and also occasionally improbable in my view) is Norman Holland's *The Dynamics of Literary Response* (New York: W. W. Norton, 1975). Also powerfully suggestive is Erik Erikson's *Identity: Youth and Crisis* (New York: W. W. Norton, 1968). R. D. Laing's *The Politics of Experience* (New York: Pantheon Books, 1967) is quite readable. The work of Jacques Lacan I find heavy sledding; for the intrepid a place to start at least is *The Language of the Self: The Function of Language in Psychoanalysis* (Baltimore: The Johns Hopkins University Press, 1968). The work is translated with extensive commentary by Anthony Wilden. Lacan's reinterpretation of Freud is indispensable for many literary critics.

My introduction to feminist criticism has come by way of *The Resisting Reader: A Feminist Approach to American Fiction* (Bloomington: Indiana University Press, 1978) by my colleague Judith Fetterley. I recommend it as an excellent starting place because it is powerful and eminently readable. While explicitly feminist readings are accepted in American high school classrooms, explicitly Marxist analyses present insuperable communal difficulties for many teachers. But it would be a shame if we teachers did not avail ourselves of Marxist insights into the relationships among art, culture, economics, and ideology. A good introduction to this thought is the work of Fredric Jameson, whose criticism is probing, thoughtful, and not doctrinaire. I would especially recommend *Marxism and Form* (Princeton: Princeton University Press, 1971) and *The Political Unconscious: Narrative as a Socially Symbolic*

Act (Ithaca: Cornell University Press, 1981). Finally, I would add to this group of avowedly polemical works Jonathan Culler's *On Deconstruction: Theory and Criticism after Structuralism* (Ithaca: Cornell University Press, 1982). It not only helps make clear the strategies of deconstructionist critics, but also discovers in their work relationships with reader-response critics, feminists, Marxists, and others.

Commentaries

At a third level are those commentaries that focus directly on Hawthorne's story. These are more numerous than one might guess — close to a hundred by my very rough count. I will name half a dozen or so that I found especially provocative and helpful. Peter Shaw in *American Patriots and the Rituals of Revolution* (Cambridge: Harvard University Press, 1981) and in "Fathers, Sons, and the Ambiguities of Revolution in 'My Kinsman, Major Molineux,' " *New England Quarterly* 49: 559–76 combines historical research with insights from psychology, anthropology, and literary criticism to illuminate Hawthorne's story. In a similar study, "Robins and Robinarchs in 'My Kinsman, Major Molineaux,' " *Nineteenth Century Fiction* 38, no. 3: 271–88, James Duban sets the stage historically, politically, and anthropologically for the story. Both writers offer interesting speculations about the names Robin and Molineux.

Roy Harvey Pearce's "Robin Molineux on the Analyst's Couch: A Note on the Limits of Psychoanalytic Criticism" in *Historicism Once More* (Princeton: Princeton University Press, 1969) is interesting in its use of Erik Erikson's work to moderate the sometimes conflicting interpretive claims of psychology and history.

The most genial psychoanalytic treatment of the story is in Simon O. Lesser's chapter "Conscious and Unconscious Perception" in his *Fiction and the Unconscious,* cited above. Frederick Crews in *The Sins of the Fathers: Hawthorne's Psychological Themes* (New York: Oxford University Press, 1966) takes the Oedipal conflict further, discovering hints of incestuous undercurrents in the association of mother and sister with the great tree and thus by figurative extension with Robin's cudgel. Dennis Brown in "Literature and Existential Psychoanalysis: 'My Kinsman, Major Molineux' and 'Young Goodman Brown,' " *The Canadian Review of American Studies* 4, no. 1: 65–73, argues that the work of R. D. Laing can be brought to bear on the story with profit.

In closing this postscript, I will not apologize for this eclectic, personal, and perhaps eccentrically unscholarly bibliography. It was not meant to be a balanced or comprehensive set of annotations. It is quite frankly the bibliographic trail of one teacher weaving his way through the voluminous materials available, trying to get a feel for the territory and an instinct for those seminal works that will ignite one's critical intelligence and enable one to be more alert to the possibilities in the encounters one's students have with texts. In light of that, and despite the fact that my job in this essay has been critical rather than pedagogical, I want to leave some record of works on the teaching of literature that have given me guidance. Because other contributors to this volume will be more detailed in this area, I will simply name them.

Works on the Teaching of Literature

Is There a Text in this Class? by Stanley Fish (Cambridge: Harvard University Press, 1980).

The Reader, the Text, the Poem, by Louise Rosenblatt (Carbondale: Southern Illinois University Press, 1978).

Reading and Writing Differently: Deconstruction and the Teaching of Composition and Literature, ed. C. Douglas Atkins and Michael L. Johnson (Lawrence: University Press of Kansas, 1985).

Researching Response to Literature and the Teaching of Literature: Points of Departure, ed. Charles R. Cooper (Norwood, N. J.: Ablex, 1985).

Textual Power: Literary Theory and the Teaching of English, by Robert Scholes (New Haven: Yale University Press, 1985).

Every reader's track will be different from mine. In teaching as in other matters, *vive la différence.* On the other hand, if we were each totally idiosyncratic, we could not communicate. I hope, therefore, that I have provided a few crossings.

8 Readers Making Meaning: From Response to Interpretation

Patricia G. Hansbury
Canajoharie High School
Canajoharie, New York

It seems odd, somehow, that I had not thought of this before — that readers make meaning. Or maybe I did know it all along but was not prepared to abandon my formalist training, methods, and textbooks to an approach that might result in chaos. After all, what would an untrained reader do to Shakespeare, Hawthorne, Twain? Well, probably read them and respond to them. Argue about them. Maybe ask some questions about their works and why they are considered important. And that is what has been happening in my literature classes for the past few years. From my first tentative forays into the practice of reader-response theory, to surer steps (and many fumbles), I have been excited by watching students see their responses to literature take shape, have significance, and become skilled.

Bringing Meaning to Texts: Internal and External Schemata

Just as they have learned that meaning evolves during the writing process, students can learn to see reading as a similar activity. They discover that readers bring to the text a whole set of influences that will help shape the poem they create from that text. As Stanley Fish (1980) puts it, "Interpretation is not the art of construing, but the art of constructing. Interpreters do not decode poems; they make them" (p. 327). In fact, response theorists have suggested that individual readers will create individual poems from the same text, depending on such factors as personality, mood, and age — what Anthony Petrosky (1985) labels "internal influences" — and that even the same reader will create a different poem from the same text at different times. We have all noticed how much a great work of literature can grow: each time we return to *Hamlet* we find something different, something new to be pondered. Other factors, too, shape our response to literature: the "external influences" of culture and instruction. As a result of these influences, readers consciously or unconsciously choose particular aspects of a text from which to build their poem; and so, because "one text is potentially capable of several different realizations, . . . no reading can ever exhaust the full potential" (Iser 1980, p. 55).

Important to the English classroom is the idea that, as the reader incorporates textual aspects into a coherent whole, the consistency-building which marks the reading experience tends to create "a kind of incomplete, 'blocked' reading" that needs to be enlarged (Atkins and Johnson 1985, p. 4). Asking readers to discuss their responses to a text opens the variety of reading experiences to the class as a whole and opens up the text in ways that individual readers would not have seen. When the internal and external schemata that students bring to and impose on texts are made conscious, they can be shared, questioned, refined, and expanded. Group discussion and analysis bring the student beyond his or her first reading: each "may learn . . . about others' experiences with the text, . . . may come to see that his own was confused or impoverished; [the student] may then be stimulated to attempt to call forth from the text a better poem. But this he must do himself" (Rosenblatt 1978, p. 45).

My goal as a teacher is to teach students ways to read literature, to offer them schemata, or modes of perception (Purves 1985), that can be applied to the works they encounter. Robert Scholes defines the role of the literature teacher: "Our job is not to produce 'readings' for our students but to give them the tools for producing their own" (Scholes 1985, p. 24). Successful application of such tools will depend on the individual's own experience as a reader. Working towards this goal, I have restructured literature lessons so that texts and readers — all kinds of readers, from student to teacher to professional critic — interact in a conversation that can only exist because of the rich depth of the literary experience. In fact, often the experience almost demands discussion, as all our memories of eager students talkative after a particularly moving reading will attest. Iser puts it this way:

> In the literary text we have the strange situation that the reader cannot know what his participation actually entails. We know that we share in certain experiences, but we do not know what happens to us in the course of this process. This is why, when we have been particularly impressed by a book, we feel the need to talk about it; we do not want to get away from it by talking about it — we simply want to understand more clearly what it is in

which we have been entangled. We have undergone an experience, and now we want to know consciously *what* we have experienced. (1980, p. 64)

Thus armed with readings from Rosenblatt, Iser, and others, I set out to discover if I could make the actual reading experience more lively, more immediate, and more conscious for my students, as the theorists promise. The idea of letting the lesson go in the direction of student response can be a little unsettling to any teacher like me who relies on a moderately structured, ordered, planned-to-the-last-detail kind of approach. Although I had been pleased with my students' technical or formalist kind of literary skill, I knew something was still missing from literature for most of them, and I hoped reader response would help me to help them find it.

Eliciting Personal Response: "Eveline"

In his book *Readings and Feelings* (1975), David Bleich offers several specific techniques that emphasize the subjectivity of any reading experience. He tells us, "Framing the interpretive problem in terms of 'importance'. . . enlarges our critical perspective so that it may include the key influence of our emotional response" (p. 63). One of his suggestions is to ask students to choose the most important word in a text. This idea intrigued me. Bleich's emphasis on the subjectivity of literary response leads him to conclude that even seemingly objective analysis of a work is grounded in explaining or justifying one's initial emotional response: "The separation of conscious judgement from its subjective roots is false and artificial" (p. 49). Following Bleich's suggestion, I asked students to answer this question after reading "Eveline" by James Joyce: "What do you think is the most important word in this story, and why is it so important?"

In first trying this activity with the Joyce story, I was curious what words students would pick and what criteria they would use to support their choices. In fact, I was sure that *home* was the most important word and that no one could see it any other way. It seemed so obvious to me. Only after the students presented their words, which they earnestly believed to be the "right" answer with a justifiable explanation, did I begin to believe in reader-response theory. The words they chose ranged from *promise, escape,* and *dust* to *mist, invade, tired,* and *change.* From our discussion of these words and their significance to us as readers, along with the explanations offered, several major questions emerged that needed further exploration. In general, they centered on Eveline's promise to her mother, the role of her father and Frank in her life, and her failure to move at the end of the story.

We discovered that individual students' interpretations of Eveline's behavior at the dock — hands gripping the railing, eyes showing "no sign of love or farewell or recognition" — depended largely on their initial responses to the story. A boy whose mother had recently died focused on Eveline's promise: to him it seemed that Eveline chose to stay home in order not to break that promise. Another student believed that Eveline's life was suffocating her — recall the word *dusty* — and that it was too late for her to escape: she could not consciously take action. Some students were simply surprised that after all that planning, Eveline does not go with Frank.

Eliciting personal response, though significant and necessary, is not sufficient if we are to help students become better interpreters. From here we looked at some other methods of analysis to see if we could agree about what was happening in the last scene of the story. We tried a formalist perspective, a psychological one based on the human developmental stages described by Erik Erikson (1978), and a feminist approach based loosely on a model created by Barbara Hill Rigney (1978). Each perspective gave us more information about Eveline's situation; each student found something from at least one of the perspectives that would help support her or his original reading of the story. Rather than eliminating the ambiguities of this text, our explorations made it clear that the story could not be pinned to a single meaning. Recognizing the ambiguities and what we made of them became an important part of our interpretations.

At this point I chose not to offer other readings proposed by scholars; I wanted the students to have a sense of the richness of this text, to have confidence in their own ability to interpret, and to be open to the interpretations of other students. Bringing in an outside authority might curtail the students' own explorations, might limit their own ideas. Of course, students need to test their perceptions against those of others, and so, as they became more skilled and confident in their reading, we frequently consulted the known critics of a literary work. For each piece, however, we first worked through our own questions and tried to form some consensus regarding the issues raised by the text, as well as some viable interpretations.

Georges Poulet (1980) writes of the reading experience:

> To be sure, nothing is unimportant for understanding the work, and a mass of biographical, bibliographical, textual, and general critical information is indispensable to me. And yet this knowledge does not coincide with the internal knowledge of the work.

> Whatever may be the sum of the information I acquire on Baudelaire or Racine, in whatever degree of intimacy I may live with their genius, I am aware that this contribution does not suffice to illuminate for me in its own inner meaning, in its formal perfection, and in the subjective principle which animates it, the particular work of Baudelaire or of Racine the reading of which now absorbs me. At this moment what matters to me is to live, from the inside, in a certain identity with the work and the work alone. (p. 46)

That "certain identity with the work . . . alone" is what I tried to stress in experiments with reader-response theory, acknowledging also of course, as Louise Rosenblatt puts it, that "the ordinary reader who thinks his interpretation of *The Tempest* as 'good' as G. W. Knight's is . . . fatuous." But Rosenblatt adds, "Yet there is a sense in which his reading is indeed as good: Drawing on the reservoir of his past life and reading, he has lived through the experience himself, he has struggled to organize it, felt it in his own pulse" (1978, p. 14).

Exploring Ambiguities: "An Occurrence at Owl Creek Bridge"

The reactions and questions that naturally arise when students become engaged in texts are effective resources in beginning the study of the work. Usually during the preliminary discussions of our responses to the work, we discover several major issues to explore, as we did with "Eveline." We formulate these into critical questions or issues, similar in a way to choosing what Bleich would call the most important aspect of a work. Often as part of a reading assignment, I ask students to write their own questions, which we then use as a basis to begin discussion, as suggested by Rosenblatt in *Literature as Exploration.* Students record their questions or issues in journals. Class then begins by having each student write one issue on a slip of paper to hand in or by asking students to read one issue aloud from their journals. There are advantages to either method. Given a bundle of papers, I can more easily choose an issue I consider important, but by asking students to raise an issue from their journals I feel closer in spirit to "authentic" reader response. Not knowing exactly what issues will be raised means giving up a little control; it means reading and researching ahead of time to anticipate possible issues; it means sometimes exploring a new issue together in class. As teacher and student respond to the text — predicting, questioning, guessing, modifying — the classroom experience itself begins to parallel the activity of reading, and something exciting begins to happen as spectators are moved to become participants. Interpreting is contagious.

The following list is an example of the kinds of questions that students raise about text. It was generated in class after an assignment on Ambrose Bierce's "An Occurrence at Owl Creek Bridge." My specific directions were as follows:

> After reading the story, write one or more questions that you think would be important to ask in order to understand the story's meaning. In other words, what issues should we discuss? What seems to be puzzling or somehow important to the story? (You may write a question even if you think you know the answer.)

The questions that the students raised (in their own words) were varied:

What is the significance of the dream sequence?

How do the separate sections fit together?

Why must he die at the end?

How does the writer's technique show that the man is imagining his escape?

Why does the action jump around?

What effect does the order of the story have?

Is part II necessary?

Why is it written in a dream pattern?

When does the reader first suspect that the escape is only a dream? When does he know for sure?

How significant is the narrative stance? [that is, third person]

Is the dream sequence foreshadowed?

What about the ticking of his watch?

What techniques are used to form one theme?

Why did the author not tell how Peyton was caught?

What does the story tell us of Peyton's character?

How long, in physical time, is the dream?

Some of these questions are a little stilted, concocted perhaps by students eager to show off their knowledge of the story. Such questions confirm David Kaufer and Gary Waller's (1985) observation that all too often students "do not see texts as occasions for being provoked, extracting information, sifting, interpreting, or regenerating it. They rather see them as occasions (even pretexts) for displaying knowledge" (p. 72). The idea applies equally to the texts that students produce as well as those they read. A corollary is that many students have learned to see each literary text as a "locked box.... The theme is the key that opens this box in an act called understanding" (Kaufer and Waller, p. 72). By asking students to rely more on their own observations about texts and by using their responses to direct our discussions, I have found that students become more comfortable sharing their own genuine responses rather than creating something they thought I wanted to hear. The students also begin to view texts as opportunities for provocation and exploration.

Although some of the questions in the list resemble the discussion topics in the textbook, eventually most of these students learned to depend more on their own responses. Overall, though, these questions reflected a thoughtful reaction to the initial impact of the story, a second step in the process of responding. I asked the students to put their responses in the form of a question because I wanted them to say something about the issue, rather than simply list items such as "point of view" or "the watch ticking."

After this list was compiled, we narrowed it down to the ideas they felt were most important: the structure of the story (order of narration) was the issue most students wanted to address, followed by (with a little prodding from me) the narrative stance and its effect on the reader. The other questions followed from these major issues. Generating this list and the concurrent discussion occupied most of one class period; another period was spent discussing ways to address the issues. For this story we decided that a close reading, focusing on the three parts of the work and the point of view (a formalist approach), would give us the best results.

Focusing on the Reading Experience: "A Modest Proposal"

Activities such as choosing important passages or raising interpretive questions address one aspect of reader response; other issues are raised when we focus on the reading experience itself. As students become conscious of what they do to a text and of what a text does to a reader, they begin to explore some of the more sophisticated literary conventions. Russell Hunt's (1982) suggestion that students be asked to stop reading at particular places in a text to answer specific questions seemed a perfect technique to try with Jonathan Swift's satiric essay "A Modest Proposal." Teaching students, even advanced juniors, to look for the subtle signals that differentiate Swift the writer from his cleverly designed narrator can be difficult. Without such a distinction, however, the essay fails to be effective: students do not recognize the dissonance between the shared norms of the writer and the audience. Using the following procedure led to better results than I was used to seeing in classes that studied this essay.

I gave students copies of the first ten paragraphs of the essay (ending with the words "especially in winter") and asked them to follow along as I read it aloud. I decided to read aloud for several reasons. One, hearing the differing emphasis between main and subordinate clauses helped students overcome the difficulty of Swift's long and complicated sentences. Two, by reading aloud I could control the situation to some extent so that we could stop at particular places to write and talk. To start, I read only the first three paragraphs and then asked students to write answers to any one of the questions I wrote on the board:

What is your reaction to this speaker?

Who is he? (describe him)

Do you like him? Why or why not?

What might he say next?

It seemed important that students write their answers before we discussed the questions so that each person could formulate an opinion. Then we discussed what they had written. At this point in the essay, most agreed that the speaker seemed to be a humanitarian, concerned, if a bit stuffy; however, Jeff, the rebel in most discussions, argued that there was "something about this guy" that he did not trust. Unfortunately, when asked to cite specific phrases that led him to that opinion, he was silent. Although students were used to Jeff's negativity, his statement seemed to alert some readers to other possibilities.

I read aloud the next two paragraphs and again asked students to write answers to the same questions. In the discussion that followed this reading, more students began to share Jeff's opinion, and such phrases as "child just dropped from its dam" were offered as evidence. The discussion was important because some readers were prepared to accept anything that this seemingly humanitarian narrator of the first few paragraphs might propose. Not everyone noticed immediately the speaker's obvious change in diction. Because of our discussion, however, most students soon became aware of Swift's game and were ready to play it. I read the next two paragraphs and then the final three from that section, and we wrote and discussed after each reading. By then, students were in control of the idea of this essay and were ready to finish reading it for homework.

During the next class we discussed the historical context of the essay, and we looked more closely at Swift's ironic use of a speaker who does not share the views of the implied author. The discussion was not so different from my previous lessons on this essay except for two important factors: there were no suspicious and frustrated readers, and the topics arose from students' enthusiastic questions about the work. Not all my experiments were so successful of course, but in this case the students were able to experience part of the fun of satire because they had been guided to discover it on their own. They were rewarded with that superior feeling satire bestows on the reader who "gets it." In addition, by learning for themselves some variations on the distinction between author and narrator, they had acquired new schemata to apply to other works.

Interpreting Details in Retrospect: "The Lottery"

The interaction between texts and readers is often highly emotional, and writers rely on that to achieve a variety of purposes. A story that always elicits a strong response from students is Shirley Jackson's "The Lottery." Because of the special nature of this story, it seemed ideal for demonstrating another way that texts manipulate their readers and for emphasizing the tendency of readers to create their own story out of a text. Reading is a sense-making activity. As we read, our expectations are either satisfied or modified, and in the process there is a "retrospective effect on what has already been read. This may now take on a different significance from that which it had at the moment of reading" (Iser 1980, p. 54). The power of "The Lottery" is derived in part from just such a situation. As the reader progresses through the story, on a journey from innocence to knowledge, the seemingly ordinary details of children playing with stones, housewives tarrying over dishes, and the hometown quality of annual traditions take on in retrospect an aspect of horror that is invisible in the context of the first reading. The student who approaches the story a second time is a different reader, alert to details other than those in the first reading and aware of the difference in significance of these details.

In beginning "The Lottery," we modified somewhat the approach used for Swift to meet the demands of this particular story and the purposes of the lesson. I read the story to the students, stopping five times to allow five minutes for written response to any of the following questions:

How does the passage make you feel?

What details or features stand out the most? Why?

Does the passage remind you of any experience you've had? Of any other work you've read?

What might happen next? How might the story end?

What questions do you have about the characters? the action? the setting?

These questions were designed to be useful during both readings and were reviewed with the students before beginning the story. I wanted them to write responses at natural breaks in the story, so I stopped reading and gave them time to write at each of these places:

1. ". . . get home for noon dinner."
2. ". . . between his father and his oldest brother."
3. ". . . talked interminably to Mr. Graves and the Martins."
4. "Zanini."
5. End of the text

At the end of the story, which was also the end of the class period, the students were eager to discuss what had happened, and I was wishing for a double period. I announced the homework assignment: they were to write their immediate reactions, responses, and ideas to be shared the next day. They were also to reread the story, respond at the same places (a list was given to them), and be prepared to compare the two readings in class.

This lesson was a team effort; a colleague conducted the class the next day, while I observed and recorded what happened. Two significant ideas arose in this discussion. First, the students discovered that there are no free or irrelevant details in literature. When asked what the biggest difference between the two readings was, the students agreed that their reaction to specific details was definitely different each time. Such items as the title, the town gathering, the smooth round rocks, the places characters chose to stand, the sense of anticipation, the focus on Tessie, all took on a different significance during the second reading. The students saw how Jackson manipulated the reader's response by omitting certain details, creating suspense.

Several students reported that during the first reading they had suspected early that something bad or ironic would happen, but the details they had emphasized in their responses were the happy mood, the tradition of the lottery. Some students had wondered why children were putting stones in piles, while others saw this as a perfectly natural activity. Those who questioned the stone-gathering were probably already aware of the second idea that arose during discussion: the existence of a literary convention stipulating that all serious pieces of fiction contain some tension or conflict. The more skilled readers in this group were anticipating and looking for evidence of conflict during the first reading.

Other details that took on a special significance in the second reading were the general avoidance of the black box and the sense of closeness among the members of the community. Students noticed the attitude of social duty mingled with fear and, realizing that someone in the town was killed each time the ritual was conducted, they knew why the oldest son in one family draws as the head of the household.

Observing this discussion, I noticed that after the second reading the focus of students' reactions had moved from within the story — questions about detail, motivation — to larger implications outside the text. Uneasy about unresolved problems, the students wanted to know if the Hutchinsons or anyone would move to some other town, maybe one where the lottery no longer existed. They wanted to know how well the corn would grow that year and what would happen to the lottery if the crops failed. An overwhelming question for many was whether the story "could really take place today."

To address these issues, the students were asked to consider the tradition of sacrifice and the use of scapegoats. Their thoughts (and fears) varied as to whether the situation portrayed in the story was realistic. This activity was evidence that the text itself may be finite, but the literary work created by each student's interaction with the text implied a world that was enlarged with further discussion. In other words, the work did not end with the last sentence; instead, both the story and its effect kept unfolding in the reader's mind.

Using Journals: *1984* and *The Adventures of Huckleberry Finn*

Students' reactions to and ideas about each work are valuable throughout the lesson. An effective way for them to record these thoughts and interpretations is by keeping response journals, which we use regularly as resources for class discussion or individual essay topics. When we study longer works, I ask students to keep a journal separate from class notes or to use a double-entry system — a journal on one page, relevant class notes on the facing page — so that they have a complete record of their reading experience. For students who do not know what to write (a large group when we first began this practice), I provide the following general questions:

> What does this remind you of? from your own experience? from other works of literature?

How do you feel about a particular character, his or her actions, an event, a setting, a situation?

Does this story seem realistic?

What do you think will happen next?

One of the first times I asked students to keep a journal was while we were studying *The Adventures of Huckleberry Finn*. They were familiar with the procedure and the general questions, so I asked them to have their journals by them as they read and to write when they felt compelled to respond, or at least every few chapters. Excited by the results during the more structured response activities, I thought this time I may have given them a task too demanding to accomplish successfully on their own. Some of the students found the reading itself to be more difficult than I had expected. When the journals were turned in, I was sadly disappointed. Although daily class discussions were lively enough, most students had written very little and so had little to draw from for further study. Most of the entries were short, superficial, specious. Several students wrote simply, "I wonder what will happen next?"

Although several factors played a determining role — the time of year, frustration over the book — the results were nevertheless disappointing. The exercise was also a learning experience for me. To be truly effective at the high school level, journal assignments need to be at least a little bit directed and structured. I found them more successful if we used them in class or as assignments throughout the reading of a longer work. We would begin by reading aloud in class and writing directed responses. I designed the questions and writing activities to be specific enough so that students know what to do, yet not so directed as to interfere with their own response to the work.

For example, at the beginning of *1984*, the students were asked to describe and respond to the atmosphere created by Orwell's opening paragraphs. The assignment elicited an immediate response and helped the students become aware of the atmosphere created by the physical description and its relation to the events in the book. Throughout our study of the novel, we wrote responses to a variety of questions or directions. Sometimes I asked students to predict what a character might do next and to tell what that action would reveal about the character, or to guess what might happen next and to describe what that would mean for the work as a whole. We could then compare and contrast our predictions with what really happens and draw conclusions about the differences. Or I asked students to choose an important or provocative word or action or setting and to explain why they chose it. Class discussion might begin by sharing what we had written, comparing our reactions, and returning to the text to verify, confirm, or support our ideas. Students' responses determined what was important for us to explore about the work and what kind of outside help such as historical, literary, or critical information would be necessary. In most cases, what we uncovered in our study of a literary work was in fact quite similar to what had been "covered" in the more teacher-centered classes. Most texts seem to demand certain approaches, as students' responses and questions demonstrated.

Writing to Discover and Interpret

The importance of writing throughout this experience became clear. Although the initial reading experience is, as Rosenblatt writes, of such an "ineffable and inward character" that the personal experience cannot be shared, the aesthetic event can be reported in a form that is actually the beginning of an interpretation (1978, p. 132). To discuss the aesthetic event, one must be able to define it; the definition arises in the act of recognition — writing. We accept the fact that the experience cannot be shared, but also that in writing about it one necessarily changes it by choosing how to tell it. Only by doing so, however, can interpretation begin. The activity of interpretation, as Rosenblatt sees it, consists of five steps:

1. Characterizing the work in terms of emotional response
2. Reporting the sequence of ideas and the attitude of the persona
3. Describing the characters — details, actions, psychology
4. Discussing the structure of the work
5. Emphasizing the symbolic content. (1978, p. 136)

I saw that the threads of most of these activities were spun in the classroom during the initial response to the work; they began to be sorted out as interpretation proceeded. My joining students in writing responses was important, too. It was tempting at first to try to grade a few papers or outline another lesson while they wrote, but I found that by writing with them, I could more easily share their experience. We became a group of scholars reading together in an atmosphere that proved stimulating for both students and teacher.

Responding to the Text: A Way into the Work

By asking students to focus on the process of reading as an integral part of interpretation, I found that lessons in many literary conventions evolved. Their responses to a text were therefore a necessary step in acquiring new schemata. Such concepts as suspense, satire, persona, and implied reader, and such critical methods as formalist, psychological, or archetypal analysis became part of students' repertoire of literary skills more easily than I had seen before. Through their own questions about a text, the students had demanded the new models and concepts.

Out of these experiments with reader response has evolved a procedural model that parallels Rosenblatt's three-step process: (1) evocation, which is the act of creating a poem from a text; (2) interpretation; and (3) evaluation (1978, chapter 7). Although these activities can occur almost simultaneously, each is a separate aspect of the reading process, and each calls for recognition and attention from the student of literature. To address each of the three stages, I lead students through these activities:

1. Responding to the work

2. Raising critical questions and defining issues of significance

3. Group work in analysis and research to explore the issues

4. Reports from groups

5. Final discussion

Each student must then complete a synthesizing or evaluative activity, usually written, to reach some closure with the work, a step as important as the initial response. Most students soon realize that closure does not mean that all of their questions have been answered, but it helps them find a significance in their work and to put the parts — response, questions, interpretation — together again. I try to vary the final assignments so that the students can practice writing for various purposes and audiences while experiencing a sense of closure with the work. Assignments can be tailored to the individual styles of teacher and student, but the following types of task have generally elicited interest and interesting results:

1. Write a narrative describing the life of a character ten years from now (for example, Eveline).

2. Compare or contrast a character, image, style, or theme of one work with that of another.

3. Write your own. . . . (for example, Modest Proposal).

4. Write an interpretive essay using one or more critical perspectives on the work.

5. Compare or contrast the effectiveness of specific critical methods in clarifying the ambiguities of a particular work.

6. Write a new ending for the work and suggest how it changes the possibilities for interpretation (for example, "The Lottery," "An Occurrence at Owl Creek Bridge").

Reader response, then, is more than simply asking students to describe their emotional reactions to a work of literature. In redesigning literature classes, I have looked for specific techniques to help students see reading as a process, to be conscious of what they as readers do to a text and of what a text does to a reader, as theorists such as Fish and Iser have suggested. I want students to be aware of the predictions, guesses, and reversals that constitute active reading. Knowledge and evaluation of this activity is important to understanding many of the conventions of literature that frequently elude unwary readers.

Finally, response to a work is a way into that work. When discussion begins with students' questions instead of the teachers' questions, the direction of study begins to take shape. As a group we determine which aspects of the text we will explore, which informational sources we will consult, and which methods of analysis we will apply. Allowing students to see that their responses and questions are legitimate and helping them to succeed at interpretive activity fosters sensitivity to texts. And so I have seen enthusiasm, heard heated discussion, and listened to thoughtful questions from students who were moved by the literature they had read. More than that, they were learning to look beyond their own responses to the text and to explore what in the text or in themselves created a reading. Scholes reminds us that "reading and writing are important because we read and write our world as well as our texts, and are read and written by them as well" (1985, p. xi).

The truth of texts is infinite, is partial. Exploring literature, losing oneself or finding oneself, is an experience we can share with our students, but we need to remember that

> if wisdom, or some less grandiose notion such as heightened awareness, is to be the end of our endeavors, we shall have to see it not as something transmitted from the text to the student but as something developed in the student by questioning the text. (Scholes 1985, p. 14)

If we help our students become more aware of textuality, of their role in creating their world, then we have done the very thing for which we love literature in the first place: we have shared experiences, expanded horizons, created connections.

References

Atkins, G. D. and M. L. Johnson. 1985. Introduction. *Writing and Reading Differently.* ed. G. D. Atkins and M. L. Johnson. Lawrence: University Press of Kansas.

Bleich, D. 1975. *Readings and Feelings: An Introduction to Subjective Criticism.* Urbana, Ill.: National Council of Teachers of English.

Cooper, C. R., ed. 1985. *Researching Response to Literature and the Teaching of Literature.* Norwood, N.J.: Ablex.

Erikson, E. 1978. *Childhood and Society.* 2d ed. New York: W. W. Norton & Co.

Fish, S. 1980. *Is There a Text in this Class?* Cambridge: Harvard University Press.

Hunt, R. A. 1982. Toward a Process-Intervention Model in Literature Teaching. *College English* 44: 345–57.

Iser, W. 1980. The Reading Process: A Phenomenological Approach. In *Reader-Response Criticism,* ed. J. Tompkins. Baltimore: The Johns Hopkins University Press.

Kaufer, D., and G. Waller. 1985. To Write Is to Read Is to Write, Right? In *Writing and Reading Differently,* ed. G. D. Atkins and M. L. Johnson. Lawrence: University Press of Kansas.

Petrosky, A. R. 1985. Response: A Way of Knowing. In *Researching Response to Literature and the Teaching of Literature,* ed. C. R. Cooper. Norwood, N.J.: Ablex.

Poulet, G. 1980. Criticism and the Experience of Interiority. In *Reader-Response Criticism,* ed. J. Tompkins. Baltimore: The Johns Hopkins University Press.

Purves, A. C. 1985. That Sunny Dome: Those Caves of Ice. In *Researching Response to Literature and the Teaching of Literature,* ed. C. R. Cooper. Norwood, N.J.: Ablex.

Rigney, B. H. 1978. *Madness and Sexual Politics in the Feminist Novel.* Madison: The University of Wisconsin Press.

Rosenblatt, L. M. 1976. *Literature as Exploration.* 3rd ed. New York: Noble and Noble.

———. 1978. *The Reader, the Text, the Poem: The Transactional Theory of the Literary Work.* Carbondale: Southern Illinois University Press.

Scholes, R. 1985. *Textual Power: Literary Theory and the Teaching of English.* New Haven: Yale University Press.

Tompkins, J. P., ed. 1980. *Reader-Response Criticism: From Formalism to Post-Structuralism.* Baltimore: The Johns Hopkins University Press.

9 Seventh Graders Making Meaning: A Historical-Cultural Approach to Ray Bradbury

James Butterfield
Sand Creek School
Albany, New York

Seventh grade is a good time to experiment with a historical-cultural approach to reading and responding to literature. This approach can help students understand that works of literature legitimately may be seen from different perspectives (Guerin and Labor 1979). A different approach gives readers a new way of looking at things, a "competitive world of new views . . . shaping everyday life by providing new models for our experience" (Suleiman and Crosman 1980). The more that a student can derive from literature, the more relevant the text will seem, with feelings, images, even personal recollections contributing to the truth of the work being read.

The students to whom the following lesson was presented were in a high-average, seventh-grade English class. Using the historical-cultural approach, we focused on reading a short story from Ray Bradbury's *Dandelion Wine*. I selected "The Whole Town's Sleeping" (included in one of the anthologies available for our class use) for two reasons: because so much can be done with the text in the classroom and because of the nostalgic realism that Bradbury so carefully constructs. He goes to great lengths to create a definite time frame for the story.

Set in 1928, the story focuses on an unknown killer whom the town has named "Lonely One." One evening Lavinia Nebbs, a "maiden lady" who refuses to be intimidated by the fear that has this small Illinois town terrified, plans to go to a movie with two friends, Helen and Francine. On the way to pick up Helen, Lavinia and Francine discover the body of Lonely One's latest victim, Elizabeth Ramsell, who "had laid herself out to enjoy the soft stars and easy wind, her hands at either side of her like the oars of a delicate craft . . . her face moonlit, her eyes wide and like flint, her tongue sticking from her mouth." Lavinia insists they continue on to the movie.

Adding to the story's terror is a dark ravine, a "black dynamo that never stopped humming," which cuts the town in two. Lavinia must cross the ravine alone on her way home from the show. After walking Helen and Francine home and refusing to stay the night with either, Lavinia continues homeward. Shortly, she come upon Officer Kennedy, who offers to walk with her. Once again she refuses, saying to herself that she would not walk home with any man, not knowing who the Lonely One might be. Through the darkness she walks down the ravine steps and finally convinces herself that someone is following her. She listens; her heart starts pounding. Fear takes over and she begins running for her life while hearing sounds behind her. She runs hysterically up the hill toward the street to her house and safety. Barely managing to put the key into the lock, Lavinia opens, slams, and locks the door — safe at last. She soon realizes, however, that she is not alone. Before she can turn on a light, somewhere behind her in the darkness "someone cleared his throat."

The lesson consisted of five parts: (1) prereading, (2) a reading and discussion of the story, (3) group work in response to the reading, (4) a look at Bradbury and history in a follow-up discussion, and (5) writing activities. Taking for granted that the lesson was a seventh grader's first encounter with a historical-cultural approach, I used a step-by-step process. I told the class that we would read a short story, using an approach called historical-cultural, and that each prereading activity would take them closer to a new understanding of the story — beyond plot and character.

Answering the question "What is your definition of history?" was the first task that faced the class. Student responses, which were written on the board, included the following: the story of man, things that happened a long time ago, the study of dinosaurs, studying different countries and things that happened in them long ago, different wars and effects on people, famous people and what they left for us, my story, the story of my family, and where I came from. We used these definitions as handy reference points throughout the lesson.

The next two prereading activities demonstrated what Bradbury calls "sense impressions" that we, as individuals, receive from history. Five taped pieces of music were played in mixed order: something on a harpsichord, a Charleston, "Boogie-Woogie Bugle Boy," Elvis's "Jail House Rock," and a current rock song. Students orally arranged the music in historical order. Although the class found this first exercise rather easy, they saw that their sense impressions relied on specific words from the lyrics, identifying rhythms as different in time, or forming some visual image from television or movies to help with chronological arrangement.

The second activity used pictures, each with a varied background scene with dress styles of the late 1700s, late 1800s, early 1900s, and 1980s. I opened the discussion by asking, "What leads you to believe this person's dress came historically before this other person's dress?" Students responded with comparisons they used to arrange the pictures in historical order, including clothing length, earrings, hair styles, a person's stance, shoes, and customs as shown from the backgrounds. This led to a discussion of an author's sense of history and how authors might weave their own sense impressions into a work. I read to the class a bit from Bradbury's introduction: "First I rummaged my mind for words that could describe . . . and shaped stories from these." The students began to see themselves in terms of Bradbury, "rummaging" their minds for memories that allowed them to place the pictures in order.

"Define culture" was the next assignment. No response. Blank faces. No contact. I had anticipated this reaction, so we consulted our dictionaries (readily available at each desk because they prove invaluable, especially in the later group work). We took the time to note all definitions. "Which definition applies to your sense impressions of music and dress styles?" The class chose a fitting definition: the "integrated pattern of human knowledge, belief, and behavior that depends on man's capacity for learning and transmitting knowledge to succeeding generations." This exercise led nicely into the final prereading activity.

A challenging homework activity was purposely the most complex of the warm-ups. Its objective was to demonstrate how history produces cultural elements. Each student received a sheet with the following headings written above four columns: Wars, Chronological or Historical Order, Years, Cultural Items. Listed randomly in the first column were the American Civil War, the Vietnam conflict, World War I, the American Revolution, and World War II. The students were asked to place the wars in correct historical order in the second column. Once the items were arranged, the students were directed to assign a year to each war in the third column; for example, any year from 1963 to 1975 was acceptable for Vietnam. Association of sense impressions was next; an object, custom, person, way of life, anything cultural was listed in the last column. Answers provided an interesting insight into seventh graders' knowledge of history and their cultural awareness.

One quiet boy mentioned that his father wore camouflage fatigues to repair the family car. The ensuing discussion of Vietnam and the boy's knowledge of the war through his father brought other students to an increased awareness. Other students whose fathers had fought in the war added their own bits and pieces that gave the whole class a brief but realistic picture of the conflict. Another boy had grandparents who met in France during World War II and waited for one another after the war. A girl said that the American Revolution brought to mind our "greatest president," George Washington. She remembered him as our first president because his picture appears on every one-dollar bill.

All their seemingly simple responses forced the students to think, to become more aware of history and its projection of attitudes, customs, and values handed down to them. Finally, the homework sheets were collected, and select responses were discussed and listed on the board. At first I thought the students would make fun of one another's responses, but just the opposite occurred; the students were enthusiastic because each response triggered an intelligent comment.

I introduced "The Whole Town's Sleeping" as a mystery that involved a particular time and place. The first few pages were read aloud (up to the discovery of the body in the ravine). I then assigned an independent reading of the story and reminded the students that "history" was still the important item on the agenda.

A very general discussion of the story focused on plot, character, and a literal understanding of the work to make sure students knew who was who and what was going on in the story. The class was then divided into small groups and assigned to reread a section of the story carefully. A group secretary recorded anything the group found unusual or confusing about character development, setting, vocabulary, dialogue, and attitudes, all the while relying on the definitions of history and the warm-up activities. Each secretary presented the group's findings to the class, eliciting further questions and responses. From the presentations, the students realized that they were looking at the story from two points of view — as a person living in 1928 and as a person living in 1985. Following are a sampling of the notes and some student comments:

1. *Group noted:* The names Lavinia, Francine, Helen.
   Comment: Old fashioned names, especially Lavinia.

2. *Group noted:* Francine is "dressed in snow white."
   Comment: Who dresses like that to go to a movie? My mother doesn't like to go to a movie with me (or any place else) unless I look nice; she says that's how her mother brought her up.

3. *Group noted:* The name Douglas Spalding.
   Comment: Why isn't he called "Doug"? Was it a custom to call people by their whole first name and not use a nickname?

4. *Group noted:* Miss Fern and Miss Roberta.
   Comment: Unusual names . . . old fashioned. Today we don't put

"Miss" in front of first names . . . isn't anybody married in this town?

5. *Group noted:* The word "bosh."
   Comment: Never heard this word. . . . Dad said his grandpa used it.

6. *Group noted:* Lavinia asks for "a nickel's worth of peppermint chews."
   Comment: A nickel? We would probably get one chew for that much today . . . things were cheap in those days.

7. *Group noted:* The druggist shovels the candy.
   Comment: Weren't there any bags of candy they could buy? Or couldn't the girls buy candy at the movie . . . maybe candy wasn't sold at the movies in those days.

8. *Group noted:* "Maiden lady."
   Comment: Old fashioned way of saying "not married" . . . like an old maid, but Lavinia doesn't seem that old.

9. *Group noted:* The movie only costs $.41.
   Comment: Where? . . . *obviously* a long time ago.

10. *Group noted:* "You're so fine and nice. . . ."
    Comment: Would a friend talk like this? . . . might say, "you're a great person, you're cool," or something like that . . . these characters seem to have nice manners.

11. *Group noted:* Character of Lavinia Nebbs.
    Comment: She reminds me of my sister, not afraid of anything. . . . I think most girls today are like her . . . women's lib and that freedom.

12. *Group noted:* Ray Bradbury, author.
    Comment: How does this man know so much about this place, this town? These women? The ravine? And all those other things like old songs, 1928?

13. *Group noted:* Lavinia's trip through the ravine.
    Comment: When Lavinia went through the ravine and was thinking back to childhood about the guy coming up to her room while she was in bed reminded me when I was small and I was afraid to drop my arm over the side of my bed because I thought someone or something was going to grab me and pull me under the bed.

The group findings introduced the students to a third point of view, that of Bradbury the author, referred to in group note number twelve.

Little had been said about Bradbury other than his being a modern writer of both science fiction and mystery. A short talk about several of his works provided some insight into his varied literature. I asked the class, "How do you suppose someone like Bradbury wrote so carefully and realistically about this time period, these characters, and this particular situation?" The class responded with answers like "He researched history books," "A relative told him what it [the time] was like," "He lived in those times," "The story was real."

Reading "Just This Side of Byzantium," Bradbury's nostalgic introduction to *Dandelion Wine*, provided an excellent wrap-up. In the introduction, Bradbury says he "rummaged" his mind to derive any horrible occurrences and fears from his childhood and then set to work writing the stories, not simply from one year, but from memories from "all the lawns of the summers" in which he grew up. He calls the book a "gathering of dandelions from all those years."

Once the students began to get a glimpse of the story as part of the whole recollection, they saw the strong forces of the past that acted on Bradbury. He mentions remembering simple items, among them a half-burnt firecracker, a rusted toy, or a fragment of a letter, trying to coax remembrances "of his past, his life, his people, his joys, and his drenching sorrows."

"Our past is a strong force that none of us can really forget." I wrote this statement on the board and asked the class what I meant. Responses centered on the fact that we all remember our past, not all of it, but certainly bits and pieces, some happy, some not so joyous. As a group, we continued discussing highlights of Bradbury's introduction. The students began to see how the author used *his* bits and pieces, even the not-so-happy bits of stored information — the deep, dark ravine where Bradbury's brother Skip would hide and jump out and grab him, the depressing coal docks and railyards and, of course, the Lonely One, a real individual whom the author, even though he was only six years old at the time, remembers frightening everyone and never being caught — great ingredients for a great story.

After discussing the introduction, I reread what I believed to be an important point of Bradbury's, a point that is necessary in understanding any story in relation to its author. He says that certain elements may seem depressing, ugly, or even irrelevant, but they are "not ugly to children; ugliness is a concept that we happen on later." Even unpleasant sense impressions are important in literature and the writing process. After completing this wonderful reminiscence, my seventh graders saw Bradbury's story as much more than a conglomeration of words centering on plot and character, but rather as a reflection of Bradbury's life and times.

The final activity consisted of a writing task through which the class, divided into thirds, looked at the story from one of three perspectives: (1) seeing Lavinia Nebbs through the eyes of a friend living in 1928; (2) viewing Lavinia through Ray Bradbury's eyes after reading the complete introduction to *Dandelion Wine;* (3) seeing Lavinia through their own eyes, 1985 readers. Once the compositions were corrected, exemplary writings from each perspective were read aloud, and the class discussed key points that demonstrated the importance of the historical-cultural approach. Sample excerpts follow (any errors have been reproduced):

Perspective One

"Why, Miss Lavinia, you look so pretty today. And isn't that a new straw hat?" asked Sam Parkson, the town druggist.

"Why, Sam Parkson, I've worn this hat dozens of times. I'll have none of your billarny. Good day, Sam."

That little so-and-so thought Sam. For years she's been a-comen into my store with her high and might attitude. Maybe that stranger who was in askin' 'bout her will wisk her away. Poor fella. She's a cold fish, that one is. Not afraid of anything-any man fer sure. Some day she'll be payed back for her holier than thou ways. . . .

Perspective Two

I have often wondered how an author can make a story so real and after reading Mr. Bradbury's introduction to *Dandelion Wine* title Just This Side of Byzantium, it gave me a better view of Lavina Neebs, the main charactor.

I think Mr. Bradbury either knew someone like Lavinia or formed her out of some character he knew. He uses the word rummage when talking about looking back for words to describe his passed, and I think Mr. Bradbury did this when he created the charactor of Lavinia Nebbs. Her name fits her to a t, being a maiden lady and very head strong. If married, she certainly would be bossin the family. I think Mr. Bradbury wanted to show Lavinia as this strong willed, though foolish, independant person, not afraid of anyone or anything. . . .

Perspective Three

Lavinia Nebbs, 20th Century Woman's Woman (title)

Even though "The Whole Town's Sleeping" takes place in 1928, he could be writing about 1985. Lavinia Nebbs, the main character, represents women's lib. She has a lot of nerve, and no man is going to intimate her into hiding away from Lonely One. Sometimes I got the impression that she was almost excited by the thought that he might go after her. Lavinia takes control; she is her own woman. What does she do? After finding the body in the ravine, she continues on to the movie, sure that Lonely One won't strike again so soon. She decides not to stay over at her friends' houses, and she won't walk home with any man even when one offers to walk her. Lavinia even remembers, while walking through the ravine, a childhood fear about a "dark man" coming up to her room while she slept, and while running through the ravine, she convinces herself "he's" following. An award should be given to Lavinia for having sense to fight back and cowering to a man. . . .

I was pleased with the results of the writings. Students thought for themselves, delved into the text for facts, looked carefully at Bradbury's methods and reasons for writing the story and, where applicable, even attempted to place themselves into the book's setting to add realism to their own writing.

We English teachers should help our students achieve an awareness of literature beyond the basic plot of a text, expand their knowledge, and see that literature encompasses one's life and times, a reminder "of his past, his people, his joys, and his sorrows." I am confident my seventh graders benefited from the use of a historical-cultural approach.

Bibliography

Bradbury, R. 1975. *Dandelion Wine.* New York: Bantam.

Cooper, C. R., ed. 1985. *Researching Response to Literature and the Teaching of Literature: Points of Departure.* Norwood, N.J.: Ablex.

Geertz, C. 1973. *The Interpretation of Cultures.* New York: Basic.

Guerin, W., and E. Labor. 1979. *A Handbook of Critical Approaches to Literature.* New York: Harper.

Rosenblatt, L. M. 1978. *The Reader, the Text, the Poem.* Carbondale: Southern Illinois University Press.

Suleiman, S. R., and I. Crosman, eds. 1980. *The Reader in the Text.* Princeton: Princeton University Press.

10 Ninth Graders Making Meaning: A Structuralist Activity with *Of Mice and Men*

Doris M. Quick
Burnt Hills Schools
Burnt Hills, New York

As a first-year teacher twenty-five years ago, I taught a class in ninth-grade English. Then, I perceived my role as English teacher to be mainly a purveyor of literature and my method that of skillful questioner. The answers to my carefully orchestrated series of questions would lead the class, I hoped, to an appreciation or perhaps a better understanding of the literature under discussion. In planning my questions, I was not consciously aware of being influenced by any particular school of literary theory except New Criticism, which had been the backbone of my own training. I hoped that through osmosis or transfer of training my students would like the literature I presented. I never asked myself what strategies or skills they had learned as a result of my instruction that might help them to encounter the next piece of literature without my skillful questioning.

Now, twenty-five years later, I am teaching another ninth-grade class. I could write a very long article on many teaching strategies that did not work with this group. Instead, I prefer to tell about a happy marriage between John Steinbeck's *Of Mice and Men* and Roland Barthes's description of a structuralist activity. After the experiment, I concluded that this mixed-ability group of ninth graders had gone through a process that provided them with an orderly procedure for rereading a text closely. In addition, the process seems compatible with their developmental ability to encounter a text, for it trades on knowledge they are likely to have intuitively. This structuralist activity, if practiced often in the classroom with a variety of texts in a variety of genres, might well provide even inexperienced readers with strategies for analyzing texts on their own. Most important, readers are held responsible for generating their own observations about what seems important in a text rather than responding to questions the teacher deems important.

I do not wish to mislead you, however. I was originally going to entitle this article "Ninth-Grade Structuralists Read *Of Mice and Men.*" I like the title, but unfortunately it promised more than it delivered. My ninth graders are not transmogrified into structuralists. They have never to my knowledge heard the word "structuralism" and would probably be mildly alarmed if I suggested they were of that ilk. Nor have I thrown out all of the other good stuff we teachers do. I still ask questions designed to see if they comprehend (or indeed if they read the assignment at all). I still have students keep a reader-response journal as they read. The structuralist activity described here is an adjunct that gives students a structure for close rereading. It is not the primary focus of a classroom by any means, nor should it be.

First, let me describe some of the tenets of structuralism and the structuralist activity as set forth by Barthes. Then, I will tell how I applied his ideas to a rereading of one section of *Of Mice and Men* and talk about some of the students' reactions. Finally, I will be honest about what parts of this activity did not live up to my expectations.

Like most linguists, structuralists see certain unconscious rules operating in the structure of language and literature. In language we do not need to be conscious of the grammatical rules of the spoken language in order to construct English sentences that convey meaning. Similarly, in literature we do not necessarily need to be conscious of the "codes" that Barthes says underlie the structure of literature. But we might be more analytical in our thinking about literature if we consider the five operant codes, as revealed in words, phrases, and sentences that (1) move the plot along (the action code); (2) arouse or satisfy the reader's curiosity (the enigmatic code); (3) "resonate with symbolic overtones" (the symbolic code, Barthes 1977, p. 1); (4) relate to the cultural background of the reader or writer for their meaning (cultural code); and (5) inform us about the understood relationship between narrator and reader (the communication code).

The structuralist's job as described by Barthes consists of "restructuring an object so as to reveal the principles of its functioning and thus render it intelligible" (1971, p. 1196). As readers, we take apart a piece of literature to see how it works, but then we have an obligation to reformulate it in a way that makes sense to us. Particularly appealing to ninth graders is the fact that they are not being called upon to judge or criticize but rather to describe.

The structuralist's activity of carefully reading a text word by word to identify those linguistic features that mark the codes is very slow, very painstaking. Thus it usually lends itself to analysis of poetry. However, a short prose passage (a paragraph or two) works as well. Structuralists read line by line, taking the data as presented to them. They stop to comment wherever they intuitively sense a place in the text that advances one of the codes. At the end of this analytic game, structuralists reorder the work to talk about how the text makes sense to them. It is important to note that structuralists do not interpret texts, nor do they search for *the* meaning. Rather, they describe how the codes function in the text.

An element of structuralism that appeals to ninth graders particularly is the assumption that each reader decides where to stop in the text to comment. Each reader is free to intuit the passages that function to move the text along. I am continually amazed that even young readers have an intuitive sense of what is important. They frequently choose common passages to comment on, a fact that gives credence to the structuralist assumption that we are unconsciously aware of the codes that are important. When students are divided into small groups to discuss the codes, they see that they tend to stop at the same places and that they share ideas about the importance of these stopping places in a mini-community of interpreters. More about that later.

How does a structuralist activity apply to *Of Mice and Men*? It seems a natural union. First, the novel is short, so ninth graders are caught off guard right away. It is also a significant piece of literature carefully crafted by a well-known author, two criteria I consider important in selecting literature for study. It is at once rich, complex, and accessible. Students had almost no problems with the first read-through for comprehension, and in fact some read ahead of the daily assigned reading. The novel is tidily structured around six tightly written chapters, each of which advances the narrative of two loners, Lennie, a huge retarded man, and George, his caretaking companion. Both men are in quest of their dream to own a farm. Several clearly drawn minor characters contribute to two major themes: (1) our dreams often do not work out as we planned (the best laid plans of mice and men often go awry), and (2) in modern American society there are outcasts who feel alienated from the mainstream society.

Let me quickly point out that I usually let students grapple with the problem of identifying the theme. What is this novel, play, or poem all about? For this experiment, however, I deviated from my usual strategy. I presented the two major themes (dreams deferred and alienation) and said that our task would be to determine how the author worked his material to convey these themes, in other words, how the five codes function to add up to the themes. It would be more honest but trickier for relatively inexperienced readers to let them read for comprehension, apply the codes to sections of the work, and finally arrive at their own conclusion of what the work is about.

In an early series of lessons, I prepared the students to be receptive to the two major themes. We had previously read Lorraine Hansberry's *Raisin in the Sun*, and the students had written a piece about their own failed dreams and their reactions to their experiences. I now had them reread and free-write in their journals about the feelings associated with deferred dreams by way of suggesting that this theme would recur in the current novel. Then I showed a series of five slides that depicted people seemingly alone and desolate. I asked the students to jot-list their reactions to the slides, and we shared the lists on the blackboard. We noted the remarkable similarities in the words selected (*suicide, aching, terrible, frightening, cold*) to show that we all are familiar with the despair of loneliness. Students accepted the idea that these two themes could be tracked in the novel they were about to read. (They are well bred enough to take the teacher's word about matters that are likely to save them work and headaches).

Six readings were assigned, one chapter per night for homework. The students were also asked to do free writing in their reader-response journals to record their impressions, questions, observations, speculations, and insights into what seemed important. These journals and my questions became the basis for class discussion for the first read-through. Nothing remarkable here. After the initial reading, however, we returned for a close rereading and trotted out a structuralist activity. It proceeded this way.

The objective in this part of the teaching was to help the students, who already had accepted a statement about the themes, try to discover how the work achieved its purpose, that is, how the five codes identified earlier function in this novel.

Incidentally, I omitted a discussion of the cultural code (elements that depend on the particular cultural background of the reader or writer for their meaning), sensing that this category would be too difficult for ninth graders to work with. I may have been wrong, because in their journal questions the students asked about the significance of the novel being set in the West (an outpost for outcasts, as it were) and in the Great Depression; they were obviously prepared to accept the possibility that both contributed to a sense of alienation. So be it. Another time, I would keep that category.

I distributed a ditto that looked like this:

Close Rereading of *Of Mice and Men*

Today, I will ask you to work in groups of 6. Each group will be assigned a different code to study. You are to quickly skim the last chapter in the novel. Then, working in your group, decide on what words, phrases, sentences, images contribute to the code you have been assigned. Make a list of the citations you find on the chart below. You should have a minimum of 10 citations. Then, in your group discuss the importance of the citations you listed. As a group, write a statement to the larger group about what you believe to be the significance of the code you studied.

Group 1:	Group 2:	Group 3:	Group 4: Communication
Action Code	Enigma Code	Word Code	Code
What words, images, phrases, sentences tell us what is happening?	Words, images, phrases, sentences that arouse or satisfy the reader's curiosity?	Words, images, phrases, sentences that seem rich, complex, to have symbolic overtones?	Words, images, phrases, sentences, that tell about the understood relationship between narrator-reader?

The groups worked silently for about twenty-five minutes, each student reading, skimming, jot-listing places in the text where he or she found words, phrases, sentences, images that seemed to fit the code to which the group had been assigned. The last chapter opens with a description of the Salinas River, where Lennie has come to hide after accidentally killing Curley's wife. Later in the chapter, George, the caretaker, will kill Lennie, partly out of concern that he is unable to fit into society and partly to save him from a mob of ranch hands. Here is Jeremy's list under the enigma code:

why a snake?

a heron?

heron eat snake. why?

periscope, 2nd snake

"George gonna give me hell"

"George gonna whish he was alone an' not have me bother him"

Why George said he isn't mad at Lennie?

How could George kill his best friend?

Group 2 was assigned to discuss enigmatic detail. I joined them, leaving the other groups temporarily on their own, a state of affairs they are accustomed to. Frankly, I thought that this group had the most interesting code and that the composition of the group made it the most likely one to come up with something worthwhile.

One student read aloud and the group passed over the first paragraph describing a pool of water. The students already know that later on in the chapter George will shoot the retarded Lennie, who has, unaware of his own strength, killed a young woman while attempting to stroke her hair. Lennie previously killed a mouse and a kitten in a similar way. The reader understands that George shoots Lennie to save him from a mob and because Lennie simply cannot function in society. Here is the second paragraph, which leads to a lively discussion:

> A water snake glided smoothly up the pool, twisting its periscope head from side to side; and it swam the length of the pool and came to the legs of a motionless heron that stood in the shallows. A silent head and beak lanced down and plucked it out by the head, and the beak swallowed the little snake while its tail waved frantically.

During the reading, group members interrupt the reader. I now invite you to listen in on the tape-recorded conversation:

Jennifer: I stopped to wonder about the snake. Why did Steinbeck put the snake in there?

Teacher: Any speculations? [silence] What kinds of associations do you have with "snake"?

Others [pretty much in unison]: Slimy, scary, death, poisonous, Adam and Eve.

Teacher: Let's go on. What happens?

Patrick [reads and stops]: So he dies. Swims over to the heron.

Jeff: He dies? Do you think the snake ate the bird?

Patrick: No. The bird ate the snake. [reads] It's the other way around.

Jeff: Do you think he's dead?

Patrick: He ate him. [reads] Here. Now. The heron kills the snake.

Teacher: You stopped here. What do you make of this?

Jeremy: The snake is small compared to the heron. But the snake has power. George is small compared to Lennie. George has stronger power than Lennie and he's more intelligent.

Teacher: Are you saying that the snake is like George?

Jennifer: But Lennie is more like the snake. Lennie does evil things, but he doesn't really mean to, and at the end of the book, George kills Lennie.

Jeremy: So Lennie is like the snake?

Patrick: But Lennie didn't know he was evil. He didn't mean to be evil.

Jennifer [laughs]: Neither did the snake! And the snake in the garden! The snake in the garden didn't mean to be evil.

Patrick [laughs]: He just was there.

Patrick [continues to read passage]: Another snake. Another repetition of the periscope head.

Jennifer [begins reading after a long silence]: Lennie appears. [reads] "Suddenly Lennie appeared out of the brush, and he came as silently as a creeping bear moves. The heron pounded the air with its wings, jacked itself clear out of the water and flew off down river. The little snake slid in among the reeds at the pool's side."

Jeff: Lennie appears just like the snake.

Jeremy: But he is silently creeping like a bear.

Jennifer [laughs]: So Lennie is like a bear and a snake at the same time.

Jeremy: Well, he is sort of big and he is clumsy. And he's evil though he doesn't mean to be.

Teacher [after long silence]: Anything else? Is there any other place you want to stop? Any other puzzle?

Jeremy [jumping ahead several paragraphs in the text, reads]: "Lennie said softly, 'I didn't forget, you bet, God damn. Hide in the brush and wait for George.' He pulled his hat down low over his eyes. 'George gonna give me hell,' he said." George is going to give him *hell.* That's like the snake and evil. Why did Lennie think that? Why right here? [silence] I always thought George liked him. I didn't expect him to expect George to be angry. [silence]

At this point in the tape, the intercom is heard booming out the daily announcements, and the students achieved no closure on the interesting issues they were wondering about. Those of you who teach in secondary school will understand the situation.

The next day I reminded the students of some observations they had made:

1. There is recurrent animal imagery.

2. Lennie (and maybe George, too) is compared to both a snake and a bear (evil, but unintentionally; clumsy).

3. Lennie makes a reference to being "given hell," so perhaps he is at some level aware he has done wrong, at least in George's eyes.

I pressed the students to think about the title (the best laid plans of mice and men often go awry) and the two themes of dreams deferred and alienation and to speculate on why the places they found puzzling contributed to the themes. They tried to write a sentence or two to share with the class:

> We were puzzled by the snake being eaten by the heron. Lennie is compared to the snake since he is evil without meaning to be. He is also compared to a bear since he is clumsy. Lennie is killed by George (like the snake getting killed). This shows his dream (of owning a ranch) will be deferred.

This may not strike you as an amazing insight. And you may ask yourself if it was worth more than two days of class time to do the group work and the reporting. Surely I could have brought them to a similar statement by the skillful questioning I did twenty-five years ago. But let me remind you that structuralist activity is *slow*. I argue that the process of choosing their own places in the text to puzzle over and of sharing questions and answers is worth the time. I would also argue that the five codes give students a structure, a heuristic method, a probe to accomplish this critical process of questioning, sharing tentative answers, arriving at conclusions about literature.

At least five other interesting things worth noting are going on in this snip of conversation. First, students are helping each other to learn, a good example of the collaborative learning we teachers are reading about in our journals. Notice that Jeff was mistaken about the heron killing the snake. He had it the other way around. I suspect that most readers would expect the snake to be the predator and the heron the victim. Part of the power of this brief passage is the unexpected and ironic twist that parallels the later twist in the plot when George, the weaker partner, kills Lennie. The students corrected Jeff's misreading without much fanfare, and they supported their correction by referring to the textual evidence, a process most teachers hold dear.

Second, the group of student readers is acting as a community of interpreters. That is, as individuals they can only speculate on Steinbeck's intention in writing the snake-heron passage, but by trying ideas out on each other, they are able to validate their own guesses as they see how their hypotheses fly with their peers.

Third, the students are building on their past readings. The class had read mythology and talked about universal symbols like snakes representing evil. Their willingness to read the snake as a sort of archetypal symbol does not come out of left field, but is based on previous experiences with literature.

Fourth, students know intuitively where to stop to comment. Of the five students in this particular group, three asked questions in their jot-listing about the snake-heron passage. When it was brought up, the other two were willing to accept the passage as worth commenting on.

Fifth, students still need a teacher to prod them when they work in groups. They get stalled and are not sure they are saying important things, so a teacher must act as group facilitator. The teacher usually tries to get around to each group to probe, prod, question, keep them on track.

In summary, I would encourage other teachers to experiment with a structuralist activity in the classroom. Barthes's codes provide students as young as ninth graders with an orderly procedure for rereading a text. The process is theoretically sound and appropriate for their developmental level and allows them to make decisions based on their own intuitive sense of what is important in a text rather than relying on teacher-made questions.

References

Barthes, R. 1971. The Structuralist Activity. In *Critical Theory Since Plato*, ed. H. Adams. New York: Harcourt Brace Jovanovich. (Presents Barthes's theoretical framework.)

————. 1977. Textual Analysis of a Tale by Edgar Poe. *Poe Studies* 10, no. 1: 1–20. (Applies structuralist theory to "The Truth in the Case of M. Valdemar.")

11 Twelfth Graders Making Meaning: A Sociological Approach to *Death of a Salesman*

Carol Decker Forman
Burnt Hills–Ballston Lake High Schools
Burnt Hills, New York

As teachers of literature, we make certain assumptions about what we do in the classroom. We know that literature is rich, beyond any final interpretation, and meaningful to our students only to the extent that they are engaged in the text. And so our job seems to be that of mediator or provider of ways for students to "get into" texts. We may seem to speak out of both sides of our mouths when we say that we can begin only with student responses to literature *and* that we must structure the curriculum so that the literature is accessible to students. Are these statements contradictory? By no means. Our experience makes it possible to predict what cognitive tools our students will need to meet the demands of specific texts.

It seems safe to assume that as teachers we approach a piece of literature from a slightly different angle than we would as reader-critics alone. First we read and do our own interpretations. Then we stand back and look not only at the most problematic aspects of the work, but also at what critical paradigms we used to resolve those difficulties. We ask questions about which aspects of the work are most likely to pose problems for naive readers of a certain age, what kinds of literary questions they are most likely to raise, and what students will need to resolve those questions. For the answers to both the literary and the pedagogical problems, we look to research and theory — and then struggle with ways of translating both into practice.

By the time my college-bound seniors meet Arthur Miller's *Death of a Salesman* in the spring, they have had almost a year of applying multiple critical approaches to literature. The course is designed to help students see that no single approach is sufficient and to give them practice using different approaches. The course is also designed to help students assess the demands that a text makes on them and to select the critical paradigms that will be most useful in their interpretive process. To develop their assessment and selection skills, my students practice using critical models (culled and simplified concepts) from the formalist, psychological, archetypal, and cultural-historical schools of criticism. For example, they work with Fraser's concept of the archetypal sacrificial king, Erik Erikson's stages of psychological development, Northrop Frye's theory of genres and archetypal seasonal quest myth, as well as with the four models described later in this paper.

Death of a Salesman is complex and open to many approaches. More than any other approach, however, a sociological reading seems called for. Miller discusses drama in general this way:

> I hope I have made one thing clear . . . and it is that society is inside of man and man is inside of society, and you cannot even create a truthfully drawn psychological entity on the stage until you understand his social relations and their power to make him what he is and to prevent him from being what he is not. The fish is in the water and the water is in the fish. (1958, p. 39)

I want my students to focus on Willy Loman in relation to his society, concentrating initially on Willy and moving toward an understanding of the way society works on him. I hope, too, that the study brings my students to a broader understanding of the structures of society itself. For this, it makes sense to choose extra-literary models from sociology, models drawn from the writings of George Herbert Mead, Milton Rokeach, Emile Durkheim, and Karl Marx.

My first job is always to get the students to read the play. If I had answers to all of the questions about how to do this, I would be sunning myself in the tropics. However, I do make attempts every year. One effective motivating device is to begin with a discussion of the business world, using an article about a scam or some common but unethical business situation. This year I was particularly lucky. Near the time I was to assign the play, an article appeared in *The New York Times* about five young men who, new to the business world and anxious to get ahead, allegedly stooped to illegal information sharing. The article prompted a lively discussion between class members who held that "business is business" and those who held that moral issues supersede the dollar. The discussion was so heated that the assignment to read the play caused barely a whimper.

On the day when students are to have finished the play, I break the class into groups of four or five. I ask each group to brainstorm and produce a list of critical questions about the play, to group related questions, and to suggest an order for approaching them. This may sound like a difficult task, but my students are used to doing it. (One of my more domestic students calls it "sorting the laundry.") I introduce the technique early in the year when I discuss the idea of different critical approaches.

Students are amazingly good at grouping questions, especially when given the categories. Early on, I label categories (questions relating to characters' motivations, the historical background of the time, structural elements such as image patterns, archetypal symbols, or characters, and so forth). Later, I spend time developing categories inductively and then reemphasizing the process. Juniors and seniors can group related questions independently by the end of the year; younger students might not be able to do this task unassisted.

The class period after the lists are prepared, the small groups report to the whole class. On the blackboard I try to organize a group picture of the questions and the categories they seem to fall into. This can get confusing, so I usually ask one student to list all of the questions that are raised and another to list the categories that are mentioned. If it looks as though the process will be finished in one class period, I ask a third student to record what has been put on the blackboard. In any case, I usually do some editing and arranging before the next class.

The first time I tried the method, I was terrified. I was being observed by three professors who had introduced me to the approach. It worked beautifully, however, because the kids do tend to see the same significant questions about a particular work and the same kinds of significant questions in general. The more they do it, the more sophisticated and insightful their initial probes become. Have faith.

This year, my students raised many fine questions about the play, but they had some difficulty arranging categories of questions. The problem of Willy's suicide was on everyone's list. The other questions seemed to group around various problems that might have led to Willy's suicide. When I pointed this out, the students identified a category of questions about Willy's poor relationships: Why couldn't Willy get along with Biff? Why did he belittle Linda? Another category revolved around importance and values: Why did Willy think being a salesman was so great? Why did he place so much emphasis on being well liked? Why doesn't Howard treat Willy with more concern? A final group dealt with Miller's intentions: Why does he make the play so depressing?

The questions demonstrate that students immediately see Willy's remarkable lack of understanding of himself and his relationship to the world around him. Less able students conclude that Willy is a "wimp" and "out of it." A few more, schooled in the jargon, call him alienated.

In past years I was not very successful in getting students beyond these surface conclusions. The students who were satisfied with them could scarcely tolerate unstructured discussions on the ill-defined whys of Willy's life.

To help students get at the more profound nature of Willy's relationship with his world, I borrowed and modified the "I-me" paradigm of development and the concepts of the significant and generalized others from the sociologist George Herbert Mead. Mead (1934) contends that there is no self until society creates one in the child. Through interaction with other members of society, primarily family members, children learn to see themselves as persons. Mead calls the feedback that a person gets from others "me" images. A person is not, however, simply a sum of the "me" images collected from his or her interactions. Each person also develops an "I," which is active and self-directing. The "I" can redirect or refuse "me" images. The interaction of the "me" and the "I" elements of the personality makes the person truly human.

Mead also differentiates between the people who are important in the development of an individual's personality — the "significant" others — and the social groups to which an individual may wish to belong — the "generalized" others. Rock musicians, astronauts, world-class chess players, and yuppies are generalized others whom students might recognize as groups that influence the development of those who aspire to membership.

My students like Mead's model and show little resistance to using it. The following excerpts from their essays demonstrate the kinds of things students can do with the model:

> The Mead model can be used to explain why Willy Loman killed himself. Willy got a view of himself from the people around him. It was an unrealistic picture from his wife Linda and his children when they were young. They believed his stories and encouraged Willy to believe them by believing them. When Willy got older, everyone began to see reality except him. When Biff tried to get him to see reality, it was too much for him to handle. . . .

> Mead's concept of I-me and his idea of significant and generalized others can help us understand Willy and what he wants out of life. Willy places that image or idea of the "super-salesman" great in every respect . . . Willy wanted to be that salesman. Willy

> substituted that idea, *that* salesman, as his significant other and
> put his family (Linda, Biff, Happy) as his generalized other.
>
> In the Mead model, Willy substitutes his generalized other for his
> significant other. Willy wants the American Dream so bad that
> he puts it in front of his family.

I included this last quotation to demonstrate one monster that can
be created when trying to get students to use multiple critical approaches. What does the opening phrase indicate about this student's
understanding of the process? Is it simply an error? The same phrasing
occurs in the papers of students who have not fully grasped the
process as a process. This student can readily use Mead's concepts in
a literary situation; he might be able to use more than one approach.
What he does not have a real handle on is why a person might use
more than one approach.

Students in my classes use Mead's concepts to gain a deeper
understanding of what Willy was doing that kept him so separated
from reality and from himself. They could see that his ways of
measuring his own worth were problem ridden. And many students
want to stop the interpretive process at this point. They blame Willy
for the problems, call him a jerk, and want to move on. It is difficult
to get them to step back far enough to see Willy as a product of
something larger. Sometimes I want to attribute this resistance to
intellectual laziness, but I run across the same resistance to Winston
Smith in *1984* and Oedipus in *Oedipus the King.* High school students
strongly resist the idea that the individual might be controlled by a
larger force. I have not decided whether it is a psychological issue —
younger people struggling with their own control of the world — or
a cognitive issue based on an inability to see systems working within
systems — or both. All I know is that it takes some work to get
students to see the larger picture.

One approach that kids have used successfully to look at social and
psychological systems at work is Milton Rokeach's (1968) values
clarification model. He postulates that a value is an enduring belief
that a specific mode of conduct or end-state of existence is personally
or socially preferable to the alternatives. Once a value is internalized,
consciously or unconsciously, it becomes a standard or criterion for
guiding action, for developing and maintaining attitudes toward relevant objects and situations, for justifying actions and attitudes, for
morally judging self and others, and for comparing oneself with others.
Rokeach distinguishes between instrumental values (behaviors) and
terminal values (end-states), each of which has a kind of rank ordering

within the individual. Conflicts, says Rokeach, occur when one of the following things happens:

> A person is induced to engage in behaviors that are inconsistent with his or her attitudes or values.

> A person is exposed to new information from a significant other that is inconsistent with information already present in his or her value system.

> A person is exposed to information about states of inconsistency already existing within his or her own value system.

At one point in our work with *Death of a Salesman,* I ask students to reread the scene in which Willy goes to talk to Howard, and the following scenes with Bernard and with Charlie. I then ask them to describe the nature of the conflict in each of the scenes.

Most of my students have been in situations where they were made to feel insignificant — job interviews, interviews with their principal over infractions of rules, and the like. They recognize the conflict in the scene where Howard fires Willy immediately. With some of the students, however, the issue of humans versus machines and the significance of the individual do not become clear until they do some writing about it. When I asked them to list what is important to Willy and to Howard, they have to look hard at the issue of valuing a tape recorder more than a person's job, between valuing self-control over a lifetime of dedicated work. The juxtaposition of the two lists makes Miller's social feelings clearer to the students.

To focus more on the source and the effect of Willy's value system, the class discusses the following scenes in which Willy talks to Bernard and to Charlie. Bernard is a character type that high school kids tend to dislike, because many of them share with Willy the belief that to be well liked is to "have it made." They call Bernard a "nerd" and a "school boy" when they first encounter him and point out that Willy mocked Bernard's prophetic concern over Biff's math grade. In this scene, the students readily see another one of the Rokeach values conflicts that involves an inconsistency. Willy's primary instrumental value had been to be well liked; here he is faced with the fact that success is not at all based on popularity.

Although it is a struggle helping students see a larger system at work on Willy, I ask them to repeat the same process of identifying what is important to each character in the scene between Willy and Charlie. Here, Charlie is trying to get Willy to see reality while trying desperately to save Willy's dignity. Students invariably pick up on what they regard as an inconsistent message from Charlie. He is the one who tells Willy directly that all a man has is what he can sell, yet he also wants Willy to maintain his esteem by working for money rather than being forced to beg for it. Some students will even say that Charlie values Willy as an individual, that he is the one friend Willy has. One student said, "The ironic thing is that Charlie cares more about Willy than Willy does."

When students are asked to compare Charlie's values to Howard's, some lightbulbs go on. The students' own lists are concrete evidence of a values conflict within our society — and one that kids are confronted with in a myriad of ways. My students call Howard's values "realistic" and "street wise," practical but not very pretty. Charlie's values are "tender" (meaning wimpish) and "idealistic." Other students defend the humanism displayed by Charlie yet voice a concern that a person must be shrewdly humanistic not to be taken advantage of.

One of my objectives is to help students focus on the conflict of societal values in the play and to get them to evaluate their own stance on the issue. I therefore asked them to respond to the following passage from a Miller essay:

> The deep moral uneasiness among us, the vast sense of being only tenuously joined to the rest of our fellows, is caused, in my view, by the fact that the person has value as he fits into the pattern of efficiency, and for that alone. The reason *Death of a Salesman*, for instance, left such a strong impression was that it set forth unremittingly the picture of a man who was not even especially "good" but whose situation made clear that at bottom we are alone, valueless, without even the elements of a human person, when once we fail to fit the patterns of efficiency. . . . In short, the absolute value of the individual being is believed in only as a secondary value; it stands well below the needs of efficient production. We have finally come to serve the machine. The machine must not be stopped, marred, left dirty, or outmoded. Only men can be left marred, stopped, dirty, and alone. (1955, p. 10)

Without question, some students resist Miller's interpretation of the values of society and say that, while it sounds great to reject the materialistic business code of values, it is simply not practical. Others are more sensitive to the human cost that such a code demands. Many in their essays referred to Biff's statement that Willy "had the wrong dreams" and to the suicide itself to justify their contention that the cost was just too high. The point of the exercise is not to force agreement but to focus attention on how the values of a society affect the lives of its members. The Rokeach model is a useful tool for gathering and for structuring the interpretation of "data." Here are some responses to Miller's words:

> Willy's terminal value in life is to be financially secure and to be a successful father to his wife and two sons. Willy wants especially to be a successful father so he can be happy with his family and himself. But until he finds success with the society around him, he will not be happy with himself.

> Miller's quote would describe well what I believe is true in life. This story only brings to life the impact it has made on one Willy Loman. It seems that if you aren't successful, but just able to say you've done well in life or in business, you get disregarded. You don't fit in anymore. It's as though you were put on the earth to be a piece of a giant machine and *all* must do well in order for that part's importance to continue. If one piece isn't functioning to capacity, it gets thrown away, unloved and alone. Willy Loman is that piece.

> It's a sad fact that your individuality isn't even a close second in what's important in this world. People judge you, accept you and discard you on your ability to "make it" in the world.

> Willy's main instrumental value was to be well-liked. He told his boys that Bernard would never make it in the world because he wasn't well-liked. Making it in the world was Willy's terminal value, the only thing that mattered to him. It must have really blown Willy away to meet Bernard on the way to the Supreme Court on the same day he got fired. Double teamed on the values court. I'd say this is why Willy committed suicide.

Willy's suicide is identified by students as the crucial question of the play. Students who have not delved far into the play tend to feel that his suicide confirms their estimation that he is a wimp. Even Linda's impassioned plea that "attention must be paid" doesn't seem to force further examination. Some students point to the series of events — the firing and the restaurant scenes especially — as causes for the suicide. Few students can independently point to Willy's alienation, the tragedy of losing his sense of belonging and community that permeates this play and many of Miller's other works. But the connection does come after students use some ideas from Emile Durkheim's sociological writings as probes.

Durkheim (1933) theorizes that society makes an individual conform to it through the process of internalizing values. Society works to make the individual feel a personal, moral responsibility for social facts. How successful a society is depends largely on the extent to which it is integrated. A society that is tightly knit has much more control over the individual. An integrated society also offers the individual more "protection" from the larger world, but the price is loss of individual freedom.

Anomie is Durkheim's term for the feeling of loss of connection with society. People experience anomie when they feel that society is no longer protecting them or when the social facts of society (laws, customs, and so forth) no longer make sense to them. Reminding my students of *1984* and *Lord of the Flies*, which they had read earlier in the year, helps them make the connection.

Durkheim also wrote extensively about suicide in various kinds of societies. *Altruistic* suicide occurs when the members of a society are regulated too strongly. Individuals are so attuned to the demands of the society that they are willing to take their own lives when the norms so require. Some examples are hara-kiri and kamikaze. *Anomic* suicide occurs in societies that fail to provide guidance and feelings of connectedness for their members. They feel alienated, fail to find meaning for their lives, or are overwhelmed by feelings of futility and frustration.

Willy's personal alienation from his family is apparent to most high school students, but they are confused by the why and the how. They point to Biff's attempts to reach Willy, Happy's pathetic pleas for notice, Linda's unwavering support, as well as Charlie's patience. Students have trouble understanding where the inability to connect comes from. The more perceptive ones identify it with Willy's lack of self-esteem, but few can explain this lack in terms of the larger societal picture.

I ask students to work in small groups to find scenes where Willy is shown to be most alienated from his society and his family. The firing and the restaurant scenes come up most often. Some students even suggest the scene where Willy pleads with Ben for answers and the funeral scene. Some scenes are mentioned because of specific lines in them: "Attention must be paid. . . ." "There is more of him in this front stoop than in all the sales he ever made. . . ." "He had the wrong dreams. . . ."

This discussion leads to the understanding that Willy is cut off in several ways, some because of what he has done to himself trying to be successful, some because of the lack of humanity and compassion in other people. I suggest here, if no one else does, that Willy's suicide can be seen as an example of anomic suicide. The point is not to get students to affix a label and call it an interpretation, but to give them the conceptual tools to examine the fictional world of Willy Loman and to search for the social constructions and attitudes that made his tragedy socially inevitable.

When students focus on the many ways that Miller demonstrates Willy's alienation, the term *anomie* invariably comes up. This concept reminds students to look not only at Willy's disconnectedness, but at the society that fails to include him.

Earlier in the year we study *1984*. Durkheim's concepts are an important part of that study, but the students rely more on Marx's (1909) description of social structure to understand the design of Orwell's society. In the discussion of Willy's society, students often raise questions in Marxian terms about societal elements that seem to be working against Willy. The scene with Howard as well as Biff's angry scene near the end of the play are most likely to provoke this kind of questioning.

According to Marx, a society has a base and a superstructure. The base is composed of the activities we undertake to sustain us and the employee-employer relationships we develop for necessary production. The superstructure is composed of the mental processes that legitimate the base — noblesse oblige, for example. The ideas of any society come predominantly from the ruling class because it controls the means of producing literature, art, history — the means by which a society objectifies and thus understands itself. At this point I want students to probe further into the play, using Marx's concepts to see Willy as a product of his society and to develop some understanding of the play as social criticism. I also want them to recall where we have been. Initially we focus on Willy, the individual in society; then we move toward an understanding of the nature of society and its effects on its members.

This sounds like a lot to ask of high school students, and for some it is. They do need a format to work with to do it all. An effective tactic is to list the five kinds of alienation that Paul Blumberg discusses in his essay "Work as Alienation in the Plays of Arthur Miller":

> Sociologically conceived, the alienation of labor has many dimensions and has been dramatically treated by Miller in the following ways:
>
> 1. Alienation as a perversion or misuse of the products of one's own labor.
> 2. Alienation as the estrangement from community or Gemeinschaft values; it is the retreat in one's work into a superprivatized world where one feels no responsibility to anyone except one's immediate family or circle of friends regardless of the possible destructive social consequences of one's work. . . .
> 3. Alienation as the transformation of oneself into an otherdirected organizational man; one who sells his integrity, the genuine and unique core of one's personality in order to please

others and to achieve success in the new middle-salaried world of the large organization.

4. Alienation as the destruction of social relationships and of one's self-respect arising out of the self-hatred caused by the knowledge of failure to achieve material success.

5. The classic form of work alienation described by Marx, the alienation of the manual worker: the necessity to thrust oneself constantly into a form of toil which is dull, routine, repetitive, uncreative and stultifying. (Blumberg 1969)

I ask students to list at least one aspect of the play that corresponds to each kind of alienation and to free-write a response to the play, focusing on one aspect. The sharing of these lists and responses shows that students can see the workings of the larger social system on Willy and on his family. They see Howard as a person so estranged from humanity that he felt no moral responsibility for the humiliation he was inflicting on Willy. In discussing the organizational man who sells his own integrity, my students suddenly see more clearly the relationship between Willy and his sons. From this angle, they understand the irony of Willy's being such a fine carpenter but being unable to acknowledge his skill as a valuable personal attribute: "Even your grandfather was better than a carpenter." Biff's rebellion against the rigidly prescribed modes of behavior and hierarchy of the business world takes on more validity for students when they compare it to Happy's self-abasement. Students understand, too, why Willy cannot understand Biff's resistance to Willy's way of looking at the world. To Willy, no other way seemed available.

I feel good about what happened in my classroom with *Death of a Salesman* this year. Everything did not go precisely as planned, but much of what I wanted to happen did happen. My students really did grasp the concepts of the sociological models provided. Not only did they use them to interpret literature, but a few students began thinking about life in terms of the models. One student introduced a handsome young man to me as her "significant other." More importantly, students began to see connections between their study of *Death of a Salesman* and what they were doing in their sociology and film classes.

It came as no surprise that the students felt most comfortable with Mead's model: it is the most personal and, because of the way it was presented, the least abstract. On the final exam, students were instructed to select one of six full-length works, identify a critical question, and resolve the question, using two approaches studied this year. Forty-five of fifty students used Mead's concepts in their answers; thirty-three chose to write about *Death of a Salesman,* and all of them used Mead's model for part of their answer.

I wish I could say that each of my students came to see the characters and the play as part of a larger construct and that independently they drew several layers of interpretation, but that did not happen. Working independently, many students preferred to look at Willy as an individual character. When encouraged to use these models, however, more students worked on higher abstract levels — seeing social systems at work. The extra-literary models made the "figure-ground" relationships of Willy to his society and Willy's society to our society accessible to more students because the models provided the conceptual tools and the vocabulary needed for this kind of thinking.

Objections can easily be raised that this unit focused too narrowly on a sociological reading. However, other units in the course were studied from different literary perspectives. At the end of the year, the students were more confident and certainly more capable in assessing the demands of a text. Although they chose more personal, less abstract models when working independently, very few of the students applied the models inappropriately or chose inappropriate approaches to any work. Only the better students could compare various critical approaches, but most of my students could apply the models successfully by the end of the year. Working with *Death of a Salesman* convinced me that high school students can use conceptual tools systematically to broaden and deepen their reading and interpretive skills.

References

Blumberg, P. 1969. Work as Alienation in the Plays of Arthur Miller. *American Quarterly* 21, no. 2, pt. 2: 291–310.

Durkheim, E. 1933. *The Division of Labor in Society.* Glencoe, Ill.: The Free Press.

Eagleton, T. 1983. *Literary Theory: An Introduction.* Minneapolis: University of Minnesota Press.

Marx, K. 1909. *Capital.* New York: Kerr.

Mead, G. H. 1934. *Mind, Self and Society.* Ed. C. W. Morris. Chicago: The University of Chicago Press.

Miller, A. 1955. On Social Plays. In *Two One-Act Plays.* Englewood Cliffs, N.J.: Prentice-Hall.

———. 1958. The Shadows of the Gods: A Critical View of the American Theater. *Harper's Magazine,* August, 35–43.

Rokeach, M. 1968. *Beliefs, Attitudes and Values.* San Francisco: Jossey-Bass.

12 College-Bound Seniors Studying *Jane Eyre*: A Feminist Perspective

Roseanne Y. DeFabio
Saratoga Central Catholic High School
Saratoga Springs, New York

One of my most satisfying experiences in applying critical approaches to literature in the classroom came in reading *Jane Eyre* with a group of advanced-placement seniors. In the past I had taught *Jane Eyre* from a basically formalist approach, paying some attention to historical-cultural concerns, especially the roles and expectations forced on women in Victorian society. The inevitable agreement between me and my students that the plight of women in that unenlightened society was indeed hard constituted for me a sufficiently "feminist" reading. I congratulated myself on having raised the consciousness of those young readers.

A few years ago, however, I investigated "feminist criticism" while preparing a presentation to a group of teachers. In the course of that investigation, I discovered the complexity of the topic and became especially intrigued with feminine archetypes. In my reading I happened on Barbara Hill Rigney's *Madness and Sexual Politics in the Feminist Novel* (1969), which presents a wonderfully detailed psychoanalytic analysis of *Jane Eyre*. Fascinated with the concept of feminine archetypes and feminist perspective on literature, I went back to the classroom, determined to see what new discoveries students could make by reading *Jane Eyre* from this perspective.

What is it that teachers of high school literature courses teach? I think the answer is twofold. We provide the opportunity for students to experience some of the valued literary texts of our culture, and we provide opportunities for them to develop textual skills. In his book *Textual Power: Literary Theory and the Teaching of English* (1985), Robert Scholes raises the same fundamental question. His response is, "The object of such study ought to be textuality: textual knowledge and textual skills" (p. 20). He goes on to distinguish three basic skills: reading, interpretation, and criticism.

I came upon Scholes's book on textual power recently, after having experimented for three years with a literature program relying on reader-response techniques and multiple critical approaches to literary texts. Scholes affirmed the practice, which I had found highly successful in my own classroom.

In brief, the general classroom procedure I follow starts with the students' responses to the text and moves through an application of critical models to a final resymbolization, or written interpretation, of the text. To answer critical questions, the students need to apply material from outside. In some cases, they are able to find their own critical strategies or interpretive paradigms. At other times, they look to the teacher for the tools to unlock meaning. But note that the teacher's role is to supply the tools, not to answer the questions, not to define the meaning.

Having read *Jane Eyre* with classes before, I was aware of some critical questions prompted by the text and could prepare for them. What I had now was a new assortment of critical material for the students to apply in seeking answers to these questions — material that I believed would force them to look at this text as well as others in a new way.

The critical material that I wanted the students to apply fell, as I saw it, into three categories. In the first category were archetypes of mythic hero and quest that my students were familiar with but had never before applied to the feminine experience. In the second category were archetypes belonging specifically to the feminine principle; these concepts were new to my students. Finally, I distinguished a category of material based on modern political feminism; much of this material is related to the madness commonly found in female literary characters or attributed to them.

We began reading *Jane Eyre* in class, following the usual procedure. I assigned sections of the text to be read for each class meeting and asked the students to keep a response journal throughout the reading. At the beginning of each class, each of us chose a passage we considered especially significant, and we wrote about it for a few minutes, making observations, posing questions, comparing it to what had come before, speculating on where it might lead. In class discussion we shared our written responses with the class and responded to each other's journals.

As the two weeks allowed for reading the text passed, many of the questions were resolved to the satisfaction of the group, but others stood out as significant critical questions that required further investigation. At the conclusion of the reading, the students formed small groups. Each group selected one of five critical questions from the group discussion:

1. Does the story of *Jane Eyre* fit the pattern of the mythic heroic quest?
2. What do we know about Jane from her relationships with the other characters?
3. What is the significance of the recurring fire and ice images?
4. To what extent are weather and nature important thematic elements?
5. What religious view emerges in the text?

As the groups began to work on their questions, they looked for familiar strategies to produce an interpretation. During these sessions I moved around the room, reminding the students of techniques or critical models that might be helpful and asking questions that would force the students to look deeper into the text. The following describes some of the findings and procedures of each of the groups.

The Quest Pattern

The group investigating the quest pattern thought that they had an easy task. They were sure from the beginning that the story would fall into the pattern without complication. The class had an outline of the heroic quest pattern, which they had previously used to analyze many other stories. That outline, a simplified description of the heroic quest found in Northrop Frye (1957), Joseph Campbell (1968), and Otto Rank (1959), looks like this:

1. Origin of the hero: obscure parentage; foster parents; danger; exile.
2. Journey: education and preparation for the test; obscurity; travel into unknown lands.
3. Quest: noble goal; community benefit; conflict with monsters; temptations.
4. Supernatural aid: divine intervention.
5. Reward: heroic qualities; self-knowledge; marriage.

As the group worked through this outline, the noise level rose, indicating that the task was not going smoothly. Lively arguments broke out. The main disagreement centered on the specific nature of Jane's quest. According to the archetypal pattern, the goal of the quest should benefit the community. However, Jane's goal (self-realization, independence, liberty, the attainment of knowledge) seemed personal rather than social.

The students also argued about Jane's innocence, whether she had given in to temptation at any point. Using Jane's own words, some contended that she had sinned in putting Rochester before God: "He stood between me and every thought of religion, as an eclipse intervenes between man and the broad sun. I could not, in those days, see God for His creature: of whom I had made an idol." Other students argued that this was evidence of Jane's scrupulosity and of the temptation that Rochester represented, which Jane ultimately resisted.

Characters

The second group used several critical strategies to analyze the characters. They looked at all of them as either "flat" or "round," either "static" or "developing." They considered the possibility that some characters might be seen as "foils" to Jane. And they also decided that there was a clear division of characters into villains or helpers.

The students made up a chart on which each character was listed either as a "helper" or as an "obstacle" to Jane. At first the chart had most of the characters on the obstacle side. In the helper column the students initially put Bessie, Helen Burns, Miss Temple, Mrs. Fairfax, and the Rivers sisters. Then one student objected that Helen Burns, though Jane loved and admired her, could not be seen as a helper because Helen represented a life of resignation to suffering that was incompatible with Jane's search for liberty. So Helen Burns was moved to the obstacle column. Another student objected that if this line of reasoning were followed, all of the characters could be seen as obstacles. The group then drew up a new chart, listing each character with the role that was not to Jane's advantage. When the group presented this chart to the class, they argued that it showed Jane as a person with an unresolved identity crisis because of conflicting and unacceptable role expectations. (The students had often used Erikson's [1964] theory of the stages of psychological development to analyze literary characters.)

Fire and Ice Imagery

The group that was looking into the images of fire and ice used the common structuralist technique of observing repetitions and opposi- tions in the text. One student was struck from the beginning by the frequent repetition of fire images balanced by equally prevalent images of ice and stone. At my suggestion, the group went back to the text to find specific instances of the images, identifying the places and characters with which they were associated. They concluded that this underlying opposition between fire and ice reached its peak in the opposition between Rochester, who is continually associated with fire, and St. John Rivers, who is described repeatedly as cold, hard, and icy. According to the group's reading, the basic conflict for Jane throughout the story was between an excess of passion and emotion on the one hand and a complete lack of human warmth and emotion on the other. They were concerned by the fact that both extremes were obviously to be avoided but that no middle way seemed to be offered. Characters associated with neither fire nor ice (for example, Mrs. Fairfax and Bessie) were unappealing to the students.

The group members were dissatisfied with their inability to account adequately for Bertha Mason. They agreed that she was a grotesque example of the "fiery" nature, but they found no equally grotesque manifestation of a "frozen" nature. In their report to the class, they said this problem needed to be solved to fully explain the opposition of fire and ice.

Weather and Nature

The students in the weather and nature group found their work overlapping with the fire and ice group. In their report to the class, they too suggested that certain places and people were associated with excessive heat or cold (especially St. John Rivers). This group also pointed out that little of what we call fair weather occurred in the story. Most of the scenes take place in the dreary fall and winter months. Even those seasons that we would expect to be fair are not. The summer months at Lowood are full of pestilence and death, and the May days at Gateshead when Jane returns to visit her dying aunt are so cold and stormy that fires are needed. A period of fair weather follows Jane's return to Thornfield, but it ends abruptly in a violent storm after she accepts Rochester's proposal. The storm seemed to the students to be an important indicator of the evil of that intended union. Storms follow Jane to Marsh End. Significantly, she says to Rochester the morning after she is reunited with him, "It is a bright, sunny morning, sir. The rain is over and gone, and there is a tender shining after it."

I asked these students to look at the opposition between natural scenes and houses in the novel. At Lowood Jane found in the woods and gardens around the school a haven of beauty and sweet scents that were in marked contrast to the stench and decay of the pestilence within the school. At Thornfield Rochester calls Jane out into the "freshness" of the garden where "all is real, sweet and pure" and away from the house, which he calls "a mere dungeon." When Jane protests that the house seems to be "a splendid mansion," he replies, "You cannot discern that the gilding is slime and the silk draperies cobwebs; that the marble is sordid slate." The students observed an exception to this pattern: the houses at Marsh End and Ferndean seem almost indistinguishable from the natural setting. The students were troubled that this seemed true of both places because only one place, they felt, could be Jane's proper home. And why, they wondered, does Moor House not reflect the lack of human warmth of its master?

Religion

Students in the religion group found in the text a great number of positive and negative references to Christian religious traditions, but they also found suggestions of what they termed *primitive nature worship* and classical mythology. The students agreed that, in spite of the apparent opposition of these religious views, they do not seem to be in conflict in the text. Rather, the personal religious experience of Jane Eyre incorporates elements of all these traditions.

To help explain this blending of traditions, I gave the group some historical material, including a biographical sketch of Charlotte Brontë and a historical introduction to nineteenth century literature from a college textbook. This material convinced them that Jane's attitude toward nature as a living spirit and her emphasis on individual imagination and intuition were more indicative of the Romanticism current during Brontë's formative years than of the realism and social emphasis of the Victorian period in which she wrote.

Some members of the group investigated character names at the suggestion of one student who was struck by the appropriateness of the names Maria Temple, Helen Burns, and St. John Rivers. Equipped with a dictionary of names, a copy of *The Lives of the Saints,* and a volume of Edith Hamilton's *Mythology,* they found that the mixture of names from classical mythology and Christian tradition echoed the harmonious blending of pagan and Christian religious elements they had already observed. The class and even some group members themselves were skeptical about the validity of their interpretation and thought it should be disregarded.

The work described so far was done before I presented the feminist archetypal material that I wanted the students to apply. The actual amount of class time devoted to this early group work was only two periods. During the first period the students worked together applying whatever critical material they could find to answer their questions, and during the second period they reported their findings to the class.

I then asked the class to consider *Jane Eyre* as a feminist novel and to investigate their questions again from that perspective. After a very short discussion, the class agreed to accept Rigney's definition of feminist novels as those "which present studies of alienated female consciousnesses in opposition to a male society or to individual male authority figures" (p. 10).

I introduced the feminist approach by explaining Rigney's application of R. D. Laing's theory of madness to the characters in feminist novels. Laing's theory sees madness as a "spiritual journey" similar to the archetypal pattern of the quest. Some of Laing's key observations that Rigney (pp. 7–11) finds useful are the following:

1. Psychosis is a sane response to life in a destructive society.

2. Madness is but a stage in the evolution of a conscious, truly sane person. (Note: Jung's mythic heroes pass through a phase of withdrawal and deep introspection before returning as lawgivers.)

3. "Superior sanity" is achieved through recognizing the general illness of society and the implications of that illness for the individual.

4. Both men and women are existential entities, but role prescriptions cause a division of the self in some cases.

5. The division of the self is expressed through the presence of a doppelgänger, which represents the recognition of one's own tragic fragmentation and alienation.

6. Ontologically insecure people are in constant dread of engulfment (the sense that one may lose oneself in the identity of another), which is commonly expressed in images of burning, drowning, and bondage.

Applying these observations to the characters in feminist novels, Rigney (pp. 7–11) identified this common pattern for feminist novels:

1. Rejection of father figure and dread of engulfment.
2. Expression of the divided self in the form of a doppelgänger.
3. Annihilation of male authority figures and of the doppelgänger.
4. Search for the metaphoric mother and discovery of the mother within the self.
5. Return from psychosis.

After discussing Laing's theory of madness and the common pattern of feminist novels, I gave the class the following outline for a feminist archetypal interpretation of *Jane Eyre*:

   I. The male authority figures (see worksheet, p. 161)
  II. The doppelgänger — Bertha Mason as Jane's double
      A. Qualities
         1. Androgynous (the unfeminine in Jane)
         2. Violent
         3. Passionate; unchaste
      B. Annihilation
 III. Search for the mother
      A. The human disappointments
         1. Mrs. Reed
         2. Bessie
         3. Helen Burns
         4. Miss Temple
         5. Mrs. Fairfax
         6. The Rivers sisters
      B. Metaphorical mothers
         1. The moon
         2. The earth
      C. Self as mother
  IV. Return from psychosis
      A. The integrated self
      B. Relationship with Rochester
      C. Attitude toward St. John Rivers

With these new materials the students returned to their groups to see what further insights could be obtained from this new perspective. As they worked, I went to each group, supplying other specific material for them to consider.

The quest group tried to match Rigney's five-step pattern of feminist novels with the quest pattern and with Jane's experiences. They produced the following chart:

QUEST	FEMINIST NOVELS	JANE EYRE
1. Origin: foster parents	Rejection of father fig. Dread of engulfment	Jane rebels against Reeds Has "fit" in red chamber
2. Journey & preparation	Divided self & doppelgänger	Jane's role confusion Bertha Mason as doppelgänger
3. Quest	Annihilation of male auth. figures and doppelgänger	Reed, Brocklehurst, Rivers, Bertha — all removed Rochester made dependent
4. Supernatural aid	Search for the metaphoric mother	Moon and Earth mothers
5. Reward	Return fr. psychosis	Marriage to Rochester Jane — "altogether a human being"

In formulating this chart, the group agreed on points that had troubled them before. They now were able to agree that the object of Jane's quest was to achieve integration of the self and overcome forces that threatened to engulf her. The personal nature of her quest might, they thought, significantly distinguish the feminine experience from the traditionally social nature of the male mythic hero's quest.

One aspect of the feminist reading that some members of this group rejected was the characterization of Jane's behavior as madness. They did agree that she was alienated from her society and dreaded engulfment, but they did not agree that these constituted madness either in her own eyes or in the eyes of those who knew her. This position was debated in the general class discussion, with the fire and ice group arguing that the division of self, symbolized by the fire and ice imagery, constitutes the kind of madness defined by Laing and Rigney.

The group studying characters had a very large task. Half of them concentrated on John Reed, Reverend Brocklehurst, St. John Rivers, and Rochester as male authority figures who pose a threat to Jane's identity. I gave this group a worksheet listing the male characters and the traits common to them as male authority figures:

1. Titles of authority and a position of authority over Jane

  2. Association with murder
  3. Response provoked in Jane that indicates fear
  4. Images related to the dread of engulfment:
     a. burning
     b. bondage
  5. Annihilation

Worksheet 1, reproduced on page 161, indicates some of the group's findings.

The other half of this group considered Mrs. Reed, Helen Burns, Miss Temple, Mrs. Fairfax, and the Rivers sisters as possible mother figures for Jane (section III of the outline). In each case they found that Jane was disappointed. Mrs. Reed had promised to act as Jane's mother, but, like the wicked stepmother in fairy tales, she resented the child and tried to destroy her. Helen Burns was for a time a comfort and a loving companion to Jane, but she was too saintly and too sickly to be a mother figure, and she died shortly after they met. Miss Temple, in Jane's own words, stood "in the stead of mother" for several years, but when Miss Temple married a clergyman from a distant county, Jane was again motherless. In Mrs. Fairfax and the Rivers sisters Jane found agreeable companions, but at Thornfield and at Moor House the women were too ineffectual to help her. In both cases she was forced to flee for her own safety.

The search for the mother was continued by the religion group, which analyzed the metaphorical mothers in the text. I supplied this group with a summary of some of the feminine archetypal material in works by Annis Pratt (1981) and M. E. Harding (1971). Some of the myths I referred them to were the Isis-Osiris and Demeter-Kore myths and the Grail legends, which introduced the concepts of the matrilineal line, the earth goddess, the moon goddess, and the Magna Mater. This material helped the students explain why Jane referred to the moon and the earth as "Mother," but it also helped explain why Jane found more support and guidance in these ancient feminine deities than in the patriarchal religion represented by Brocklehurst and Rivers.

The moon goddess myths were especially interesting to the student who had argued the significance of the character names. She was excited to discover that the goddess Diana in the Isis myth and Mary the mother of Jesus belong to the same mythological tradition. The other class members remained unconvinced, but they did agree that the novel was richer in meaning because of its mythological elements.

The myth of Eros and Psyche supplied new insight for the fire and

Male	Terms of Authority	Association with Murder	Response of Jane	Engulfment Images		
				Burning	Bondage	Annihilation
John Reed	Cousin Only male "Young master"	"You are like a murderer."	Jane strikes him, is banished to red room	Red room	"You are like a slave driver."	Suicide
Rev. Brocklehurst	Master of school Male only	Causes death of Helen and others	Jane escapes to woods	Hell fire	Absolute power	Discredited Disappeared
St. John Rivers	Only male "Exacting master"	"If I were to marry you, you would kill me. You're killing me now."	Jane leaves to find Rochester	Hell fire, but more often <u>ice</u>	"When he said 'Go' I went but didn't love my servitude."	Gone to India Near death
Rochester	Only male "My master"	Adele says, "You will starve her." "I had no intention of dying with him."	Jane leaves Thornfield "I will not be yours."	Calls Jane to fire "His touch and glance burn like coals." Burned in fire	Says to Jane, "I'll attach you to a chain." Binds Bertha with a rope	Blind Maimed Dependent

Worksheet 1. Half of the small group studying characters in *Jane Eyre* completed this chart of the major male characters and the traits common to them as authority figures.

ice group. After reading an analysis of the archetypal elements of that myth in Erich Neumann's *Amor and Psyche: The Psychological Development of the Feminine* (1956), the students began to see the conflict between passion and emotional frigidity as representative of fragmented aspects of Jane's own personality. This group was more impressed than the quest group by the theory of madness, because it seemed to explain the extremes of temperament that Jane found in other people. In danger of fragmentation herself, she failed to find balance in others.

This group spent a great deal of time discussing Bertha Mason. Troubled by the character earlier, they welcomed the concept of the doppelgänger as a way of making sense of her. For Jane, they now saw the absence of a balancing character of ice as evidence that the passionate side of her nature (an expression of the feminine principle of Eros) dominated and needed to be kept in balance. Her attraction to Rochester, but also her outbursts of anger or rebellion, indicated this need. In Jane's relationship with Rivers, the danger was that his coldness would destroy her natural warmth. The group concluded that the fundamental opposition, expressed in the images of fire and ice, is not the external forces threatening Jane but the feminine and masculine principles within her.

The thematic elements of weather and nature were also clarified by applying archetypal patterns and imagery of the seasons, the vegetable world, and houses. The students started with a quotation from Northrop Frye, defining the quest romance in ritual terms as "the victory of fertility over the waste land" (p. 193). Summaries of the fertility myths (Demeter-Kore and Grail) provided an understanding of the Green World and Wasteland archetypes. With this background, the students found an explanation for the prevalence of bad weather in *Jane Eyre*. They also thought it significant that bad weather and infertility are associated with the sinfulness of the king (male authority figure).

The same material along with the biblical story of Eden clarified the significance of the gardens. The garden around Thornfield, for example, is a place of natural beauty and a haven for Jane from the unhappiness of human society, but it is also a place of temptation. The worst temptations occur in the gardens at Thornfield and Moor House, where Rochester and Rivers try to tempt Jane into evil marriages — the one because it was bigamous, the other because it was loveless. The final garden scene at Ferndean seemed to come from the Green World epiphany, in which the power of the goddess restores to life the "dying god" and also renews the natural world.

The houses in *Jane Eyre* are for the most part associated with human evil and pride, and in each case the evil is connected with the sinfulness of the "master." The students returned to an earlier question: Why does Moor House appear natural and alluring despite its master? In his analysis of Eros and Psyche, Neumann points out that in feminine literature the danger of engulfment is often disguised as a regression to paradise, an appealing place that conceals a devouring monster.

Unlike the other houses, Ferndean conceals no evil secrets. To Jane, it seems so much a part of the wood around it that it is scarcely "distinguishable from the trees." She comes to this natural setting, no longer dependent or fragmented, but independent and whole, able to support and guide the maimed and blinded Rochester.

When the groups reported to the class after this second investigation, the results were very satisfying. Rather than the five individual interpretations that can emerge from group work, each group contributed to a unified interpretation of the novel. The findings of the other groups also added to their insight into their own question. For example, the quest group expanded their development of each step of the pattern as they listened to the reports of the others.

Let me now stress that writing at each step in the process is essential. The group reports, although less formal than final essays, must be made in writing. Each group produced a chart, outline, or summary, which it shared with the class. The great value of this exercise is that, first, it forces precision and agreement among group members and, second, it provides a useful analysis for other readers. The final essays demonstrated the students' impressive ability to incorporate group findings into individual interpretations.

What, then, did I teach when I taught *Jane Eyre* to this class? What was accomplished by the involved approach just described? Using Scholes's criteria, I would say, first, that my students gained textual knowledge. They were able to demonstrate a rich understanding of this demanding novel. Second, they developed textual skills. Not only did they get practice in reading, interpretation, and criticism, but they also expanded their critical repertoire for use in future reading. As their essays on *Hedda Gabler* and *A Doll's House* indicated, students were able to apply on their own the feminist archetypal approach that we had used together.

Walt Whitman said in "Song of Myself," "I teach straying from me." I think that is what teachers of literature teach.

References

Campbell, J. 1968. *The Hero with a Thousand Faces.* Rev. ed. Princeton: Princeton University Press.

Erikson, E. H. 1964. *Childhood and Society.* New York: Norton.

Frye, N. 1957. *Anatomy of Criticism: Four Essays.* Princeton: Princeton University Press.

Harding, M. 1971. *Women's Mysteries Ancient and Modern: A Psychological Interpretation of the Feminine Principle as Portrayed in Myth, Story, and Dreams.* New York: G. P. Putnam's Sons.

Laing, R. D. 1969. *The Divided Self.* New York: Random House.

Neumann, E. 1956. *Amor and Psyche: The Psychic Development of the Feminine: A Commentary on the Tale by Apuleius.* New York: Pantheon Books.

Pratt, A. 1981. *Archetypal Patterns in Women's Fiction.* Bloomington: Indiana University Press.

Rank, O. 1959. *The Myth of the Birth of the Hero.* New York: Vintage Books.

Rigney, B. H. 1969. *Madness and Sexual Politics in the Feminist Novel.* Madison: The University of Wisconsin Press.

Scholes, R. 1985. *Textual Power: Literary Theory and the Teaching of English.* New Haven: Yale University Press.

III Contexts: Social Dimensions of Literature

13 Literature in a Multiethnic Culture

Mary Hawley Sasse
Carbondale Community High School
Carbondale, Illinois

Twenty-odd years ago — during that pivotal, crazy, exhilarating decade of the 1960s — educational institutions were jarred into rethinking their attitudes about and practices toward ethnic minority groups. In classrooms across the nation, responsive teachers sought out courses and instructors to help them learn about America's ethnic diversity, scrambled for materials that reflected ethnic contributions to American society, and instituted various ethnic study units and elective courses. Those tasks, especially for English teachers, were seldom easy.

They often found desired materials in short supply, out of print, or systematically excluded from standard anthologies and texts. Courses needed to supplement their college majors, confined largely to English and Anglo-American literature, were hard to find. College instructors, sometimes enticed to become instant experts, were often as frustrated as their students with the oversights of publishers and the deficiencies in library collections, even as they identified the wealth and significance of previously ignored minority-racial-ethnic literary achievement. To complicate matters, many English teachers — born and bred in formalist criticism — were committed to philosophical approaches that did not always fit the newly discovered literatures. They practiced methods, often unknowingly, that reflected ethnocentric bias or revered the canon of American literature as something handed down from God.

In response to growing concerns, some positive steps were taken to address the situation English teachers experienced, particularly as it pertained to teaching materials. For example, in 1970 NCTE's Board of Directors adopted and disseminated a policy statement, *Criteria for Teaching Materials in Reading and Literature,* the work of its Task Force on Racism and Bias in the Teaching of English. Recognizing the "inadequate representation of literary works by members of nonwhite

167

minorities" in materials used in "most elementary, secondary, and college English courses," "representation of minority groups which is demeaning, insensitive, or unflattering to the culture," and "the inclusion of only popular works by a limited number of 'acceptable' writers" (pp. 2–3), the task force addressed its criteria to publishers of anthologies, basic texts, and learning programs, and to teachers who used them.

Many teachers welcomed these words. Long saddled with antiquated anthologies, they were only too aware of the need for change. For example, the widely used high school literature text *Adventures in American Literature* (Harcourt, Brace and World, 1963) devoted just ten of its 827 pages to nonwhite writers of the United States. Included were three spirituals and a poem by black Americans; and a lament, a song, and a two-page "story" by Native Americans. The 1963 edition of *The United States in Literature* (Scott, Foresman) included even less: three spirituals and two poems by black American writers (James Weldon Johnson's "The Creation" and Gwendolyn Brooks's "The Explorer"). While the whole NCTE *Criteria* is worth repeating, in brief the task force urged "fair (more than token representation) and balanced (reflecting diversity of style, subject matter, and social and cultural view) inclusion of the work of nonwhite minority group members" in texts, and "editorial and critical commentary" that did not "ignore the role played by nonwhite minority writers in the continuing literary development" (pp. 3–4).

Recognizing the new market for ethnic materials, publishers began to compensate for the paucity of materials with a spate of specialized texts. In addition, standard anthologies received at least a face-lift, if not real revision, with the addition of more ethnic selections and, in a few notable instances, editorial apparatus that recognizes the ethnicity of authors and makes explicit note of the contributions of ethnic groups to American literature. In spite of these positive gains in published materials, however, most students and scholars of multiethnic literature continue to call for increased availability of ethnic-specific and multiethnic texts; inclusion of more ethnic writers, represented by more than token short selections, in anthologies; and other support materials. In addition, teachers worry about the current tendencies toward the use of mandated anthologies and standard texts (which may or may not represent ethnic contributions fairly); the emphasis on excellence in education, which gives little consideration to the needs of literary study because programs stress "mastery" at the end of each lesson;

the emphasis on teaching reading comprehension rather than responses to literature; and the de-emphasis of literature as a whole, as writing consumes a greater and greater part of the time available to instruction.

Significant for both prospective and practicing teachers of ethnic literatures is the work of the NCTE Standing Committee on Teacher Preparation and Certification. The 1986 *Guidelines for the Preparation of Teachers of English Language Arts* states that teachers of English language arts need to know about "an extensive body of literature and literary types in English and in translation"; that is, literature "by people of many racial and ethnic groups, and by authors from many countries and cultures" (p. 9). They must also be able to "use a variety of effective instructional strategies appropriate to diverse cultural groups and individual learning styles." Specifically, teachers are to "be aware that learning styles and ethnic backgrounds, for example, influence students' language experiences and development" and to "become knowledgeable about the various cultural backgrounds and cognitive characteristics of their students" (p. 11). Finally, the guidelines stress teacher attitudes, specifically "a desire to use the English language arts curriculum for helping students become familiar with diverse peoples and cultures":

> In a multicultural society, teachers must be able to help students achieve cross-cultural understanding and appreciation. Teachers must be willing to seek and to use materials which represent linguistic and artistic achievements from a variety of ethnic and cultural perspectives. In such diverse cultural contexts, students explore their own perceptions and values. (p. 14)

That is the trick — to be *willing* to *seek* and to *use* materials that represent linguistic and artistic achievements from a variety of ethnic and cultural perspectives. Teachers must have the attitudes, the knowledge, and the pedagogical skills necessary to teach all of American literature, as an NCTE flyer urged over ten years ago.

The first task for most English teachers is getting in touch with their own and their students' ethnicity. In 1981 about 82 percent of the public school staff was white. According to Robert A. Cervantes (1984), this figure has varied but slightly for the past several years (p. 284). Those teachers who have not yet examined their "Anglo-conformity" biases predicated upon an "ethnocentric ideology" and "ethnocentric pedagogy"(pp. 275–76), and minority teachers as well, must develop a better understanding of their own ethnic backgrounds so that they can transcend whatever biases distort the value of all literatures and hamper positive teacher-student relationships.

Because the ethnic disparity between teachers and students is rapidly increasing, as demographers point out, teachers can no longer hold only a "rural mindset" or base curriculum "on rural-agrarian values and beliefs" that do not "provide reasonable solutions" for a population that is 75 percent urban and changing radically in its ethnic mix (Unks 1984, pp. 443–45). Comparative figures should be of no little interest to all teachers:

1. In 1951, only 11 percent of all immigrants came from Latin America, Asia, and Africa; by 1976, 79 percent came from these areas. In 1951, 89 percent of all immigrants were from Europe and the rest of the world; in 1976, only 21 percent came from these areas (New Faces, pp. 28–32).

2. In 1986, about 50 million or 21 percent of America's 240 million people were of Hispanic, Asian, or black descent; "shortly after the year 2000 one out of three Americans will be nonwhite" (Demographic Portrait, pp. 16, 18).

3. "In 1950, all but one of the nation's 25 largest city school systems had a white student majority. By 1980, all but two had a majority of minorities" (Ornstein 1984, p. 478).

4. "The Hispanic population should reach 30 million in the year 2000 (10.8% of the total population) and 46 million in 2020 (14.7%), surpassing the U.S. black population (14.0%) as the largest minority group. . . . [The Asian population] is expected to total 12 million in 2000 (4.3%) and 20 million in 2020 (6.4%) compared to four million (2.0%) in 1980" (Ornstein 1984, p. 486).

These statistics, while they pertain to only a few of the more than three hundred ethnic groups, should put teachers on notice that changes in attitude are essential as they "lead the nation in purging itself of the notion of superior and inferior languages and cultures" (Unks 1984, p. 458).

For some teachers, that might mean learning Spanish as a second language to bring a better understanding to Hispanic American literatures, which often employ a bilingual approach. For others, that will mean abandoning a stranglehold on the traditional white canon or a totally black literature program. For all, that will mean an understanding of the definition of *ethnic* — a nation, a people, a language group, a sociologically defined race, a group bound by religion, or a group having certain genetic or physical traits (Montagu 1974, p. 441) — as revealed in both teachers themselves and in their students, who must live in an increasingly heterogeneous world. It will also mean gaining an understanding of the "marginal" person, one who is not easily classifiable or who resists classification for whatever reason. With those understandings comes an acceptance of the universality of human experience, which teachers can use as a bridge between themselves and other ethnic peoples and as a recognition of the richness and diversity of American ethnic literatures.

The second task, especially for English teachers who have neglected the field or whose academic preparations predate the "discovery" of ethnic literatures, involves learning — something that must be continuous and long term, as Bob H. Suzuki (1984) points out (p. 307). While some may take a college course or two, a workshop here or there, to aid in the task, the best bet may be self-directed reading. Because it is impossible "for any teacher to incorporate the experiences and perspectives of all the ethnic groups . . . into the curriculum" (p. 312), teachers might begin with the literatures of the groups they teach. All sorts of bibliographies of primary texts and critical resources now exist to expedite the location of appropriate materials. That, of course, is a decided improvement from just a few years ago.

To use a personal example, when I began teaching in a racially mixed high school (meaning 10 percent black minority) some twenty years ago, I could locate only one slim text, *The Negro in American Literature and a Bibliography of Literature By and About Negro Americans* (1966). This volume, prepared by Abraham Chapman, who would later edit *Black Voices* (1968), was designed for a college course. Armed with that text and only a fair personal reading background in black literature, I began my own list of books that students might enjoy. As it turned out, with not a single black student in my pilot project, thirty white students sought out — from libraries, attics, basements, book-stores — and read, discussed, argued over, and wrote about ninety different titles by black authors. Their selections included far more than those on my original list. From the students I learned a valuable lesson: learning together is a lot of fun. I subscribe to the position that Henry F. Beechhold and John L. Behling (1972) take in *The Science of Language and the Art of Teaching:* "Teachers don't know everything and shouldn't be required to conduct their classes under the tacit assumption that they do. There is much for the teacher to learn from the student. Education is (or should be) a working together to find out" (p. 41). In subsequent years, my black students often taught me more about their particular literature than the words of black literature alone could ever do. They taught me about the habits of language that define one's world view, a subject handled with scholarly skill and insight by Beechhold and Behling in their chapter "Language, Culture, and Reality" (pp. 12–44).

Since then I have expanded my reading to include Jewish American, Asian American, Hispanic American, Native American, and a smattering of European American writers, partly with the help of the resources listed at the end of this chapter. Often my students have encouraged my reading, for they reflect a far different ethnic mix than they did. In place of all white classes, I frequently enjoy American students from many ethnic backgrounds, as well as foreign students from many lands. The earlier defensiveness of black students is gone, replaced unfortunately in a few cases with an unbecoming disdain on the part of white students. On the whole, however, all students speak easily about their ethnicity, something that was difficult for them to do in earlier times, as they help one another learn about the strengths and weaknesses, the joys and the sorrows, the humanity of all peoples revealed in ethnic literature.

Finally, the third task for the English teacher involves pedagogical decisions. We must select appropriate reading materials for students. Even after having read widely in one or more ethnic literatures, teachers may find selection difficult. Teachers must come to terms with their definition of *literature*. As Werner Sollors (1984) recommends, the term "should be understood in the broadest sense to include jokes and advertising, unpublished diaries and best-sellers, folklore and movies — in addition to the more familiar literary genres" (p. 96). From the *cuentos* (parables), *dichos* (proverbs), *chistes* (jokes), and *adivinanzas* (riddles) of the Mexican American to the oral tradition, both ceremonial (sacred songs and cycles) and popular (commonplace songs and tales), of the Native American to the brand new poem in translation by a Vietnamese American, teachers have hard choices to make.

Those choices should involve three distinct criteria. First, teachers should choose selections written or composed *by* ethnic peoples. That is not to say that works written *about* them by others should be excluded, but the difference should be made clear because of possible bias or stereotyping. The distinction between *by* and *about* is further complicated by pseudo-ethnic writers who choose ethnic pseudonyms when they deal with ethnic themes. No matter how authentic their work may appear to be, Anglo writers such as "Danny Santiago" and "Amado Muro" betray one's trust. Respect should be paid also to some writers' desire to be known first of all as writers, rather than ethnics, just as attention should be given to ethnic writers who choose to write on nonethnic themes.

Second, teachers should choose selections that represent the total, dynamic nature of an ethnic group. That means selecting works from various periods. To do otherwise, as Suzuki points out, is to ignore "the continually changing nature of the subculture so it is viewed as rooted in the past and static and unchanging" (p. 300). What might have been true for a Native American born in a hogan in the eighteenth century may not be so for a modern Navaho who plays golf or herds sheep with a truck. For the same reason, selections should be drawn from writers representing both urban and rural experiences and various geographical locations. The experiences, attitudes, and ideas of modern Hispanic American writers (Puerto Rican American, Mexican American-Chicano, Cuban American, and so forth) often differ radically.

Third, teachers should choose selections that represent a broad spectrum of experiences, from the idealized to the seamy. To do otherwise is to risk a kind of "cultural relativism according to which all aspects of every ethnic subculture are seen as worth maintaining and respecting" and which "has misled some into romanticizing an ethnic subculture, even to the extent that they accept oppressive and exploitive elements of that subculture as enriching and worth respecting" (Suzuki, p. 301).

The availability of ethnic materials is crucial. Financial constraints often seem to sabotage the most thoughtful selection process. Over the years, to use another personal example, I have managed to secure classroom sets of only the following texts: *Black Voices*, the Houghton Mifflin *Multi-Ethnic Literature* series (1972), *I/You/We/They: Literature By and About Ethnic Groups* (Scott, Foresman, 1976), and Alice Marriott's and Carol K. Rachlin's *American Indian Mythology* (1968). Not to be deterred, I have continued my practice of handing out suggested reading lists and have depended on the energy of students, librarians who have enlisted the help of area and state lending agencies, and friends to secure individual titles. At first I was concerned about the limited amount of common reading and the suitability of individual titles for my students. After reading Helen C. Lee's (1973) comment in *A Humanistic Approach to Teaching Secondary School English*, however, I decided that the idea of student-selected titles, with a little help from me, worked well. She wrote, "The most important characteristic of any group of learners is how different they are from each other; hence grade levels and materials assigned to them embody myths of little validity, usually invented for purposes of financial expediency" (p. 5).

I have come to depend on my students' good sense in selecting titles appropriate for their own reading abilities and maturity. What common reading we do — often hot from the photocopy machine — provides focus and direction to additional self-directed student reading. Of course, I have an "ideal" anthology planned in my head, but it constantly changes as we run across another essay, story, poem, or new novel that simply must be added to the list. With the present situation, at least we stay current by incorporating scholars' recent discoveries and contemporary ethnic writers' work.

Finally, teachers must address curriculum arrangement and the learning environment. Under the elective system popular some years ago, ethnic literature courses (both multiethnic and ethnic-specific) were offered in many secondary schools, just as they were in some colleges. Other English programs devoted special units to the literatures. Today more integration of ethnic selections throughout the corpus of literature is evident. Experienced teachers well-versed in ethnic literature find few problems in selecting appropriate pieces for generic, thematic, or chronological approaches. However, if the literature is not treated from its ethnic perspective, some misrepresentation can occur. Care must be taken to provide a cultural "set."

To assist in that endeavor, I recommend Walter J. Ong's *Orality and Literacy: The Technologizing of the Word* (1982), which examines the organization of thought and expression in oral cultures and how literacy transforms consciousness, "traces the heavy oral residue that marks literature and thought until very recent times . . . [and] assesses some effects that the new knowledge of orality-literacy contrasts is having . . . on our understanding of what it is to be a human being, conscious of self and other" (Preface). I use some of Ong's ideas when my students study language and "purely oral art forms" (instead of the self-contradictory term "oral literature," as Ong points out). Our language study always includes serious attention to the features of dialects (pronunciation, grammar-usage, and vocabulary) as a base for a frank consideration of terms such as *wasp, dago, chink, nigger,* and *honky* when they are used in a pejorative manner. We examine connotation-denotation in series such as *neighborhood, slum, ghetto,* and *barrio;* elevation and degradation in terms such as *Negro, nigger, nigra, colored,* and *black;* and the meaning of acronyms and other abbreviations such as *WASP, NAACP, AIM, NINA,* and *BIA.* We establish the function and position of the *cantor, priest, minister, shaman, rabbi,* and *preacher;* and make lists of unfamiliar words as we read and seek their meaning (sometimes in specialized dictionaries). Always we arrive at working definitions of *race, ethnic,* and *stereotype,* and the sequential terms *alienation, accommodation,* and *assimilation* as essential to objective, analytical reading.

These language activities, too, help lead to reasoned written responses to both oral art forms and verbal art forms. In addition to reading-response journals, my students often do primary research on the nature of ethnic images in movies and on television, study the nature of satire in plays such as Luis Valdez's *Los Vendidos* and Ossie Davis's *Purlie Victorious,* and examine the nature of stereotypes in selected pieces. In the past they have generated the following topics, to name a few:

1. Frank Alpine's transformation (in Bernard Malamud's *The Assistant*)
2. Six southern black women as symbols (in Jean Toomer's *Cane*)
3. The influence of jazz and blues on imagery and theme (in Ralph Ellison's *Invisible Man*)
4. The search for self (in Maya Angelou's *I Know Why the Caged Bird Sings*)
5. An analysis of character and theme (in Elie Wiesel's *Night* and *Dawn*)
6. Tony's dreams: his path to maturity (in Rudolfo Anaya's *Bless Me, Ultima*)
7. Celie's emotional growth as revealed in the language of the letters (in Alice Walker's *The Color Purple*)
8. Significant symbols (in Richard Wright's *Bright and Morning Star*)
9. A search for identity (in Maxine Hong Kingston's *Woman Warrior*)
10. The theme of invisibility (in N. Scott Momaday's *House Made of Dawn* and Leslie Silko's *Ceremony*)

While helping students with their writing topics, I have found Robert Scholes's *Textual Power* (1985) to be exceptionally helpful. Scholes, who views reading and writing as "complementary acts that remain unfinished until completed by their reciprocals" (p. 20), identifies three related skills — reading, interpretation, and criticism, that is, "text within text," "text upon text," and "text against text" (p. 24) — and provides insights extremely valuable for the teaching-learning environment.

That environment, of course, should be as democratic and process-oriented as possible. Some tactics that Suzuki recommends are "role-playing, simulation games, nondirective styles of leading discussions, having students lead discussions, breaking the class into small discussion groups, or having students pursue individual or group projects and having them report back to the class on their findings" (p. 313); all have their place in such a context. Ethnic literature study thrives in such an environment and allows students and teachers to become truly involved with the vital, many voices of America.

References

Adventures in American Literature. 1963. New York: Harcourt, Brace and World.

Beechhold, H. F., and J. L. Behling, Jr. 1972. *The Science of Language and the Art of Teaching.* New York: Scribner's.

Cervantes, R. A. 1984. Ethnocentric Pedagogy and Minority Student Growth: Implications for the Common School. *Education and Urban Society* 16:274–93.

Chapman, A. 1968. *Black Voices.* New York: New American Library.

———, ed. 1966. *The Negro in American Literature and a Bibliography of Literature By and About Negro Americans.* Oshkosh: Wisconsin Council of Teachers of English.

Demographic Portrait: Diversity. *Education Week,* 14 May 1986, 16–18.

I/You/We/They: Literature By and About Ethnic Groups. 1976. Glenview, Ill.: Scott, Foresman.

Lee, H. C. 1973. *A Humanistic Approach to Teaching Secondary School English.* Columbus, Ohio: Charles E. Merrill.

Marriott, A., and C. K. Rachlin. 1968. *American Indian Mythology.* New York: Mentor.

Montagu, A. 1974. *Man's Most Dangerous Myth: The Fallacy of Race.* 5th ed. rev. London: Oxford University Press.

Multi-Ethnic Literature Series. 1972. Boston: Houghton Mifflin.

New Faces: How They're Changing U.S. *U.S. News and World Report,* 20 Feb. 1978, 28–32.

NCTE Standing Committee on Teacher Preparation and Certification. 1986. *Guidelines for the Preparation of Teachers of English Language Arts.* Urbana, Ill.: National Council of Teachers of English.

NCTE Task Force on Racism and Bias in the Teaching of English. 1970. *Criteria for Teaching Materials in Reading and Literature.* Urbana, Ill.: National Council of Teachers of English.

Ong, W. J. 1982. *Orality and Literacy: The Technologizing of the Word.* New York: Methuen.

Ornstein, A. C. 1984. Urban Demographics for the 1980s: Educational Implications. *Education and Urban Society* 16: 477–96.

Scholes, R. 1985. *Textual Power: Literary Theory and the Teaching of English.* New Haven: Yale University Press.

Sollors, W. 1984. Nine Suggestions for Historians of American Ethnic Literature. *MELUS* 11, no. 1: 95–96.

Suzuki, B. H. 1984. Curriculum Transformation for Multicultural Education. *Education and Urban Society* 16: 294–322.

The United States in Literature. 1963. Glenview, Ill.: Scott, Foresman.

Unks, G. 1984. The New Demography: Implications for the School Curriculum. *Education and Urban Society* 16: 443–58.

Additional Resources

Note: In addition to the many journals that students of ethnic literatures can consult, I recommend the following titles, which include bibliographies, anthologies, and criticism:

Allen, P. G., ed. 1983. *Studies in American Indian Literature: Critical Essays and Course Designs.* New York: Language Association.

Baker, H. A., Jr. 1980. *The Journey Back: Issues in Black Literature and Criticism.* Chicago: The University of Chicago Press.

———, ed. 1982. *Three American Literatures: Essays in Chicano, Native American and Asian American Literature for Teachers of American Literature.* New York: Modern Language Association.

Banks, J. A. 1984. *Teaching Strategies for Ethnic Studies.* 3rd ed. Boston: Allyn and Bacon.

Baumgarten, M. 1982. *City Scriptures: Modern Jewish Writing.* Cambridge: Harvard University Press.

Blicksilver, E., ed. 1978. *The Ethnic American Woman: Problems, Protests, Lifestyle.* Dubuque, Ia: Kendall/Hunt.

Butcher, P., ed. 1984. *The Ethnic Image in Modern American Literature: 1900–1950.* Washington: Howard University Press.

Chapman, A., ed. 1974. *Jewish-American Literature: An Anthology.* New York: NAL.

———. 1975. *Literature of the American Indians: Views and Interpretations.* New York: NAL.

Christian, B. 1980. *Black Women Novelists: The Development of a Tradition, 1892–1976.* Westport, Conn.: Greenwood Press.

Colonnese, T., and L. Owens. 1985. *American Indian Novelists: An Annotated Critical Bibliography.* New York: Garland.

Cordasco, F. 1986. *The Immigrant Woman in North America: An Annotated Bibliography of Selected References.* Metuchen, N. J.: Scarecrow Press.

Di Pietro, R. J., and E. Ifkovic, eds. 1983. *Ethnic Perspectives in American Literature: Selected Essays on the European Contribution.* New York: Modern Language Association.

Fisher, D. 1980. *The Third Woman: Minority Woman Writers of the United States.* New York: Houghton Mifflin.

————, ed. 1977. *Minority Language and Literature: Retrospective and Perspective.* New York: Modern Language Association.

Gittleman, S. 1978. *From Shtetl to Suburbia: The Family in Jewish Literary Imagination.* Boston: Beacon Press.

Green, R. 1983. *Native American Women: A Contextual Bibliography.* Bloomington: Indiana University Press.

————, ed. 1984. *That's What She Said: Contemporary Poetry and Fiction by Native American Women.* Bloomington: Indiana University Press.

Harper, M. S., and R. B. Stepto. 1979. *Chant of Saints: A Gathering of Afro-American Literature, Art, and Scholarship.* Urbana, Ill.: University of Illinois Press.

Heisley, M. 1977. *An Annotated Bibliography of Chicano Folklore from the Southwestern United States.* Los Angeles: UCLA Center for the Study of Comparative Folklore and Mythology.

Jacobson, A. 1977. *Contemporary Native American Literature: A Selected and Partially Annotated Bibliography.* Metuchen, N. J.: Scarecrow Press.

Jiménez, F. 1979. *The Identification and Analysis of Chicano Literature.* New York: Bilingual Press.

Kanellos, N., ed. 1983. *Mexican American Theatre: Then and Now.* Houston: Arte Publico Press.

Kim, E. H. 1982. *Asian American Literature.* Philadelphia: Temple University.

Kroeber, K., ed. 1981. *Traditional Literatures of the American Indian.* Lincoln: University of Nebraska Press.

Larson, C. R. 1978. *American Indian Fiction.* Albuquerque: University of New Mexico Press.

Lauter, P., ed. 1983. *Reconstructing American Literature: Courses, Syllabi, Issues.* Old Westbury, N. Y.: The Feminist Press.

Lincoln, K. 1983. *Native American Renaissance.* Berkeley: University of California Press.

Martinez, J. A., and F. A. Lomeli, eds. 1985. *Chicano Literature: A Reference Guide.* Westport, Conn.: Greenwood Press.

Miller, B., ed. 1983. *Women in Hispanic Literature.* Berkeley: University of California Press.

Miller, W. C. 1976. *A Comprehensive Bibliography for the Study of American Minorities.* New York: New York University Press.

————, ed. 1972. *A Gathering of Ghetto Writers: Irish, Italian, Jewish, Black, and Puerto Rican.* New York: New York University Press.

————, ed. 1986. *Minorities in America: The Annual Bibliography.* University Park, Pa.: The Pennsylvania State University Press.

Mohr, E. V. 1982. *The Nuyorican Experience: Literature of the Puerto Rican Minority.* Westport, Conn.: Greenwood Press.

Ramsey, J. 1983. *Reading the Fire: Essays in the Traditional Indian Literatures of the Far West.* Lincoln: University of Nebraska Press.

Rock, R. O. 1985. *The Native American in American Literature: A Selectively Annotated Bibliography.* Westport, Conn.: Greenwood Press.

Sanchez, M. E. 1986. *Contemporary Chicana Poetry: A Critical Approach to an Emerging Literature.* Berkeley: University of California Press.

14 Literature and International Understanding

Eileen Tway
Miami University

Mary Lou White
Wright State University

One means of understanding a country and its people is through literature, which embodies customs, attitudes, beliefs, and behaviors. Understanding can of course be broadened through language, artifacts, exchange visits, and other types of contact. However, literature alone is a time-honored extender of experience and allows a reader to step into another place or time for a while and even into another person's character.

Literature can cross national boundaries in many ways: when books are shipped to countries with a common language, when they are made available in translation in countries where the language is different, or when a writer from one country writes about another country, its people, and customs. Similar stories, themes, or motifs also show up in entirely different countries. Northrop Frye (1972) gives an example of a story told among a tribe of California Indians: A man follows the ghost of his wife to the land of the dead and is allowed to take her home on condition that he not touch her before getting back. Frye says, "Anyone familiar with Greek mythology would say on reading this story: 'That is the same story as the story of Orpheus and Eurydice' " (p. 5). Many "repeatable units of imaginative experience," as Frye calls them, show up in countries around the world.

For teachers of literature, the international experience is available in books and can take many routes: choosing books published abroad in a shared language and now released for sale in one's own country; selecting books in translation that reflect other cultures; finding books published in the native country that are about other countries; and looking for universal motifs or archetypes (Frye's repeatable units).

According to the editors of *Guide to World Literature*, "As we move into multi-national economic, ecological, and cultural enterprises and inter-dependencies, it becomes increasingly important for students to recognize national similarities and differences, but above all to recognize our common bond, our common lot" (p. 3). The editors go on to suggest that a study of world literature contributes "much to an appreciation and understanding of the heritage we share" (p. 3).

Young people today are living in a global community that is shrinking because of the rapid communication made possible through modern technology. At the same time, that community is being disrupted by misunderstandings and cultural differences. Representing the culture from which it springs, literature presents a compelling means for achieving cross-cultural understanding. Reading one book may not bring a great deal of enlightenment, but it is a beginning. As Warren Carrier and Kenneth Oliver say in *Guide to World Literature*, "[T]here must be a beginning if there is to be growth" (p. 12). Understanding grows when the first book is compared with a second from the same country or culture, and so on.

The NCTE committee that edited *Reading Ladders for Human Relations* (1981) took the view that one must understand oneself and learn to get along with one's immediate neighbors before attempting to understand far-away others. Consequently, the beginnings of the "Ladders" for human relations include books on "Growing into Self," "Relating to Wide Individual Differences," and "Interacting in Groups" before "Appreciating Different Cultures" and "Coping in a Changing World." No doubt it is true that the better we understand ourselves, the easier it is to understand others. But perhaps it is also possible that by testing our own identity and customs against those of others a clearer perspective on ourselves can emerge.

International understanding is a gradual accumulation of knowledge, attitudes, and opinions. Even in kindergarten, children exposed to books such as *The Wheel on the Chimney* (Hungary) can learn about people from other countries. While the concept of *nation* may not be well developed in young children, the concept of *other peoples* begins to take shape. Primary school children may learn from books such as *Moja Means One: A Swahili Counting Book* (East Africa) and from the many other picture books of international interest that are now available.

To learn what children around the world are concerned about, intermediate school children can read books such as *Sadako and the Thousand Paper Cranes* (Japan) and *A Prairie Boy's Summer* (Canada). Junior high and middle school students reading *A Life of Their Own: An Indian Family in Latin America* can see a way of life different from their own and yet recognize a common humanity. High school students have a wide range of factual and fictional material from which to choose, for example *The Sword of the Prophet: A History of the Arab World from the Time of Mohammed to the Present Day,* Colin Thiele's stories set in Australia, and classics such as *Ivanhoe.*

The term *one world* is heard often. Yet literature studies tend to focus on understanding the multicultural heritage in our own country. Important as this focus is, the world encompasses more than one country. To help young people broaden their views, teachers and librarians can make books of international interest more readily available and can guide reading toward a more global perspective.

What Has Been Done

In the 1960s the National Council of Teachers of English expanded its scope to include a more international perspective, according to J. N. Hook in *A Long Way Together* (1979). Hook says, "Not until the 1960s was the Council affluent enough for its international endeavors to amount to much" (p. 217). For example, in 1966, through the cooperation of the International Exchange and Training Branch of the Department of Health, Education, and Welfare, twenty-seven teachers from countries as diverse as Bolivia, Czechoslovakia, and Greece participated in the NCTE convention. Other efforts to reach beyond our own boundaries included cooperative ventures with other English-speaking countries and NCTE study tours abroad.

The only specific mention of literature in an international sense in *A Long Way Together* is confined to one paragraph comparing and contrasting American and British teaching preferences (p. 221). However, NCTE did concern itself with literature on an international scale in several ways. Publications such as *Reading Ladders for Human Relations* (1963, 1972, 1981) were listed with books of annotations that could promote international understanding, and *Guide to World Literature* was successful enough to warrant a second edition (1980).

Literature was an important topic at the Anglo-American Seminar on the Teaching of English, held at Dartmouth College in 1966. The study groups made a general recommendation that "the curriculum should include not only English and American literature but the 'reservoir' literature in the background of our culture (such as classical mythology, European folk and fairy tales, and the Bible), some foreign literature in translation, and some attention to other media of expression" (Muller 1967, p. 79).

Perhaps the biggest movement toward an international exchange through literature has come about through the combined efforts of librarians, publishers, and teachers. Strangely enough, though, a journalist refugee from Hitler's Germany was the catalyst for bringing these people together. Jella Lepman, after becoming a British citizen, promoted her idea that better understanding could be achieved in the world if children could get to know more about other children around the world. In 1948 Lepman founded in Munich the International Youth Library, which today contains 400,000 books in 110 languages. Bettina Hurlimann says, "From its inception, it was not simply a library, but served as a 'meeting place' for children and adults alike, for authors, illustrators, publishers, critics, politicians — anyone at all concerned with the business of children. No such library had ever existed before" (1976–77, pp. 2–3).

In 1953 Lepman founded the International Board on Books for Young People (IBBY) in Zurich. IBBY now has national sections in many countries, including the United States. As stated in its promotional flyer, IBBY encourages the establishment of national and international public and school libraries, the continuing education of those involved with children and children's literature, and the publication of imaginative and challenging books for young people. IBBY has consultative relations with UNICEF and UNESCO and is a member of the International Book Committee and the International Federation of Library Associations. The National Council of Teachers of English became a patron member in 1986.

Some may ask whether such efforts as an international youth library and an international board on books for young people are too idealistic for today's world. A child's book, *Conrad's Castle,* may help answer that question. A small boy, Conrad, is intent on building a castle in the air. When someone finally comes along and says, "Hey, you can't do that," Conrad hesitates, and in that moment of doubt the castle comes crashing down. He stands, surveying the ruins, then sets his chin and says, "I *can,* too!" He begins to build his castle again — solidly — in the air. Those who set their sights on promoting international understanding through books *can,* too. Who is to say that books cannot be a fortification against ignorance and misunderstanding? Books can help youngsters to step into another's shoes for a while, to recognize universals throughout the cultures of the world, and to appreciate similarities and differences among peoples.

Teachers who wish to promote more international understanding through literature have much support and many resources available. It only remains to raise awareness in the teaching profession of such resources.

What Can Be Done in Classrooms

When a teacher makes a commitment to teaching for a global point of view, international books can become a central focus of the curriculum. Resources and teaching techniques can be developed to implement the teaching.

Developing International Book Collections

International books can be collected in individual classrooms and in school libraries. Each collection might resemble a miniature International Youth Library with literature from many nations. Instead of using only the selection guidelines specifying a certain number of books from each country or from each genre, teachers and librarians might consider building a collection based on significant cultural influences portrayed in the books.

A recent study by one of the authors (White 1986) resulted in a description of books showing a range of cultural differences. Descriptively, international books can be placed on a culturally intensive continuum, from highly universal to strongly political, with five major groupings. On the universal side of the continuum the first grouping can be labeled "artistically playful books." These are usually picture or toy books that are gamelike or invite children to get involved. These are not stories with a plot, but simply offer opportunities for amusement. For example, a French book, *Find Me!*, encourages children to follow the story in pictures. *Peep-O*, a British picture book, is a playful romp through a series of cut-outs that invite a young reader to figure out what is on the next page after peeping through a die-cut round window.

Older children are intrigued with books featuring paper mechanics that illustrate concepts of the physical world or with flip books that allow new combinations of distorted body segments. The format of half-page books, popularized by John Goodall, has been used in many countries. Books such as these give children the opportunity to have high quality, toylike, artistic productions from many nations. Although the international concepts are minor, the books have a visual impact and can draw readers into the activity.

A second set of books forms the "world of childhood" grouping. Using universal settings, these books deal with the world of childhood, not with the geographic world. Some of them focus on real people but may also have animals as the central characters or may be fantasies set in other worlds. *Happy Children,* a Chinese picture book for preschool children, shows simple scenes of children at play, and *The Happy Dog* is a simple animal tale from Japan. Books for older children in this grouping are *Konrad,* the science fiction tale of a perfectly manufactured boy who is delivered to an eccentric woman in a less-than-perfect home, and *The Green Book,* a novel written in England but set in the future. Certain folk tales fit into this category. Although these tales can be traced to a specific nation, the translations, retellings, and illustrations often depict social groups, such as peasants or rich people, that are common in all nations.

Toward the culture-specific end of the continuum, hints of a national culture creep into the pages. The third grouping is therefore labeled "touch of culture" because the books, although based on universal concepts, offer clues to a specific culture through pictures or words. An example is *Angry Arthur,* a picture story book about a British boy who flies out of this world. Touches of British culture are apparent in mailboxes and a few articles of clothing. *May We Sleep Here Tonight?,* an animal fantasy, suggests its Japanese origin only in the book titles pictured in the background and in a few kitchen items; otherwise, the story is universal. Folk tales fall into this category also; some have one or two colorful words that suggest the country where the story was probably set. Hints of the culture can sometimes be seen in the shoes of a character, a tiny apron, or other illustrative feature. Children can be gently moved into settings that are new to them and thus acclimate themselves to unique cultural elements.

Books that are native to the culture form a fourth group labeled "culture specific." They are set in particular times and places. Both text and pictures are specific to the geographic region. Sometimes the books are fantasies, but the reader gets specific cues nonetheless. These books reflect the culture in varying degrees. In the *Weirdstone of Brisingamen,* for example, author Alan Garner writes of the stones found in Alderley Edge, the park area next to his childhood home. Novelist Alison Morgan, however, feels a distance when writing about her childhood home in Wales. She currently lives there, but her education in England made her feel like a stranger in her native town. Thus, the degree of cultural intensity may differ even in culture-specific books.

Time has much to do with cultural intensity as well. When Trina Schart Hyman traveled to Wales in 1984 to make sketches for her version of Dylan Thomas's *A Child's Christmas in Wales*, she found Swansea to be a modern industrial city far different from the town of Thomas's youth. She chose to make her sketches in Laugharne, a coastal village quite unchanged since the early 1900s. While capturing the spirit of the times, she took liberties with place in order to make the historic setting appropriate.

Other examples of culture-specific books are *Playing Beatie Bow*, set in both modern and historical Australia; *Lumberjack*, a historical pictorial concept of lumbering in Canada early in this century; and *The Emperor's Plum Tree*, a French-told folk tale set in the Orient.

The fifth and final category is the grouping called "political" books. The text and often the illustrations carry messages of political views, sometimes obvious and sometimes subtle. At times the books carry several levels of meaning. *Rose Blanche* is a German book that pictures the tragedy of war, as does *Hiroshima No Pika*. Although picture books, they are intended for audiences beyond the picture-book stage. Political messages are embedded in many culture-specific books, but when a book seems message-heavy, "political" seems a more appropriate classification than "culture specific."

With these variations, teachers can select books of different cultural intensities for classroom reading and for individual students. These categories are offered here to indicate that the request for "a book about Japan" is naive or at best only a beginning in the careful selection of books for building international understanding.

Teaching with International Books

The following examples are offered as guidelines for using literature to help children learn about the need for interdependence throughout the world.

Enlarge the Child's World View

Children need to learn a great deal about other cultures. Not only do they need an abundance of information, they need to process it in relevant ways and to view it from perspectives other than their own.

Depending on their age, children might learn about Canada, for example, from picture books:

Chester's Barn, an account of farm life on Prince Edward Island

West Coast Chinese Boy, a story about Vancouver's Chinatown in the early 1920s

The Enchanted Caribou, an Inuit legend rendered in dramatic illustrations

From novels:

Beckoning Lights
Danger on the River
Tom Penny and the Grand Canal

And from biographies and activity books:

Gretzky! Gretzky! Gretzky!
Let's Eat! Allons Manger!
Birdwatching — An Introductory Guide for Young Canadians

Global learning needs to be directed. To achieve this end, students can be given opportunities to compare and contrast information they learned about Canada. Working charts hung on walls and added to regularly would indicate the growing mass of information. When differences in information appear, as they inevitably do, children can cite statements from the various books. Life in 1920s Vancouver, for example, is different from life on a contemporary Prince Edward Island farm. From their reading, children can learn about time and about geographic, economic, and social differences. Discussions guided by the teacher and based on sound questioning techniques provide excellent learning opportunities.

Rather than focus solely on one culture, as is commonly done in social studies units, children can study broadly about a topic of interest. One fourth-grade teacher developed a strategy for encouraging children to think of structures found around the world. He put together a set of slides of bridges, tunnels, walls, gardens, and roads. While showing formal gardens of southern plantations, topiary gardens, country gardens, and city parks, he related the pictures to literature, for example, *The Garden of Abdul Gasazi* and *Tom's Midnight Garden.* He urged the children to take a topic and explore it worldwide. They could find statistics about the largest, the longest, and the highest bridges; find varied purposes for walls; learn about the construction of tunnels throughout history; and find stories that use roads symbolically. This activity was a fine way to help children de-emphasize the United States as the focus of their thinking and note how other cultures compare with ours.

Still another activity in gaining a world view is having children learn what other countries think about certain aspects of our country. The American Indian or "Red Indian" is a popular figure in literature throughout much of the world. Students might read about Native Americans in *The Robbers* and in *Little Brother without a Name*. They might also read about Native Americans in U.S. books that are distributed and in some case translated abroad.

Extend Perceptions beyond the Text

Give students that opportunity to reread or listen again to books or pertinent chapters, because much of a story is missed the first time around. Children will learn the art of savoring, reviewing, and reflecting if teachers ask them to read or hear stories more than once or twice. Keep a book like *Sir Gawain and the Loathly Lady* in the classroom several days and ask children to examine the pictures and text for details. Discuss the pictures and what they tell of medieval life. Have children share opinions on the language of the retelling. Debate the theme: Is it true even today? *The Pearl,* a picture book that is classified as a "political" book, would benefit from this kind of scrutiny and can be read on many levels. Reread it and lead discussions on more than one occasion. This is the kind of book that continues to be intriguing. Develop the symbolism of books. *Gorilla* is delightful to study because of the symbolism of the parallel pictures and parallel points of the plot.

Respond to the Books Aesthetically

Carefully view the illustrations of prize-winning, international picture books that have received awards in the Biennials of Books Bratislava and books by award-winning artists in competitions such as the Hans Christian Andersen prize. For example, Ulf Lofgren's *Harlequin* is available in an English translation, as are most of Mitsumaso Anno's books. Look for distinct features of style that the illustrator incorporates into the art. Try to train the eye to see the pleasing combinations of color, line, and shape that make these outstanding works of art even if they might not obviously appeal to American children. Examine the works of international artists who use a style unfamiliar to U.S. audiences. For example, in *The Miser Who Wanted the Sun* the illustrator borders each page and then adds fine-line drawings that seem to float in the borders. Discuss the effect of this on the viewer's perception of the art. Compare this style with others and determine its effect.

Compare different works by the same artist and note growth in the work. Lizbeth Zwerger, an Austrian artist, has done several books in a distinctive style. Follow her work in progression and note the elements she tends to include over time. Give children an opportunity to try the style or medium that Zwerger uses; they might attempt to use patterns in blouses and aprons, or they might try the gold and brown tones she uses to create an effect. These trials are just that — activities to try out the way an artist works. Original work by children may later incorporate the style, but the chance to try out the process is important in learning.

Response activities in other artistic forms also help children to gain a deepened sense of interpretation. The use of movement, dance, creative drama, puppetry, shadow plays, sculpture, assemblage, musical accompaniment to readings, and voice choirs are appropriate for literary response. Crafts are also of value: cooking, stitchery, bulletin board design, displays, and games can capture the essence of the literature and extend ideas so that children feel a relationship with the story.

Develop Language Experiences through the Text

Many books are now available in dual texts of English and another language. For example, *The Jumping Boy*, the story of a child from India, is available in Bengali and English, Urdu and English, Gujarati and English, Punjabi and English, and English alone. A number of books, such as Eric Hill's stories about Spot, are available in single-language versions in Italian, French, German, and English. Children can sample other languages and eventually learn a few words.

Readers' theater enables children to sense the drama of situations. Children can take significant scenes from several stories about World War II and read them in the order they choose. The process of selecting and fitting together specific readings is worthwhile. Any number of books might be used, for example, *Goodnight, Mr. Tom, The Island on Bird Street,* and *Upon the Head of the Goat: A Childhood in Hungary, 1939–1944.*

Sound poems are creative endeavors that require choosing a few words or a line to be chanted as background during the reading of a passage. The effect of a voice chorus in the background builds the mood. The Norwegian tale *Lanky Long Legs* can be effectively read using this technique.

Today's Concerns

A number of givens affect international literature. For example, few international books are available in the United States compared with the total number of U.S. book publications. Germany, Japan, and the United Kingdom distribute a much higher number of foreign publications than we do. Publishers need to be encouraged to import more translated, coproduced books with English texts.

Even when they are available, books from other nations often do not sell well. Many librarians look upon these books, particularly the ones in translation, as shelf sitters. Teachers need to urge school and public librarians to expand the international collections. This can be done by ordering from U.S. publishers or by purchasing library books abroad when traveling in foreign countries. Often some of the most intriguing books are available in English-speaking and non-English-speaking countries.

Compounding the problem is the fact that we have no central or compiled source for reviews of international literature. When a book is reviewed, the original source of the publication is sometimes omitted. Thus many school librarians who are responsible for ordering books have no easy way to find out what is available. Translations are seldom compared with the original, and coproductions are usually not noted. The quality of international books can be assessed by answering questions such as the following:

1. Does the book reflect the culture of origin, or has it been altered so that it seems to be an American version?
2. Does the book reflect specifics within the culture without distorting or stereotyping those elements?
3. Does the book's theme transcend time and place?
4. If the book is based primarily on universals, are they easy to understand?
5. If the book is translated, is it true to the spirit of the original and are the illustrations still appropriate?
6. If the book was first published in English outside the United States, does the editing retain the flavor of the culture of origin?

The need to promote global learning for world understanding and cooperation is not a high priority in most school curricula. However, the movement for global education is growing and will certainly attempt to bring about a change in attitude. The insularity of our country and the long-held myth that we are self-sufficient have kept us, as a nation, from developing a stronger world outlook. Major educational reform in this area is called for: the use of international literature is one avenue of change.

By independently continuing their own education, classroom teachers can become familiar with international literature. Occasionally *Language Arts* and the *English Journal* offer articles about and reviews of international books, while the *ALAN Review* and the *Bulletin of the Children's Literature Assembly* more frequently present items on international literature. Study tours and international book conferences such as the Loughborough Conference, the International Reading Association World Congresses, and the Pacific Rim Conference are advertised in columns of all four journals. Many international and national journals deal specifically with children's literature. A 1985 compilation of such journals prepared by Eileen Tway was published in the *USBBY Newsletter* (Spring, 1985). Professional organizations such as the Children's Book Council, the American Library Association, the International Reading Association, and the Children's Literature Association offer critical articles, booklists, and materials that are useful for the classroom teacher.

Although developing an international perspective is a lifelong endeavor, there is evidence that the elementary years are quite formative for global education. As Gilliom and Remy (1978) note,

> The time of middle childhood is an especially important period in children's international socialization. Indeed, the period from about eight to thirteen years of age may well be unique in that it represents a time before too many stereotypically rigid perspectives dominate children's views of the world. (p. 499)

This chapter has focused primarily on children eight to thirteen years of age. Learnings during these formative years can build a background for the English and world literature courses that have been part of the secondary curriculum for many years. International literature is a new but growing link in the study of literature and in the attainment of a world view for all children.

References

Carrier, W., and K. Oliver. 1980. *Guide to World Literature*. 2d ed. Urbana, Ill.: National Council of Teachers of English.

Frye, N. 1972. *On Teaching Literature*. New York: Harcourt Brace Jovanovich.

Gilliom, E., and R. C. Remy. 1978. Needed: A New Approach to Global Education. *Social Education* 42: 499.

Hook, J. N. 1979. *A Long Way Together.* Urbana, Ill.: National Council of Teachers of English.

Hurlimann, B. 1976–77. Jella Lepman (A Remembrance). *Friends of Newsletter* 2, no. 1: 1–4.

Muller, H. J. 1967. *The Uses of English.* New York: Holt, Rinehart and Winston.

Tway, E. 1985. The International Youth Library: Schloss Blutenberg, Munich, Germany. *USBBY Newsletter* 10, no. 1: 6, 8.

———, ed. 1981. *Reading Ladders for Human Relations.* Urbana, Ill.: NCTE/ American Council on Education.

White, M. L. 1986. *A Culturally Intensive Continuum for International Children's Books.* Unpublished study.

Children's Books

Ahlberg, Janet and Allan. 1981. *Peep-O.* London: Kestrel. (Also available as *Peek-a-Boo.* New York: Viking.)

Anno, Mitsumaso. *Anno's Alphabet.* 1975. New York: Thomas Y. Crowell.

———. 1977. *Anno's Counting Book.* New York: Thomas Y. Crowell.

———. 1981. *Anno's Journey.* New York: Philomel (imprint of Putnam).

Barrie, J. M. 1949. *Peter Pan.* Illus. Nora S. Unwin. New York: Scribner.

Bawden, Nina. 1979. *The Robbers.* New York: Lothrop, Lee & Shepard.

Böll, Heinrich. 1984. *What's to Become of the Boy? Or: Something to Do with Books.* Trans. Leila Vennewitz. New York: Knopf.

Briggs, Raymond. 1985. *The Tin-Pot Foreign General and the Old Iron Woman.* Boston: Little, Brown.

Brown, Margaret Wise. 1954. *The Wheel on the Chimney.* Philadelphia: Lippincott.

Browne, Anthony. 1984. *Gorilla.* London: MacRae. (Also New York: Franklin Watts, 1983.)

Cleaver, Elizabeth. 1985. *The Enchanted Caribou.* New York: Atheneum.

Climo, Lindee. 1982. *Chester's Barn.* Montreal, Quebec, and Plattsburgh, N. Y.: Tundra.

Coerr, Eleanor. 1977. *Sadako and the Thousand Paper Cranes.* New York: Putnam.

De Paola, Tomie. 1983. *The Legend of the Bluebonnet.* New York: Harper & Row.

Fairfield, L. 1982. *Let's Eat! Allons Manger!* Toronto: Kids Can Press.

Feelings, Muriel L. 1971. *Moja Means One: A Swahili Counting Book.* New York: Dial.

Foreman, Michael. 1977. *Panda's Puzzle and His Voyage of Discovery.* New York: Bradbury.

Gallaz, Christophe, and Roberto Innocenti. 1985. *Rose Blanche.* Illus. Roberto Innocenti. Mankato, Minn.: Creative Education.

Garner, Alan. 1979. *The Weirdstone of Brisingamen.* New York: Collins World. (Also available as *The Weirdstone; a tale of Alderley.* New York: Franklin Watts, 1961.)

German, T. 1982. *Tom Penny and the Grand Canal.* Toronto: McClelland and Stewart.

Goldston, Robert. 1979. *The Sword of the Prophet.* New York: Dial.

Hastings, Selina, reteller. 1985. *Sir Gawain and the Loathly Lady.* Illus. Juan Wijngaard. London: Walker. (Also New York: Lothrop, Lee and Shepard.)

Heine, Helme. 1985. *The Pearl.* New York: Atheneum.

Herriot, James. 1979. *James Herriot's Yorkshire.* New York: St. Martin's.

Hill, Eric. 1982. *Spot's Birthday Party.* New York: Putnam.

———. 1983. *Spot's First Christmas.* New York: Putnam.

———. 1981. *Spot's First Walk.* New York: Putnam.

———. 1980. *Where's Spot?* New York: Putnam.

Hughes, Monica. 1982. *Beckoning Lights.* Edmonton: J. M. LeBel.

Iwasaki, Chihiro. 1979. *Momoko and the Pretty Bird.* (Greek and English text.) London: Bodley Head. (Also available in English-only text. Chicago: Follett, 1973.)

Janes, R. 1982. *Danger on the River.* Toronto: Clarke, Irwin.

Jenness, Aylette. 1974. *Along the Niger River: An African Way of Life.* New York: Thomas Y. Crowell.

Jenness, Aylette, and Lisa W. Kroeber. 1975. *A Life of Their Own: An Indian Family in Latin America.* New York: Thomas Y. Crowell.

Koide, Tan. 1984. *May We Sleep Here Tonight?* Illus. Yasuko Koide. London: Faber and Faber. (Also New York: Atheneum.)

Könner, Alfred, reteller. 1983. *Little Brother without a Name.* Illus. Dieter Muller. London: Macdonald.

Kurelek, William. 1984. *Lumberjack.* Boston: Houghton Mifflin.

———. 1975. *A Prairie Boy's Summer.* Boston: Houghton Mifflin.

Lim, Sing. 1979. *West Coast Chinese Boy.* Montreal: Tundra.

Lloyd, Errol. 1979. *Nini at Carnival.* New York: Thomas Y. Crowell.

Lofgren, Ulf. 1978. *Harlequin.* Trans. Alison Winn. London: Hodder and Stoughton.

Lorentzen, Karin. 1983. *Lanky Long Legs.* Trans. Joan Tate. Illus. Jan Ormerod. New York: Atheneum.

Magorian, Michelle. 1981. *Good Night, Mr. Tom.* New York: Harper & Row.

Maruki, Toshi. 1982. *Hiroshima No Pika.* New York: Lothrop, Lee and Shepard.

Nikly, Michelle. 1982. *The Emperor's Plum Tree.* Trans. Elizabeth Shub. New York: Greenwillow.

Nostlinger, Christine. 1977. *Konrad.* Trans. Anthea Bell. New York: Franklin Watts.

Obrist, Jurg. 1983. *The Miser Who Wanted the Sun.* London: Methuen. (Also New York: Atheneum, 1984.)

Oram, Hiawyn. 1982. *Angry Arthur.* Illus. Satoski Kitamura. New York: Harcourt Brace Jovanovich.

Orlev, Uri. 1984. *The Island on Bird Street.* Trans. Hillel Halkin. Boston: Houghton Mifflin.

Park, Ruth. 1982. *Playing Beatie Bow.* New York: Atheneum.

Paton Walsh, Jill. 1982. *The Green Book.* Illus. Lloyd Bloom. New York: Farrar, Strauss & Giroux.

Pearce, Ann Philippa. 1959. *Tom's Midnight Garden.* Illus. Susan Einzig. New York: Lippincott.

Robinson, Anna. 1985. *The Jumping Boy.* Illus. Wendy Lewis. London: Mantra.

Rodgers, J. 1982. *Birdwatching — An Introductory Guide for Young Canadians.* Vancouver: Douglas and McIntyre.

Scott, Walter. 1978. *Ivanhoe.* West Haven, Conn.: Pendulum Press.

Sequin-Fontes, Marthe. 1984. *Find Me!* Trans. and adapted by Sandra Beris. New York: Larousse.

Seuss, Dr. 1984. *The Butter Battle Book.* New York: Random House.

Shecter, Ben. 1967. *Conrad's Castle.* Harper & Row.

Siegal, Aranka. 1981. *Upon the Head of the Goat: A Childhood in Hungary, 1939-1944.* New York: Farrar, Strauss & Giroux.

Tanaka, Hideyuki. 1983. *The Happy Dog.* New York: Atheneum.

Thiele, Colin. 1974. *Blue Fin.* New York: Harper & Row.

———. 1977. *The Shadow on the Hills.* New York: Harper & Row.

———. 1978. *Storm Boy.* New York: Harper & Row.

Thomas, Dylan. 1985. *A Child's Christmas in Wales.* Illus. Trina Schart Hymen. New York: Holiday House.

Van Allsburg, Chris. 1979. *The Garden of Abdul Gasazi.* Boston: Houghton Mifflin.

Vander Els, Betty. 1985. *The Bomber's Moon.* New York: Farrar, Strauss & Giroux.

Zi, Ju. 1982. *Happy Children.* Illus. Lin Wancui. Beijing: Foreign Language Press. (Also San Francisco: China Books.)

Zola, Meguido. 1982. *Gretzky! Gretzky! Gretzky!* Toronto: Grolier.

15 Teaching for a Global Society: Using Literature in the Elementary Classroom

Regina Cowin
Sunshine Elementary School
Springfield, Missouri

For years I accepted the concept of the American melting pot. Widely taught and accepted, it is a traditional theory that presents an Americanization process analogous to a chemical process. It does not take much historical study, however, to realize that the melting pot is a myth. Traveling through neighborhoods, cities, and even states effectively demonstrates that ethnic characteristics never quite disappear.

News media describe the 1980s as a time for the rebirth of American pride. I believe this rebirth is the result of three decades of searching for our roots. How can we be proud of what we are if we deny what we were and where we came from? Despite this growing sense of cultural heritage, a tendency still remains to view the world through narrow stereotypes. According to James Banks (1985), teachers must help students attain cultural excellence if they are to realize world citizenship. The twentieth century lesson clearly is that we are all citizens of a global society.

As an elementary school teacher, I struggled with my belief in the need for multicultural education versus the requirement to teach an already formidable curriculum to my fifth graders. That struggle resulted in a program that uses literature as a device to teach language arts skills while extending the social studies curriculum and helping the children attain some degree of academic excellence. At the same time, I reasoned, multicultural literature would encourage my students to respect the values and perspectives of other ethnic groups.

Teaching plans were developed for two novels, *The Sign of the Beaver* and *The Diddakoi*, which seemed to be representative of multicultural literature. The books were read to three classes of fifth graders and sixth graders, all of whom were asked to write responses to the books in their journals. Journal entries took the form of predictions, lists, summaries, and role playing and were often shared in small groups or with the entire class. The teachers were also encouraged to implement their own class activities suggested by the text of the novels.

Before we shared any multicultural literature with the classes, the children were asked to fill in the Bogardus Social Distance Scale (Bogardus 1933), which measured their attitudes toward six ethnic groups: American, English, American Indian, Afro-Caribbean, Asian Indian, and Gypsy (see Figure 1 on p. 201).

The day after the children took the pretest, I introduced them to *The Sign of the Beaver* and asked them to predict what the book might be about. Many guessed that it would be about beavers and how they live; a few thought that Indians might be involved in some way. The following comments are typical of the children's responses:

> *Malanie:* It might be about these people who are looking for a certain beaver and they find a clue that helps capture him.
>
> *Kyle:* I think the book will be about Indians and how they survive. I don't think it will be about Indians in the desert because beavers live in the woods.

After the children had shared their predictions, I showed them the cover of the book. The illustration shows a pioneer boy and an Indian boy kneeling by a stream. They are turned toward each other, and the Indian boy is whittling a stick. When I asked the children to write their thoughts now, many stuck with their original predictions, but included at least one Indian boy and the white boy who was "being helped" by the Indian.

> *Mandy:* I changed my mind. The story might be about an Indian boy that is hunting a special kind of beaver and he makes friends with a white boy and shows him how to hunt beavers and other wild animals. And he teaches him how to whittle weapons and toys.
>
> *Erica:* I think my first prediction was right, but the person is a white boy who meets an Indian boy who teaches him Indian ways.

After sharing the second set of predictions, I read the first chapter of *The Sign of the Beaver.* Afterward, the children were asked to respond in their journals to what they had heard. While a few basically wrote a summary of what had happened, others tried to imagine themselves in the white boy's place.

> *David:* If my dad left me out in the wilderness I would feel sort of scared, curious, and excited to be alone. It would probably be sort of fun to be all by yourself in the wilderness with all of the animals (except the bears).

> *Kyle:* When I'm by myself I enjoy the quiet. I think I would like
> to be where he is if he wasn't going to be there so long. I know
> that he meets an Indian boy.
>
> *Malanie:* I really think this is a good book so far. Matt sounds
> really neat. He is 12 years old. He is really lucky. He gets to stay
> by himself for 7 weeks, he gets his Dad's gun and watch, too.
> My parents wouldn't let me stay by myself for a week, especially
> with a gun.

To learn more about guns in Matt's day, we invited Steve Summers,
a local gun collector, to class. He brought guns used before and during
the Revolutionary War and spoke about the history of guns and gun
safety. He passed a horse pistol around and allowed the children to
cock and fire it. They were especially intrigued that old guns had to
be loaded each time they were fired. Mr. Summers put a small amount
of powder into one of the rifles and fired it so that the children could
see the smoke. Then he told them to imagine the amount of smoke
produced by all the guns in one battle. The children asked so many
questions about the bullets and gunpowder that Mr. Summers gave
every child a small sample of each. Here are two of the responses to
the visit:

> *Malanie:* Mr. Summers came today. He brought a pistol, Matchlock,
> and a flintlock. We got bullets and gunpowder. We got to see him
> shoot the big gun and we got to shoot the pistol. The bullet is
> heavy and . . . it's blackish-gray.
>
> *Kyle:* I liked when he fired the gun. I can imagine all the smoke
> if there was a real battle. I would not like to have to reload every
> time I fired the gun. I think its neat how they work.

As the novel progresses, Matt's gun is stolen by a white man, his
food supply is destroyed when a bear gets into the cabin, and he is
attacked by wild bees while getting honey from their tree. As a result
of the bee attack Matt almost dies, but he is saved by two Indians,
an old man and a boy about Matt's age.

At this point in the reading I asked the children to pretend they
were Matt and write about how they would feel. Nearly all of them
agreed that Matt would feel sick, confused, and worried.

After five minutes I asked them to switch roles and pretend they
were one of the Indians. The children's predictions of how the Indians
would feel toward Matt ranged from merely "curious," to a certain
amount of pity, and finally to a rather strong "he's nutty."

> *Kyle:* I think [Matt] would feel sore. The kind of sore where you
> can't move. And confused. I also think he would want to find
> the Indians that saved him. . . . I think the Indians are curious
> about Matt.

Mandy: If I were Matt I would probably feel frustrated. I know I would definitely feel weird because the Indians had touched me and cared for me. Because Matt's dad had told him that there weren't any Indians and all of a sudden I find myself being cared for by them. . . . I think that the Indians think Matt is kind of nutty because they wouldn't have to do all the stuff and get into as much trouble as Matt has.

Adriane: I feel bad for Matt. If I were him I would be thinking how did I get here, what is my dad going to say, what am I going to do. I would feel frustrated, confused and sick. I would be saying, "What am I going to do now." I would feel awful. . . . If I were the old Indian I would kind of feel sorry for him, and kind of think he was nutty, too. But mostly I would feel sorry for him.

This was the first time I had asked the children to respond from different points of view. In reading literature, we frequently identify with a certain character and tend to see the situation only through his or her eyes — modeled upon our own feelings in real life. By having the children respond from different viewpoints, I had hoped they would develop a better understanding of the differences in the two boys and judge their actions with more understanding and compassion.

In the next chapters Matt begins to recover from his injuries and meets Saknis, the older Indian, and his grandson, Attean. Saknis strikes a bargain with Matt: Attean will bring him food if Matt will teach Attean to read. Attean storms out of the cabin when Matt reluctantly agrees.

Matt is almost sure that the boy will not return, but he prepares to teach him anyway. This turn of events led to a classroom discussion of how people actually learn to read. Many of the children volunteered to help in kindergarten and first grade, a project that continued through the eight weeks of the third term. The fifth-grade students read books to the younger children and in turn listened to them read. In one first-grade class the fifth graders helped the children make books out of their own written stories.

Matt's own efforts were not quite so successful. He was teaching Attean the alphabet and reading to him from *Robinson Crusoe*. While Matt was thrilled with Daniel Defoe's story, Attean often became angry and left. Matt slowly began to see Robinson Crusoe through Attean's eyes, just as some of the students had done. Why did Crusoe need all those supplies from the ship? An Indian would not need them to get along. And why should Crusoe be the master over the native Friday? Friday would know best how to get along in his own environment, an environment very foreign to Crusoe. Why should the native, or anyone else for that matter, be another person's slave?

Adriane: I think Attean thought Robinson Crusoe was dumb because Indians survive without all of the stuff Robinson Crusoe got from the ship. Indians know how to hunt food and do a lot of other things.

Erica: Attean felt like Robinson Crusoe couldn't live on his own, like he had to have nails and things to survive. I think Matt will teach Attean to read and Attean will teach Matt things about the wilderness.

Jim Bob: Matt thought that savages would be white man's slaves. I don't think that anyone should be anyone's slave.

Katrina: Well, I guess Matt is beginning to understand that Indians don't have to be slaves and they're human beings just like me.

So we progressed chapter by chapter, each lesson often lasting an hour or more in the daily schedule. The lessons involved reading, writing, and small and large group discussions. The children became better acquainted with pioneer life, and many worked with maps to figure out exactly where Matt and his father had come from and where they built the cabin. They also worked alone and in groups to construct model cabins similar to the one Matt and his father had built. After noting that Matt made a type of bread from flour and cornmeal, we collected several johnnycake recipes from grandmothers. The children brought all of the ingredients to class and, with the help of a parent volunteer, we made cornmeal pancakes for breakfast one morning.

The chapter where Matt is stung opened the door to a science lesson on bees. Many of the children looked up facts about bees. One of the parents brought in a beehive and other equipment, explained bee-keeping, and shared pieces of a honeycomb with the class.

Toward the end of the book, Katrina made the following comments about Matt's change for the better through his relationship with the Indians and about the theme of growing up:

> When Matt's father left, Matt knew very little about the woods, and wildlife.
> But now it seems like he's a completely different person. He's learned how to cook better, to hunt, to make clothes, and the signs of the woods. Matt has changed all around, he's not the same anymore. He's more like a man. He respects the rules of the forest.
> In a way he's like an Indian boy. He hunts very well, for a white boy. He not only does it for fun he does it to stay alive. Matt is trying to do and understand more things day by day. I know Matt wanted to go with Attean but deep in his heart he knew he had to stay and wait for his family.
> Matt wants to understand why, where, his parents are. But he

wants to believe they're on their way, but some how he feels that
it's not true. He's more mature than he was when his father left.
Matt understands life more than he did before.

Just like Matt and Attean showed us, Indians and white men
can live together. There can be peace for everyone. We don't need
to fight. We need to live together in harmony.

During the teaching of the novels the children were deeply involved
in the processes of reading and writing, as well as in discovering and
creating. Because many of the children felt that the story was unresolved, one class wrote another chapter focusing on whether Matt
would ever see Attean again. Although they wanted the friendship to
continue, most of the young authors realized that Attean's way of life
was passing and that he would no longer be at home in a land now
claimed by so many white people.

While Katrina wrote about the theme of the book, Adriane reacted
to the characters:

I enjoyed this book a lot. It was about a boy named Matt. I
think the best character was Attean. He had his opinions about
everything. He expressed his feelings, thoughts, and opinions. I
really think people should do what Attean did with those thoughts.
But sometimes I think he would use his opinions as the [only]
right ones. That was not the right thing to do. The author of this
book I think had a good idea of what Attean should be like.

To supplement the short sections of *Robinson Crusoe* used in the
novel, several children brought copies of the book to class. One teacher
spent time reading chapters of the original text. Aghast at the idea of
cannibals, the children wrote and talked of little else that day. Kyle
wrote, "I think cannibals are gross. I think it would be neat to be
alone on a island for maybe a month, but not for 25 years. I'm going
to read this book." And he did try but decided, "It's just a little too
hard for me now. But in a few years. . . ."

We used a parallel procedure in teaching *The Diddakoi* by English
author Rumer Godden. Set in an English village, *The Diddakoi* is the
story of a small Gypsy girl named Kizzy, who lives in a caravan. When
her Gran dies, Kizzy becomes a ward of the state. The clash between
Kizzy and the adults in authority and between her and the other
school-aged children proved to be a story our students easily identified
with.

Once the second book had been studied and shared, the children
were again given the Bogardus Social Distance Scale. Figure 1 shows
both the pretest and the post-test results; for all groups the pretest
mean is the top number and the post-test mean is the bottom number.

8. Would exclude from my country...
Would accept:
7. As visitors to my country..........
6. To citizenship in my country.......
5. To employment in my occupation ..
4. To my school as classmates........ 3.89
3. To my street as neighbors..........   2.70 2.55
2. To my club as personal chums..... 2.45   1.77 1.59
1. To close kinship by marriage 2.15 2.17 1.50 1.22 1.01
                                         1.00

Levels of acceptance: the lower the number, the higher the acceptance for the particular group.	Gypsy	Asian Indian	Afro-Carib-bean	Amer. Indian	En-glish	Amer.

Figure 1. Responses of 64 students to the Bogardus Social Distance Scale, mean scores before and after reading the two novels.

As Figure 1 indicates, after sharing the two multicultural novels, the children had higher levels of acceptance for all six groups, even though the novels deal only with American, American Indian, English, and Gypsy cultures.

The table on p. 202 lists the children's responses to the six ethnic groups considered in the study, beginning with the most socially distant group.

From the beginning it was obvious that American children would feel closest to the group typified as "Americans." For the English and for the American Indian, the median score indicates that the children would like to be close personal friends with people in these groups, many indicating that marriage to members of these groups would be acceptable. The children felt further removed from the Afro-Caribbean and the Asian Indian groups, but they could become friends with these people and would definitely welcome them into their neighbor-hoods.

The children felt the most social distance between themselves and the Gypsy group. The pretest median, nearly at 4, indicates that Gypsies would be acceptable as schoolmates, but not as neighbors. The difference in the pretest and the post-test medians is 1.44, nearly three times the next highest difference, indicating that the children experienced the greatest change in attitude toward this group. The post-test median at 2.45 indicates that the children would now welcome Gypsies into their neighborhood and maybe even want them as friends.

I attribute the greater acceptance of the Gypsy group directly to the teaching of *The Diddakoi*. Before the novel was read to the children, they were asked to write down all they knew about Gypsies. Out of

Children's Responses to Six Ethnic Groups

Ethnic Groups	Pretest Means	Post-test Means	Differences
Gypsy	3.89	2.45	1.44
Asian Indian	2.70	2.15	.55
Afro-Caribbean	2.55	2.17	.38
American Indian	1.77	1.50	.27
English	1.59	1.22	.37
American	1.01	1.00	.01

this small sampling, we saw the stereotypic Gypsy: magical powers; crystal ball; funny clothes and lots of big jewelry; bandannas or turbans with a diamond in the middle; belief in spirits; tents and accents; carnivals; poor and dirty; many children; very artistic; strange.

According to the post-test results, however, meeting Kizzy and learning more about Gypsies gave the children a clearer picture of the Gypsy culture, or at least opened their minds to it.

The cultural group the children were exposed to in *The Sign of the Beaver* was the American Indian. The pretest median at 1.77 indicates that they felt no great social distance from Indians, probably because the children were familiar with Indian culture. Some even claimed kinship with one or more tribes. Still, the post-test median of 1.50 shows a higher acceptance level after the study had been completed.

The 1.59 mean on the pretest for the English cultural group was no surprise either. While elementary school children hear about the British as our enemies during the Revolutionary War and the War of 1812, they also realize that we are closely related in our heritage and aligned with them in current world politics. Learning more about the English through *The Diddakoi* seems to have brought us closer to them in attitude, though not by much: 1.22, for a gain of only 0.37.

Of particular interest was the children's response to the two groups that were not dealt with in the two works. The Asian Indian and the Afro-Caribbean groups were the second and third least accepted in the study. The pretest and post-test medians show that these two groups gained acceptance by the second and third greatest differences. Could it be that education in one cultural area leads to a greater acceptance of other cultures as well?

Only time will tell whether these changes in attitude are significant or lasting, but the initial results are encouraging. Although the methods we used were derived mainly from recent research in reading and writing, the wealth of multicultural literature now available makes it possible to integrate literature with other academic disciplines. The process will enable us to help children achieve academic as well as cultural excellence.

Bibliography

Banks, A. 1985. *Multicultural Education for a Global Society.* Speech given at the Multicultural Conference, April 1985, University of Missouri, Columbia, Mo.

————. 1983. Multiethnic Education and the Quest for Equality. *The Phi Delta Kappa* 64: 582–85.

Bogardus, E. S. 1933. A Social Distance Scale. *Sociology and Social Research* 17: 265–71.

Egan, K. 1983. Social Studies and the Erosion of Education. *Curriculum Inquiry* 13, no. 2.

Godden, R. 1972. *The Diddakoi.* New York: Viking.

Greene, M. 1983. Observation on the American Dream: Equality, Ambiguity, and the Persistence of Rage. *Curriculum Inquiry* 13, no. 2: 179–93.

Reynolds, R. E., M. A. Taylor, M. S. Steffensen, L. L. Shirey, and R. C. Anderson. 1982. Cultural Schemata and Reading Comprehension. *Reading Research Quarterly* 17: 353–66.

Speare, E. G. 1984. *The Sign of the Beaver.* New York: Dell.

Steffensen, M. S., C. Joag-Dev, and R. C. Anderson. 1979. A Cross Cultural Perspective on Reading Comprehension. *Reading Research Quarterly* 15: 10–29.

A special thanks to:

Mrs. Sue Arnall, fifth- and sixth-grade teacher, and Mr. Ron Hampton, sixth-grade teacher, from Bissett Elementary School in Springfield, Missouri, for all their hard work on this project.

The fifth- and sixth-grade participants at Bissett Elementary.

Mr. Roy Talent, Mrs. Ruth Martin, Mrs. Beverly Ellis, and Dr. Joel Denny, for their administrative cooperation.

My own fifth-grade class and the very supportive faculty at Sunshine Elementary School in Springfield, Missouri.

16 Students Examining Values in the Study of *Huckleberry Finn*

Sylvia White

Ruie J. Pritchard
North Carolina State University at Raleigh

In his book *The Implied Reader* (1974), Iser points out that a novel dealing with social and historical norms usually ends up questioning those norms rather than confirming their validity. This reversal has a powerful impact on readers whose familiar world is made up of the norms that the novel negates. Reading such novels can be a painful act of discovery: "The reader . . . discovers a new reality through a fiction which, at least in part, is different from the world he himself is used to; and he discovers the deficiencies inherent in prevalent norms and in his own restricted behavior" (p. xiii).

Mark Twain's *Huckleberry Finn*, which certainly fits Iser's description, is especially suitable for teaching adolescents who are themselves examining values, challenging norms and social regulations, and discovering where they stand on issues. Moreover, *Huckleberry Finn* is particularly thought-provoking for young people living in the South, for in this part of the country religious values and sometimes history dictate social mores, censorship is an educational issue, the style of living is still more rural than urban, Ku Klux Klan episodes have occurred as recently as 1986, and the plight of tobacco farmers and textile mill workers has yet to be resolved.

In teaching *Huckleberry Finn*, we want to emphasize for our students their active role in accomplishing the meaning of the novel. The success of the unit depends more on whether they develop confidence in themselves as capable learners than it does on whether they can identify the river as a symbol, cite biographical facts about the author, or label literary devices.

Central to the study is the literary learning journal. Sometimes we direct the entries so that students will focus on scenes or issues that are crucial to the development of the novel, what Iser calls "rhetorical signposts" (p. 30). At other times students respond in their own voices to lead-in sentences such as the following (Reynolds 1986): "I'm completely lost at the beginning because . . . but I will read more to. . . ." "I can (can't) really understand or identify with what is going on here because. . . ." "I like this section of writing in the story because. . . ."

Huckleberry Finn offers many concepts that most adolescents can easily grasp (for example, the influence of setting on plot, the hypocrisy), thus making the novel suitable to heterogeneously grouped classrooms. But *Huckleberry Finn* can also contribute to a more global or abstract understanding (for example, the concept that too much freedom is constricting, the effects of social and environmental contexts on our values).

We suggest that the themes of the novel be taught over the course of at least three lessons, which move learners from understanding what they themselves bring to the novel, to seeing how the novel's potential meaning is actualized through plot and characters and setting, and finally to considering such larger issues as the social context of the period and the disposition of its author. The first lesson in each thematic thread therefore focuses on the students' own beliefs, prejudices, and expectations. The second lesson then looks to the facts and characters and events in the novel itself to establish what it is that this story or this character invites us to believe. Finally, the third lesson in each thematic thread challenges the students to look beyond their own perspectives, and even beyond the views of characters in the novel, to consider universal issues such as moral development and statements about the author's society or contemporary society. The culminating activity, which considers the larger issues, is designed to put knots at the end of each thread.

In teaching *Huckleberry Finn,* we want to help our students find a way of looking at novels so that they can see themselves, the characters, and the authors as products of a culture with a set of beliefs and expectations. Through their journals and guided activities, the students learn to predict, hypothesize, speculate, and confirm or reject, thus seeing themselves as capable learners.

In the following lesson threads we will use only two themes in *Huckleberry Finn* as examples: How do one's background and environment affect one's belief system? What are the factors that move one from idealism to realism?

Theme One: Effects of Background and Environment on One's Belief System

Lesson One: Focus on the Student

By introducing a major theme in *Huckleberry Finn* into an activity before assigning the first reading, we enable our students to personalize the theme and thus grasp it on a level close to what they already know. Rather than begin the unit with a general introduction to the novel, we have found that students are more receptive to it if they have seen how their own personal issues relate to what they will read.

To prompt the students to scrutinize their own belief systems, we administer a self-survey that includes questions such as the following:

1. Do you think that everyone in America has an equal opportunity to succeed?

2. Does having money increase a person's chance for success? Why or why not?

3. Do family expectations mold a person's definition of success?

4. To what extent are your morals and values a product of your family and home environment?

5. To what extent do your friends influence your decisions and morals?

These questions can be assigned for homework or can be completed during the regular class. We usually spend one class period discussing the results of this survey, which helps students recognize opinions they never knew they held. For example, students often respond with an emphatic "yes" to the first question. After we carefully examine the other questions, however, they temper their opinions and generally become more aware of just how important one's environment is in shaping attitudes, morals, values, and success. In a usually lively, thought-provoking discussion, students comment on such influences as schools, religious beliefs, siblings, television, music, divorce, alcohol use, and of course peer pressure. This activity not only previews a theme about Huck's development, it also generates enthusiasm and group sharing.

After the class discussion, we ask students to select one major issue from the survey and elaborate on it in a nonstop writing. We encourage them to maintain their personal voices and write honest, expressive responses. Students are invited to share their writings with the class. As one student wrote:

We went to church every Sunday, but we didn't sit home and read the bible. I was taught always to be respectful to adults and to stand up for what I believe. When I moved to North Carolina from New Jersey, there was a big culture shock for me because I saw all around me the laid back Southern belles. My mother thought it was awful the way most of the women were so uninitiative [sic]. I took on the same attitude . . . the more I grow up, the more I take on my mother's attitude of "you gotta go out and get what you want from the world — the world won't hand it to you."

Lesson Two: Focus on the Novel

After these activities, students are ready to investigate how Huck's environment affects his behavior and belief system. To prepare for a discussion of this aspect of the novel, we ask students to use their reader-response journals to log examples of Huck's treatment of Jim. Students will mention Huck's taking advantage of Jim's superstitious nature and the subsequent pranks that Huck plays on Jim. In one entry a student recorded the episode in which Jim is bitten by the mate of a dead snake that Huck put on his blanket. The student concluded that Huck's treatment of Jim was sometimes immature, sometimes good, and sometimes bad. This is a signal that the student is now ready to examine why Huck is inconsistent in his behavior. To encourage speculation, we ask students to record the times when Huck's thoughts about Jim are revealed.

As students keep these logs, they begin to realize on their own that Huck's inner thoughts and feelings about Jim do not always parallel his treatment of Jim. When Huck behaves according to his personal beliefs, he treats Jim as a friend; when he follows the dictates of a prejudiced society, he treats Jim as someone's property who is in no way his equal. Students begin to see Huck's internal conflict, which drives the novel.

After the lists of Huck's behavior and thoughts are considered, we introduce an exercise on the word processor. Students are given a disk with a segment of the novel that they have not yet read. To see if they have internalized enough information to predict the changes in Huck's thoughts, we ask them to read between the lines and insert directly into Twain's text the thoughts they think Huck has — and they do so using Huck's language and Twain's style. It is best to use scenes of powerful events, such as the one in chapter 31, "You Can't Pray a Lie." In this scene Huck writes a letter to Miss Watson, telling her that Mr. Phelps has Jim and will give him up for a reward.

Students consider prior action as they author Huck's thoughts and type them into the text. For example, one student interjects:

> I'm doin' right to turn in a nigger. He's a runaway and Miss Watson paid good money for him. But, you know, it kinda bothers me 'cause Jim's been real nice to me, and many times I laugh with him and we share exciting times. Maybe I should help Jim out of this mess.

When this student called up on the computer the actual text Twain wrote, he had a check on how closely he had predicted Huck's thoughts, thus reflecting his understanding of the novel. Students find the activity satisfying and also learn another important lesson through this exercise, namely, that the novels of great artists are not sacred texts that can be translated only by experts. The readers' own responses do not violate the literature.

As a culminating activity in helping students connect with the origins of Huck's belief system, we ask them to comment in writing on how Huck's environment shapes his beliefs and behaviors. These writings reflect students' observations on Huck's home life, education, lack of parental guidance, naiveté, and the attitudes of people around him.

Lesson Three: Considering Larger Issues

Rather than deliver the usual lecture about the era in which *Huckleberry Finn* was written, we lead students to infer from clues in the novel what the prevailing attitudes were during the late nineteenth century. In groups, students brainstorm on the characteristics of the era. As they share their conclusions with the class, a student scribe records them on a transparency so that they can be referred to later. At this point we usually add items to the list and delete any unsound references so that an accurate picture of the Victorian era can be made.

After we have established a clear picture of that period, students complete another entry in their journals. We ask them to speculate on whether *Huckleberry Finn* was condemned, censored, or positively received at the time of its publication. The class is usually split in their surmises about the reception of the book. After much discussion, however, they decide that *Huckleberry Finn* was probably popular rather than offensive because the readers did not understand Twain's subtle criticism of racial prejudice. The use of a word like *nigger* did not disturb readers in the 1880s because Twain's audience was mainly white and often used the word themselves. We then examine why *Huckleberry Finn* is now considered a successful piece of social commentary on the times. The students consider which of two approaches would be more persuasive — Twain's subtle criticism advanced through an adolescent narrator or an admonition entitled "Be Nice to Blacks — They're People, Too."

During the next class period, we pass out copies of a news article with the headline "*Huckleberry Finn* Still Stirring up Trouble 100 Years after First Bedevilment" (*The Raleigh Times*). The article explains that the book was indeed banned in places during Twain's time, but because of religious controversy, not racial concerns. In the 1980s the book has been eliminated as required reading in some schools because it allegedly demeans blacks. We study the issue of why censorship related to race erupts in the twentieth century, or in our region, when it was not an issue in the 1880s.

We then ask students to respond in writing to the charge in the news article that "Black kids can be humiliated by it, white kids who are sensitive feel somehow culpable or guilty, and others have their racial biases reinforced." Reggie wrote:

> The book *Huck Finn* shouldn't be causing so much trouble I mean the man is dead that wrote it. I'm black myself and it don't bother me because I know it all happened I mean he was writing a novel and his intention was to be realistic and so therefore he had to write it as it is. As for the white kids, I like the fact that they feel guilty because it lets me know who really cared and who didn't. Even if Mark Twain was being prejudiced what difference would it make now the man is dead. It couldn't have bothered people back in those days because most slaves didn't know any better. The same stuff that was in it 100 years ago is in it now so why all of a sudden they want to do something like this. What's the use of hiding the fact that blacks was slaves back then and that is the truth and I think all blacks know that. We're not slaves any more that was then and now is now and I don't see nothing wrong with teaching it to children as a matter of fact I feel like they should know how their ancestors lived.

Responses such as this are vital to creating self-dependent learners because the ideas emerge from the students' personal knowledge of their own beliefs and values, as well as from the information the novel is presenting to them.

Theme Two: Factors That Move One from Idealism to Realism

Lesson One: Focus on the Student

The theme that we trace in this part of our study is how idealism is transformed into realism as we move from childhood's naiveté to adulthood's more realistic view of life. It is effective here for the teacher to share a personal experience that illustrates a move toward being more realistic.

We invite students to bring in examples of the wisdom that people have gained from experience. Students have shared excerpts from, for example, Frank O'Connor's "Quest of a Nation," Thoreau's *Walden,* Blake's *Songs of Innocence and Experience,* film clips of *On the Waterfront,* and even news articles such as the recent story about track star Kathy Ormsby, who renewed her faith in God and her family after a suicide attempt that left her paralyzed. These sharing sessions can be quite inspiring and stirring, something often missing in the study of novels with serious themes.

Providing prompts, we then direct students to create a journal entry about the changes brought on by a loss of innocence. When did you find out there was no Santa Claus? When did you learn that an older sibling was not a god? When did you discover that a friend had betrayed you in some way? When did you find out about the true life of a famous idol (for example, that a revered athlete takes cocaine)? Students have written insightful disclosures about an "ideal" sister coming home drunk, the divorce of parents who supposedly had a perfect marriage, the failure to win an election or make a team, the discovery of corruption in government.

Lesson Two: Focus on the Novel

After students have shared their own experiences, we guide them in taking a closer look at Huck's character. In their learner's journal we ask them to keep a record of several events that prompted Huck to compromise his idealism on certain issues and move towards a more realistic perspective. As a result of this exercise, the major ideas that students usually develop include Huck's change of attitude toward the river, adventure, independence, the glamour of the feud, and his hero worship of Tom Sawyer. For example:

> Huck sees that Tom's adventures are really not so terrific when it comes down to freeing his friend. There were many simple ways of helping Jim escape that Huck pointed out but Tom rejected them saying it was too easy, being the adventurer he was. Huck later realizes that there is no time for romantic escapades when your friend is in need of help in a life or death situation.

Lesson Three: Considering Larger Issues

A valuable method for concluding the examination of idealism versus realism is to trace how Twain changed from a writer of humorous yet serious accounts of Mississippi life to a caustic and bitter writer as he grew older. The change in America's beloved humorist can be documented through his journals, letters, and biographies. Students find it interesting that an older person's attitudes do often change, just as a teenager's do. So as not to overwhelm the students, we appoint class experts over a small domain of Twain's life (for example, ten pages in a biography), and ask them to give us another look at the man in oral reports. Since the background on Twain is not presented formally before reading the novel, this assignment is a student-directed route for more information. Finally, we ask students to create a running list of what Twain had to know in order to write *Huckleberry Finn.* They mention that he had to know about the social system in the South, the underground railroad and other historical information, the names of places, geography and topography, the terms used on a riverboat, the crops in the area, the dialect — as well as how to organize information and develop an interesting story.

It is satisfying for us as teachers to see our students come to understand and respect a great novel by a great novelist and not be intimidated. We feel that they leave this very intensive unit of study aware that although a novel imposes intentions and interpretations upon its readers, it is the readers themselves who must ultimately cooperate to compose the meaning of the work.

References

DeVoto, B. 1974. *The Portable Mark Twain.* New York: Viking.

"Huck Finn Still Stirring up Trouble 100 Years after First Bedevilment." *The Raleigh Times,* 27 April 1984, p. 10-B.

Iser, W. 1974. *The Implied Reader.* Baltimore: The Johns Hopkins University Press.

Reynolds, F. 1986. Journal entry lead-ins are adapted from those suggested by Reynolds. Rockbridge High School, Columbia, Missouri.

17 From Response to Responsibility: Recent Adolescent Novels in the Classroom

Elizabeth D. Nelms
David H. Hickman High School
Columbia, Missouri

Ben F. Nelms
University of Missouri

"Surviving adolescence is no small matter," Nancie Atwell says; "neither is surviving adolescents" (1987, p. 25). Although we call these people "young adults," those of us who live and work with them know that, in many senses, they are not yet adults. They know it themselves. But neither are they children, and they are at great pains to prove it. As with the rest of their experience, so it is with their reading.

Penny has graduated from Sweet Dreams romances to Danielle Steele; she wants to know what life is like among adults. Jan has nothing but disdain for teenage romances; she is devoted to the historical saga — those mighty tomes that make *Gone with the Wind* look like a novella; she reads them, she will tell you, because she wants to know what life was really like back then. Eric knows a lot about World War II and is plowing through *The Rise and Fall of the Third Reich*, but he takes time out for William Wharton's *A Midnight Clear*; he knows he is very much like its young protagonists. Mike tells you he does not like to read and then checks out the 711-page fantasy *The Sword of Shannara*; it is not a story for little kids, he says. Bryan is more interested in the music of Iron Maiden than in books, but he reads and respects *The Loneliness of the Long-Distance Runner* because he is a runner and because Iron Maiden has a song with the same title. Elizabeth watches *Pride and Prejudice* on PBS with her

---

Authors' note: We have shared equally in preparing this manuscript. When the first person "I" is used, however, Elizabeth Nelms is writing about her own recent experiences with students. To have used another form would have been awkward and, perhaps, misleading.

parents and then reads the book; it reminds her of K. M. Peyton's *Flambards*, which she has read time and again after also seeing it on television. You probably could not sell these young adults an unmediated *Silas Marner*, and they find *Julius Caesar* tough going, but they are readers of literature. And when they read on their own, they respond with wit and curiosity. And they expect what they read to tell them something about the world they live in.

The study of literature affects the whole person, not just bits and pieces. It may of course train the mind and sharpen the senses, but — whether we plan for it to or not — it also contributes to social vision and moral development, not necessarily in the narrow didactic or instrumental way that earlier generations expected it to, but in the growth of sensibility and the exercise of imaginative alternatives. "There's something in all of us that wants to drift toward a mob," Northrop Frye says, "where we can all say the same thing without having to think about it, because everybody is all alike except people that we can hate or persecute. Every time we use words, we're either fighting against this tendency or giving in to it. When we fight against it, we're taking the side of genuine and permanent human civilization" (1964, p. 154).

The study of literature and language — both reading and writing — should arm us for this fight. Ironically, however, both the experience and the study of literature may in two quite different ways disarm adolescents and nourish the inherent mob instinct. On the one hand, when their experience of literature is limited to formula fiction (Harlequin romances, TV sitcoms, chauvinist fantasies in print and on the screen), it may reinforce stereotypes and contribute to intellectual passivity. Teachers and librarians, recognizing the appeal of these subgenres, provide adolescents with literature that attracts them without anesthetizing them, that satisfies their interests and at the same time challenges their complacency. On the other hand, when adolescents' study of literature is limited to interpretation by formula, to the comprehension and acceptance of received interpretations whether in Cliffs Notes or a teacher's carefully structured lecture, it also contributes to passivity and intellectual authoritarianism. We all have been in classes where we excelled by learning to apply one or more literary tags: "The Romantic poets loved nature and the common man," "Hamlet's tragic flaw was procrastination (or mindless haste), excess in deliberation (or impulsiveness)," "Keats was an apostle of beauty," "Hemingway's stories revolve around a code hero," "A recurring theme in _____'s work is _____" (you fill in the blanks). It could be argued that the reduction of the literary experience to such serviceable tags is hardly less formulaic than the creaky plots and cardboard characters of pop lit.

Somewhere between a laissez-faire attitude that emancipates student readers and a critical dictatorship that imposes doctrinaire adult interpretations in the name of intellectual rigor, the teacher of adolescents must find a middle way to select and present literary texts. Most teachers in most school settings attempt to find this middle way between approaches that, on the one hand, grant students complete freedom in choosing and responding to literature and, on the other hand, confine students exclusively to teacher-selected texts and text-based interpretations as explicated by the teacher. We argue that classrooms should provide a balance between freedom and disciplined guidance in both the selection of texts and response to them. Each classroom should provide some individualized reading in which students read books of their own choice and respond in their own terms, some small-group reading in which students share responses and develop the sense of a reading community, and some common reading of both contemporary works and established classics. In all three types of activity, wise teachers use considerable tact in knowing when to let students set the terms of their own response, when to guide them indirectly to questions and issues they may not have explored on their own, and when to interject direct instruction.

Classroom strategies described and recommended in other chapters of this book go a long way toward enfranchising students in the making of meaning. However, as long as the texts selected for study consist only of received classics, students always work at a slight disadvantage. It does not take a Holden Caulfield to recognize a hint of phoniness in an attitude that presents *Macbeth* or *Great Expectations* or "The Love Song of J. Alfred Prufrock" as if it were a brand new text with no critical or interpretive baggage revolving around it, genuinely open to whatever the adolescent mind and judgment make of it. Youngsters not as acquiescent to literary gurus as some of us were may be skeptical about such "open" discussions, just as we were about the science "experiments" that always had to turn out a certain way.

Fortunately, teachers of literature do not have to choose between the solipsism of a laissez-faire approach and the reductionism of dictatorial criticism. At least part of the curriculum can be — and should be — devoted to the individual reading of texts selected by students and to group consideration of contemporary texts about which neither interpretive reading nor critical judgement has yet crystallized, that in fact are genuinely open to discussion and debate. If some of these books deal with adolescent experience in a form accessible to adolescent readers, teacher and students may have a chance to begin on even ground. Indeed, the teacher may even learn from students, whose perspectives will almost certainly be different from those of one who grew up in different circumstances, in a different generation.

More and more, teachers have available a wide repertory of creditable literature that answers to adolescent needs and expectations but also rewards interpretive and critical examination. What we attempt to do in this essay is to mention just a few of these works in the context of characteristics we have observed among the adolescents with whom we have worked and lived in recent years.

Developing Independence

Adolescents are developing independence from parents and other adult authority figures. Adolescent novels provide the opportunity for adolescents to exercise independent response and critical judgment. Robert Cormier's *After the First Death* offers such a challenge. Its topic — modern political terrorism — is both as commonplace and as exotic as the headline of today's newspaper. Its young protagonists — Kate, Miro, and Ben — are caught in the same complexities as our students, the same moral ambiguities and imperatives, only drawn more clearly by the situation in which they find themselves.

I introduce this novel by telling the students that for the first week of reading we will entertain only questions, no answers. The more questions the better, for out of this confusion will arise meaning. The first few days I have a large sheet of white paper stretched across the back of the room, with felt-tip markers ready. The students come into the room airing their frustration with the curves Cormier throws at them in his interior monologues, and they demand answers. My answer is a quick glance to the blank paper, with the reminder that they should post their questions in writing. "But remember, no answers until we've completely finished reading the book." Cormier's choice of multiple points of view forces the readers to pose questions. What does the speaker mean? Who is the speaker talking about here? What does the speaker mean by "the first death"? Help!

The reader has to finish the book to find solutions, and in this sense the book works like a good mystery story. The clues are gathered. Some say that Ben's mother makes a slip of the tongue in the first chapter when she calls Ben by his father's name. After all, don't we all do that sometimes? Others protest, pointing out that in the last chapter when the narrator Ben speaks of his schoolmates, he is mentioning friends who have been identified as his father's friends. Someone else jumps in with the reminder that Ben never went away to school at all, but attended high school on the army base. So where is the speaker, and *who* is the speaker? He talks like Ben and knows what only Ben could know. Or does he? After scrambling for a closer look at the text and poring over the pages again, the students find more clues. Maybe Ben's mother did not make a mistake; maybe she *is* talking to her husband. But why would he be writing as if he were his own son Ben? That's crazy. *Exactly.* And the excitement builds.

Peppered throughout the interior monologues are found clues that make the students question whether the narrator is at school at all. For instance, someone is administering medicine on schedule as in a hospital. Could it be that this is not a school but another kind of institution? And on and on, until students unravel the mystery and the horror of a father gone mad from his own decision to put his country above his son's life. The students gasp at this stark realization and almost thank me for letting them discover the truth on their own. They had the thrill of the hunt and they met with success. What better satisfaction is there than in a job well done. And just maybe they will be brave enough to launch out on their own without me the next time.

At the middle and junior high school level, a novel that accomplishes the same purpose is Julia Cunningham's *Dorp Dead*. One adult reader dubbed it "Kafka for kids." On the surface this short novel (88 pages) is the story of Gilly, a misfit orphan who cannot find his place in the local orphanage and seeks solace in the quiet retreat of a crumbling stone tower. When he has the opportunity to live with the town eccentric, Mr. Kobalt, he jumps at the chance. Here is a place he can be alone, mind his own business, and have no one bother him again. But that is not quite the way things turn out. Gilly changes from a bright-eyed young man into a blank-faced clone of Mr. Kobalt. Then one day he begins to discover the true nature of his new master. Once he enters the room with the ladders, his life becomes a nightmare and he must escape or lose everything. The students read with wide eyes, watching Gilly go through his daily routine, not recognizing the danger signals.

Some critics reviewed this novel and rejected it as simplistic and contrived. I read one particular review to my seventh graders. They responded with anger toward the reviewer and a request to draft a letter to Julia Cunningham in defense of her novel. They told her how much they had enjoyed the story and specifically mentioned the parts

that intrigued them. The names she chose — Gilly, Kobalt, Mash —
held meaning for them, they said. The cage without a door was a
clear clue to interpreting Gilly's refusal to leave Kobalt's backyard after
his first few jaunts into town. The fast-paced ending with its building
of suspense kept their attention, and the final scene brought satisfaction
and vindication for the protagonist. They asked, however, about the
strange Hunter who appears only once in the novel. The author replied
in a letter to the students:

> The poor Hunter has been accused of being a stand-in for Jesus
> and, the most mild, a supernatural being, a No-name, when all I
> meant him to be was that one or maybe two persons who at
> some time, if we are lucky, passed through our lives, leaving
> behind a tremendous influence for good — a teacher, an aunt or
> perhaps just a single conversation in a strange room.

The students were thanked in return by the author. They had read
her book and expressed appreciation. They had discovered a meaning
for themselves that was rich and full. Here is her thanks to them:

> A writer is, admittedly by choice, a loner him- or herself, at least
> to the extent that the work must be thought about and done in
> solitude. And this solitariness also carries over after a book is
> published, with the exception of the reviewers and, after all, they
> have other purposes than to displease or delight the writer. Praise
> and interest, expressed by someone like you, break and illuminate
> this professional aloneness. My gratitude is real.

Author and reader meet and make meaning, and the readers go away
more content and somewhat more civilized.

Both of these books, however, provide more than just mysteries
upon which adolescents try out their interpretive skills. Both present
adolescent characters to whom they can relate. In their own way,
young people all know about the separateness of adolescent and adult
worlds and the possible alienation of the one from the other, about
the inner conflict between a sense of responsibility and a need to be
free, about being alone and the ultimate loneliness of each individual
forced to make decisions when there are no appealing alternatives.
This is heavy stuff, they will tell you, but it is not foreign to their
experience. In one way or another, it is part of the background of experience they bring to these texts, and the leap from their own
experience to that of the protagonist is neither as great nor apparently
as presumptuous as it would be in the case of a Hemingway or a
Faulkner novel.

The emergence of a genuine adolescent culture or subculture may
be a unique twentieth century phenomenon. In the discussion of novels

that purport to deal with the psychological, social, and moral imperatives of that culture, adolescents are not aliens groping to understand the basic premises of the book; in fact they may prove to be unique informants on the situations and scenes depicted. Thus the teacher's natural tendency to dominate may be curtailed. As Robert Scholes has observed, "The more culturally at home in a text our students become, the less dependent they will be on guidance from the instructor. I hate to say it, but I must observe that one of the reasons we teachers favor the big anthology is that it keeps our students dependent upon us, justifying our existence" (1985, p. 27).

Students reading contemporary adolescent fiction with us — whether in individualized reading, in small groups, or as a whole class — are culturally at home, and they are quite willing to assert their independence. Contemporary adolescent novels may thus provide ideal opportunities for students to exert their inner resources in responding to literature and to relate what they read to a world outside the book. Interacting with the text, students make meaning and are capable of using that new-made meaning to judge the world created by the author and at the same time to look critically at the world outside the book. Do Cormier and Cunningham have it right in what they imply of human experience and social reality? Maybe or maybe not. It is an open question, not one that any of us can easily answer. Asking the question allows us simultaneously to judge the world of the text and the world to which it apparently refers. It is one possible version of the world in which we live.

Participating in Community Learning

The adolescent is thus a member of a well-defined and increasingly autonomous community. Adolescent novels promote social interaction and community learning, even among recalcitrant learners and potential dropouts or discipline problems. The students in my tenth-grade Exploring Literature classes boasted that they hated to read and had never completed a book. The title of the course was apt, for I began to realize that these reluctant learners were really exploring whether to continue in school at all and more particularly whether to tolerate yet another English teacher.

Harry Mazer's *The Island Keeper* helped change all of that. I introduced the students to Cleo, a character who also felt estranged from the adults in her life and wished to be left alone. Her wish became reality when she ran away to her father's private island in

Canada to think and to sort out her feelings. A poor little rich girl, overweight and overindulged, Cleo had never had to lift a finger to help herself. And therein lay her lack of self-confidence. Not until she was left to fend for herself did she realize that she could take care of herself. The challenge of the island called on all of her abilities and gave her a new self-respect. When she was ready to go home, she found that her walkabout was just beginning and that she would have to survive the winter alone on the island.

The pages are filled with intriguing information on survival, and the students — even the most reluctant — enjoy predicting what will happen in the next chapter. They write what they would do in the same predicament and watch as Cleo grows up into a self-reliant young woman. They wish for a more powerful ending and dislike immensely the grandmother who is as stuffy at the conclusion of the book as she had been at the beginning. They relate to Cleo, for she has trouble communicating with her busy father and harbors feelings of resentment that she is not more a part of his life. In the end, the students rejoice in her new goals and sense of pride in herself.

But mainly they are ready to explore more about survival on their own, and they are fascinated by the mysteries of living in the woods away from civilization. One young man told me as he handed in his book that he too knew how to trap wild animals. I took that information as an invitation to ask him more. Our conversation led to a wonderful day in which he and his father demonstrated for the class the way to skin a muskrat and shared with us some cooked wild meat — muskrat, turtle, and deer. The father and I both beamed when Brian stood proudly before the group and showed his expertise in the art of trapping.

That personal sharing led us into more research on natural foods, folk arts, and survival techniques. We used handbooks written by nature enthusiasts and perused the *Foxfire* books as well as Missouri's local *Bittersweet* magazine. We asked our own elders about the way things used to be and invited elderly guests to class to show us the crafts of yesteryear. Our principal demonstrated his art of wood carving, and we all carved apples, hung them to dry on a wire across the front of the room, and later made them into applehead dolls.

A book had opened new worlds to these nonreaders, and together we plunged in headfirst. Students wrote to Harry Mazer, sharing their appreciation. From their letters I learned how far-reaching the effects really were:

> You gave me some ideas to think about like how I should be
> more responsible and live up to things in life with a feeling of

bravery, honesty, and effort to try harder. If Cleo can do it, maybe I can too.

And this letter from a student recently from Laos:

> Cleo had a situation that I have. I mean, here I am a foreigner to this country in Columbia, MO. There are no Laos families. I feel very lonely here in United States. I have no best friend to talk to when I need someone to talk to. I would not want to talk to my parents because they wouldn't understand. So, it's just like Cleo. She lost her two best people. And I lost all my friends, relatives, and my country. I wanted to leave Columbia for a while, just like Cleo. To get out of the house and go somewhere that will make me happy for a while and get all the problems solved. The thing that I will remember from reading your books is that I should never leave from home too long because I might miss my family.

This student's writing led two other students to write of their flights from Cambodia and Vietnam, of their lives before and after the exodus. We brainstormed a list of other books to read, books in which young people must survive on their own. The list included Robb White's *Deathwatch*, the Cleavers' *Where the Lilies Bloom*, Elizabeth George Speare's *The Sign of the Beaver*, Jean Craighead George's *Julie of the Wolves*, and Mazer's two other stories of young people surviving without adults, *Snow Bound* and *When the Phone Rang*.

Because they are invited to begin with a book that touches their inner lives and to respond in their own way, these reluctant, potentially alienated students are able to reach out to one another and to form an appreciative, tolerant community of readers. With just a little encouragement, they are also able to broaden that circle to include individuals to whom they do not always relate very well — parents, the school principal, older citizens in their community, immigrants new to this country. Ironically, through the process they also become more tolerant of literature itself — poems, stories, plays, films as "arty" as *The Loneliness of the Long-Distance Runner*. By making connections between these imaginary worlds and their "real" world, between the inner world of their response and the outer world in which they live, they open themselves more readily to the experience of the imaginary and inner worlds.

Experiencing Diversity

Adolescents are open to considering divergent points of view. Adolescent novels provide vicarious experience of diverse ethnic, geographical, and

historical life styles and serious consideration of recurring moral dilemmas.
We are often told at conferences on adolescent literature, especially
by publishers and book editors, that contemporary American adolescents want to read books about characters like themselves, contemporary American adolescents facing the same problems that many of
them face — peer pressure, teenage pregnancy, drug addiction, parental
abuse, and the like. We do not know which paperback books teenagers
are willing to spend $3.95 for, but generally the titles are not those
that youngsters in our classes choose for pleasure reading. Rather, they
choose escape books — romances such as Silhouette and Harlequin;
suspense stories such as Tom Clancy's *The Hunt for Red October;* the
gothic stories such as Stephen King or V. C. Andrews; and sci-fi and
fantasy, mostly space operas with titles such as *Sundrinker, Godslayer,*
and *Trekmaster.*

Students are quite aware that they are reading for escape, just as
we adults are when we settle down with a good mystery or a historical
saga. On the other hand, when they look for more serious reading,
they tell us they want to learn something. They find most teenage
problem novels simplistic (one student referred to them as "those
teeny-bopper" books), and they often do not choose to read books
about problems they confront personally (Marla lives in what some
might consider a racial ghetto, but she chose to read *Children of War,*
set in today's Northern Ireland; when she finished it she gave it to
Tony, who sits next to her).

Youngsters in middle adolescence frequently choose books on topics
we call "the uses of adversity," stories of young people who are
handicapped or face almost insurmountable obstacles. Some favorites
in my class recently have been *Winning* by Robin Brancato, *Tell Me
That You Love Me, Junie Moon* by Marjorie Kellogg, and *Flowers for
Algernon* by Daniel Keyes. The students also like stories about young
people growing up in hard times, especially those in which young
people are left to make it on their own, books like Robert Newton
Peck's *A Day No Pigs Would Die.*

Students often look for a story about characters in a setting unlike
their own (a different part of the world, a different culture, or a
situation unlike one they have faced or are likely to face), a story
about young people facing real problems, even life-threatening problems, and a story of moral courage. It is almost as if they want to test
themselves vicariously — their values, their integrity, their strength —
against the experiences of characters with whom they can identify.

They want a challenge. We think that is one of the values of good literature. Below I have described just a handful of such books that students in my class are reading now.

Not many young people we know actually get to meet an Australian aborigine, but they come face to face with an unforgettable young man in *Walkabout*. They ponder the sacrifice he makes for the British children and marvel at the strength of purpose and concern demonstrated by a character they once might have thought uncivilized. The terrain, sights, and sounds of Australia whet their appetite for more, and some students continue to research the country after the book is finished. In history classes, students study about the horrors of Hitler's Germany and the consequent death camps. But it is not until they meet Piri Davidowitz in *Upon the Head of the Goat* and Elie in *Night* that they realize what it would have been like to be herded like animals, hauled far away from home and family to wait for death in a godforsaken existence. And it is Jeanne in *Farewell to Manzanar* who reminds them not to be too complacent, for in our own country we too were guilty of herding people together and taking all their possessions when we put Japanese-Americans into walled-in camps after the bombing of Pearl Harbor. William Wharton's *A Midnight Clear* shows us fine young German and American soldiers face to face on a war front in a bitter winter, each side desperately trying to avoid the death that awaited them, seeking friendship across enemy lines at Christmas time. *My Sweet Charlie* introduces the students to an educated young black man who has gone south to help the cause of civil rights during the 1960s. There he meets "poor white trash," and their prejudices clash under the one roof where they both seek refuge.

When the Legends Die, Deathwatch, Beyond the Divide, Prairie Songs, and *Shane* all take readers to settings in the western United States, to deserts and mountains, harsh landscapes that try even the strongest souls. In each, the setting is a proper backdrop for the human dramas being lived out by each character. In *When the Legends Die* a young American Indian's search for his identity leads him on the demanding rodeo circuit until he finds where his true home really is. *Deathwatch* provides suspense and nonstop drama as the wealthy Madec hunts young Ben in the desert of Arizona. The bighorn sheep are not worthy challenges, so Madec takes on human prey. All at once we are searching for buttes and saguaro cactus and drinking as much water as we can because all of these things are of utmost importance if Ben is to survive Madec's madness. In *Beyond the Divide*, Kathryn Lasky gives a view of the wagon train and its hardships, especially on pioneer women. Meribah leaves her Mennonite family in the East and heads toward California with her father. The physical hardships of the trek are no greater a challenge than the hypocrisy, danger, and corruption within the company itself. The Yahi Indians provide one of the few respites in this bitter experience. Pam Conrad in *Prairie Songs* has written a young person's version of *Giants in the Earth,* a story of the psychological trauma of life in sod huts surrounded by the vast, lonely prairie, especially its effects on two women. In *Shane* the Homestead Act takes on new dimensions as we read of Joe's family trying to tame the arid lands of Wyoming while defending themselves from the land-hunger of cattle ranchers.

For middle school readers, *One-Eyed Cat,* which takes place in a pastoral setting on the banks of the Hudson River in the 1930s, is a remarkable story of the loss of innocence, of the sense of guilt and the need for forgiveness that almost inevitably accompany the moral coming of age. Somewhat slow-paced, the book should perhaps be read aloud by the teacher, at least until the story gets under way. Ned Wallis receives an air rifle as a gift from his uncle and, against his father's orders, fires it into the dark. It is a small, relatively innocent infraction, but its consequences weigh on Ned's conscience and ultimately play a big part in his growing up. The relationships between Ned and his stern but patient father, his invalid mother, his somewhat exotic, world-traveling uncle, and old Mr. Scully, for whom he does chores, introduce youngsters to the complexity and ambiguity of human relationships.

The theme of *One-Eyed Cat* and of most of the other books discussed in this section is the growth of a sense of responsibility. It is a theme that concerns most young readers, but one that they can discuss more freely when distanced a bit from their everyday life. Already aware of the tension between personal freedom and personal responsibility, they are willing to explore its sources and implications when discussing Adam Cooper's dealings with his family in the early days of the American Revolution in *April Morning,* or Anne Frank's frustrations and dreams while she is confined in the attic apartment in Amsterdam, or the struggles of the black Logan family in the Depression-era South in Mildred Taylor's books *Let the Circle Be Unbroken* and *Roll of Thunder, Hear My Cry.*

Just as youngsters explore the theme of responsibility in books they read, in our classes we try to lead them to a sense of responsibility in their reading. We want them to become strong, self-reliant readers, not dependent upon a teacher's assignments or study guide. This means that they must (1) choose books for themselves and respond to them actively and thoughtfully, (2) be willing to share their honest responses with a community of readers, their peers, becoming tolerant of differences of opinion while holding on to their own convictions, and (3) realize that they may question texts and use what they learn from them to question their own values. Achieving this sense of responsibility as readers requires an organization of classroom and curriculum that, at least part of the time, goes beyond teacher-assigned common reading and teacher-directed discussion of literature. Small-group activities and independent reading within a thematic unit provide ways to broaden classroom experiences.

Struggling with Universal Concerns

Adolescents are struggling with the almost universal concerns of growing up and accepting adult roles. Adolescent novels, like the great classics of literature, deal seriously and responsibly with these recurring concerns. The great themes of literature in many cases are also the obsessive themes of adolescence. We know from the last twenty-five years of developmental psychology and from our own experience with adolescents that certain themes occupy the minds and emotions and daily conversation of teenagers. They may not have been able yet to express these themes coherently, but they are recurring motifs in their expression and behavior. It is surprising how many of these coincide with the great themes of the greatest literature of the Western World. Maybe it should not be so surprising, for literature reflects and integrates the human condition. Why should it surprise us that it articulates in its wisdom what we are unable to articulate in our youth?

For example, one of the recurrent tensions in adolescence is the conflict between individuals and society. At least in our culture, it is important for young people to break away, to assert themselves, to establish their personal stance vis-à-vis the status quo in their world. For an earlier generation, the vulnerable but charismatic individual whose iconoclasm was so attractive was symbolized by a James Dean or an Elvis Presley or, in literature, a Holden Caulfield. The rebel without a cause, the man in the blue suede shoes, the catcher in the rye were somehow outside of and better than the norms of the Establishment, more honest and more sensitive. The sixties produced the flower child, the generation gap, Dustin Hoffman in *The Graduate* and *Midnight Cowboy*, the Rolling Stones and *Rolling Stone* — and S. E. Hinton's *The Outsiders*. More recently we have had Sean Penn and

Madonna, young Matt Dillon and a whole host of rebels without a cause, as in *The Breakfast Club* and *Sixteen Candles,* and a whole library shelf filled with outsiders in adolescent fiction.

One of the reasons that *Antigone* appeals so much to certain young readers is that they see in the heroine a young person standing alone against an uncaring adult society, a mindless bureaucracy that puts public respectability above personal values and emotions. It is Antigone against the Others, and the Others oppose her pride, her sense of self and of justice, and her individual integrity.

This, of course, is a familiar theme in the contemporary adolescent novel. Let us take two old favorites. *The Chocolate War* revolves around the motto, "Do I dare disturb the universe?" It is Jerry Renault against a corrupt, tyrannical, and capricious system. The larger system — the institution of the school — spawns an underground system, equally impersonal and unfair, in Archie and the Vigils. As in most of Cormier's work one senses that these two systems in the inner world of the novel merely reflect larger and even more treacherous systems in the outer world of twentieth century America. Similarly, in *The Pigman* by Paul Zindel, John and Lorraine confront society — not with a capital S, Society, but with a little s — embodied in their parents, their school, and even their thoughtless, conforming friends led by Norton. Their idyllic relationship with Mr. Pignati underscores by contrast problems in their "real" world, but what they eventually learn is that they too are implicated in this callous society that they so abhor.

We could go on with other, more recent adolescent novels that develop a similar theme, and with other themes of concern to adolescent readers that inform recent fiction as well as the greatest world literature. Our point is that grappling with these themes in adolescent fiction not only matches the students' needs and interests, but is also the best preparation for appreciating the treatment of the themes in the world's classics. The reading ladder is still the handiest tool in the high school literature teacher's toolbox. These themes may be treated as strands recurring in a year's reading, or they may give rise to thematic units. Our approach is to start with books and stories that we know will interest adolescents and then to capitalize on whatever topics emerge throughout the year, building and shaping strands and units around those themes that are most engaging for any particular group in any particular year.

The advantages of the thematic unit have been catalogued in professional publications at least since the Experience Curriculum of the thirties. The unit allows teachers to address the immediate and long-range interests of adolescents, to integrate the language arts (reading, writing, listening, speaking) around one central topic, to balance imaginative literature with discursive prose, to provide for individual differences in ability and maturity, to relate literature and writing to current media and the arts, to provide independent small-group and large-group activities unified around a single concern, and to provide practice in using language and thinking skills in something approaching "real-world" situations.

The planning of the thematic unit was well described in the fifties in a chapter called "Building Instructional Units" in *The English Language Arts in the Secondary School* (Commission on the English Curriculum 1956). The chapter unfortunately used as its topic "Back-Country America" at a time when Americans were more interested in urban America, progress, and the future, and also used an apparently unacademic topic at a time when the Curriculum Reform Movement began to put more emphasis on academic rigor and respectability. Even so, the chapter is still a landmark in explaining and defending the thematic unit. Alan Madsen, in "That Starlit Corridor" in the *English Journal* in 1964, demonstrated the same organizational patterns applied to a topic of more current interest to adolescents.

Later in the sixties, the Project English Centers at Florida State and Carnegie-Mellon developed thematic units for junior high school students and college-bound senior high school students, respectively. The latter is particularly interesting in its adaptation of the method to a rigorous, academic curriculum for honors students. For example, the year-long study of literature in the tenth grade is organized around six topics: social concerns, love, reality and illusion, heroism, human weakness, and the search for wisdom. American literature for eleventh graders is similarly organized around six recurrent themes: the Puritan attitude, the drive for success, idealism, the darker spirit, social protest, and the quest for identity.

Commercial efforts, most notably the Scholastic Literature Units and McGraw-Hill's Themes and Writers Series, simplified the development of thematic units for teachers and popularized the method. Such packaged materials are a boon to busy and less experienced teachers, but there is still no substitute for individual teachers choosing texts they know will work with their students and exploring the topics and themes that emerge naturally from those texts. An abundance of paperback novels, poetry and short-story anthologies, and works of nonfiction makes this possible on a reasonable budget.

Forming Lifelong Reading Habits

Adolescents are developing habits that will last a lifetime. Adolescent novels can help develop a lifelong habit of reading for personal pleasure. Teachers may arrange instruction that will produce responsive and

responsible reading in their classrooms; however, the real test of a
literary education is whether these adolescents become responsive and
responsible adult readers — readers who seek out quality literature for
personal reading, who respond actively and independently to that
literature, and who share their responses with a community of adult
readers. Such habits do not spring full-blown in the lives of educated
persons when they reach their majority; they are more likely to result
from years of pleasant, rewarding experience with books and readers.
Thus an active, well-planned individual reading program should not
be on the periphery of the high school literature curriculum — one
book report a month if we finish our other work in time. Rather, it
should be the heart of the curriculum.

Dick Abrahamson and Eleanor Tyson (1986) have collected an
impressive array of studies of directed individualized reading, beginning
with Lou LaBrant's landmark study, *An Evaluation of the Free Reading
in Grades Ten, Eleven, and Twelve.* For three years LaBrant used free
reading as the literature program for a group of students at Ohio State
University Lab School, documenting their achievement through careful
research. Abrahamson and Tyson summarize one of the most impressive aspects of LaBrant's findings:

> What makes LaBrant's work especially impressive is that she kept
> track of these students long after they graduated from high school.
> She interviewed them years later, and her findings were published
> in *The Guinea Pigs after Twenty Years.* There were two very
> impressive findings. First, she found that her guinea pigs, as
> adults, did markedly more reading than most other groups of
> adults examined [including graduates of Ivy League colleges]. That
> is, free reading helped to create active, adult readers. Her second
> finding, perhaps more important, was that her grown students
> expressed a strong concern for, and were active participants in,
> the development of their children's reading habits. The guinea
> pigs as adults read to and with their children, took trips to the
> library and encouraged their children to pick books that keyed
> into their individual interests. The concern for the child's attitude
> toward books and reading was not just the province of the mothers
> responding to LaBrant's study. As the researcher writes, "In
> general, it may be said that all of the thirteen fathers seemed to
> accept responsibility for reading habits as a part of family living."
> (p. 55)

One could hardly find a more apt description of what we hope a high
school literature curriculum will ultimately accomplish.

Furthermore, Bruce Appleby's 1967 dissertation (*The Effects of Individualized Reading on Certain Aspects of Literature Study with High
School Seniors*) shows that directed, individualized reading was just as

effective, at least for one semester, in achieving the goals of a conventional literature course. He concluded that instruction in literature, whether through individualized reading or a conventional literature course, had positive effects on students' ability to interpret literary materials, yet the students in individualized reading found more satisfaction in reading literature, including satisfaction in such purely literary matters as style, characterization, and technique. They also expressed significantly fewer dislikes for fiction. "This implies," Appleby suggests, "that individualized reading has a definite effect on whether or not students will view literature favorably after high school graduation."

We have been using individualized reading units for almost twenty-five years with the same ground rules. Our experience corroborates the research. Students do read more and with greater enjoyment and sensitivity when reading is individualized. We think it also promotes a better attitude toward literature chosen for class study. The essential elements of the program as we practice it are listed below; however, articles by Ley (1979) and by Appleby and Conner (1965) and the review of research mentioned previously outline the program in more detail.

1. With rare exceptions, class time is devoted to quiet reading during individualized reading. We have discovered that adolescents' time, like that of adults, is fragmented by jobs, study, school activities, dating and social commitments, and family responsibilities. For some busy teenagers, the hour in class is one of the few quiet times they have for sustained reading.

2. No books are required; no books are prohibited. There is no list from which books must be chosen. We make suggestions and, in conferences, guide students' reading, but the choice is theirs. However, we saturate their environment with good books: library books, paperback racks, booklists, bulletin boards, book talks. Our room becomes one big commercial for good literature that will appeal to adolescents.

3. There are no formal book reports — written or oral. Through the years our research with adult readers has revealed that one of the most dreadful memories they have of English classes is the required book report or project. Even when they enjoyed the books, they hated the artificiality and boredom of the reports.

4. Instead, we schedule regular book conferences with each student. Usually these conferences last about ten minutes and consist of informal conversations about the books the students have read. The conferences

may be held individually or, if several students have read the same book, in small groups. We usually try to confer with each student after each book, but some of our colleagues talk with each student regularly no matter how many books the student has finished — one, two, three, or none — since the last conference.

5. We are well informed about the books that students read. Either we have read them ourselves or we skim them carefully before the conference. We do not pretend to know as much about the book as the student who has just finished it, but we do feel obligated to know enough to participate knowledgeably in a conversation. Conferences are not tests; they are dialogues. They proceed along lines established by the student.

6. Students are asked to do short, focused writings about each book. Usually, we ask them to prepare a 4 × 6 book card after each conference on some aspect of their reading that we have mutually agreed upon. However, some teachers prefer to use reading logs or regular in-class focus writings. The point is that the writings should not be burdensome and should encourage independent thinking and evaluation. We ask students to write for their peers and use these writings as a way for students to share books with one another.

7. Evaluation of student progress is informal. We would prefer not to assign grades to individualized reading units; however, grading has always been a fact of life in every school where we have taught. Hence, we have to provide a grading system that rewards the most diligent, perceptive readers without penalizing those for whom reading is still somewhat onerous. We usually take into consideration such factors as the amount and challenge of reading, the thoughtfulness of the response, and the student's self-evaluation based on self-selected goals. All students are able to do well in individualized reading; hence, grading practices should encourage even the most reluctant reader.

8. One of our most important tasks is to establish and maintain a climate for reading. Interruptions are kept to a minimum. Students are encouraged to share books with one another. Parents are kept informed and sometimes actually read books along with their children. Librarians help with book talks, displays, and a steady supply of good, new books. Colleagues in other departments tell us about their favorite books and sometimes volunteer to have conferences with students on books they have enjoyed (this week an assistant principal is talking with a student about Tom Clancy's *Red Storm Rising*). We haunt garage sales and Friends of the Library sales for good books to have on hand (last week thirty dollars bought 120 books at twenty-five cents apiece

at a Friends' sale). We encourage students to trade books with one another. We post articles and reviews on books and writers from local and national newspapers and magazines. When reluctant students, such as those in my Exploring Literature class, cannot profitably devote the whole hour to individual reading, I initiate a program of sustained, silent reading for whatever period of time they can tolerate and gradually increase the time through the year. In other words, we demonstrate that we expect students to read widely and well, and they do.

9. And we model reading ourselves. We read and enjoy many of the books that the students read, including ones they recommend to us, and we talk about books we read on our own, just as we do with our own children at home. In this sense at least, we think of ourselves as serving in loco parentis.

Conclusion

Sylvia Ashton-Warner in *Spearpoint* (1972) captures just what is meant by inviting students to be independent thinkers. She pictures the students' minds as houses lining a street along which we, the teachers, come walking. Each house is owned by a student's soul,

> inhabited by his instincts; his wants, fears, desires and loves, his hates and happinesses. A merry, motley, moving company, some potential homicides, others pure saints, rubbing shoulders and elbows with one another, all together going for it, like a carnival of celebrants dancing madly. At times, from the pressures within, they venture outside into the street for a breath of fresh air, exercise themselves and encounter others, bring back food and something new to talk about, returning somewhat civilised.

She goes on to tell us that the unskilled teacher comes along, "gate-crashing" each house, taking over occupancy, replacing the imagery of what was within with images of his or her own:

> What's wrong with it . . . it's imagery, isn't it? But the thing is that the replacing imagery is not alive as the native inhabitants were. It is static. It can't dance. It can only do what it's told to do and what it sees to copy. It doesn't go out and see the world and make a contribution. It can't make you think and do things. . . . Simultaneously the teacher takes over occupancy of the other children in his class, so that now we have the same kind of imagery in every one of the houses, all copies of the teacher, in a street named Conformity.

Then along comes the enlightened teacher,

> strolling in the street, agog with interest in whom he meets, engaging in conversation. An interesting person at the least, so that people from the houses, the native inhabitants, are disposed to come out and meet him, exchange greetings and ideas with him. Sometimes with him and often without him, they feel free to think and do things . . . outside in the world. A street named Variation. (pp. 33–34)

The development of independent readers demands variation. Students must be given freedom to select at least some of their own reading and to respond to it freely. At the same time, they must be given the responsibility to read actively, to share their responses with peers, and to explore a variety of texts in a variety of ways. This movement from response to responsibility sets the rhythm of the literature classroom, a workshop with new challenges every day. This may mean that teachers must relinquish some control over the selection of texts and the direction of discussion. At the same time, it makes great demands on their energy, imagination, and professionalism, for they must be rigorous in their expectations of students and unswerving in their determination that these expectations be met. They have two crucial allies in this quest: one, a wealth of exciting texts from which to choose, including a growing number of fine adolescent novels and, two, the energy and adaptability of each new set of adolescents they meet. Citizenship in such a classroom prepares our students for citizenship in the community of readers and thinkers necessary to the preservation of literacy and liberty.

References

Atwell, N. 1987. *In the Middle: Writing, Reading, and Learning with Adolescents.* Portsmouth, N.H.: Boynton/Cook.

Abrahamson, D., and E. Tyson. 1986. What Every English Teacher Should Know about Free Reading. *The ALAN Review* 14, no. 1: 54–58, 69.

Appleby, B. 1967. *The Effects of Individualized Reading on Certain Aspects of Literature Study with High School Seniors.* Unpublished doctoral dissertation. University of Iowa.

Appleby, B. C., and J. W. Conner. 1965. Well, What Did You Think of It? *English Journal* 54: 606–12.

Ashton-Warner, S. 1972. *Spearpoint: "Teacher" in America.* New York: Knopf.

The Commission on the English Curriculum. 1956. *The English Language Arts in the Secondary School.* NCTE Curriculum Series, Vol. 3. New York: Appleton-Century-Crofts.

Cunningham, J. Letter to writer. 7 July 1966.

Frye, N. 1964. *The Educated Imagination*. Bloomington: Indiana University Press.

LaBrant, L. L. 1936. *An Evaluation of the Free Readings in Grades Ten, Eleven, and Twelve*. The Ohio State University Studies, Contributions in Education, No. 2. Columbus: Ohio State University Press.

Ley, T. C. 1979. How To Set Up and Evaluate a DIR Program. *Media and Methods* 15, no. 8: 20–22, 24, 52.

Madsen, A. 1964. That Starlit Corridor. *English Journal* 53: 405–12.

Scholes, R. 1985. *Textual Power: Literary Theory and the Teaching of English*. New Haven: Yale University Press.

Adolescent Novels Cited

Borland, Hal. 1964. *When the Legends Die*. New York: Bantam.

Brancato, Robin. 1978. *Winning*. New York: Bantam.

Brooks, Terry. 1983. *The Sword of Shannara*. New York: Ballantine.

Clancy, Tom. 1985. *The Hunt for Red October*. New York: Berkley.

———. 1986. *Red Storm Rising*. New York: Putnam.

Cleaver, Vera and Bill. 1974. *Where the Lilies Bloom*. New York: Signet.

Conrad, Pam. 1985. *Prairie Songs*. Harper & Row.

Cormier, Robert. 1980. *After the First Death*. New York: Avon.

———. 1974. *The Chocolate War*. New York: Dell.

Cunningham, Julia. 1987. *Dorp Dead*. New York: Knopf.

Fast, Howard. 1962. *April Morning*. New York: Bantam.

Fox, Paula. 1985. *One-Eyed Cat*. New York: Dell.

George, Jean Craighead. 1972. *Julie of the Wolves*. Harper & Row.

Hinton, S. E. 1982. *The Outsiders*. New York: Dell.

Houston, Jeanne Wakatsuki, and James Houston. 1974. *Farewell to Manzanar*. New York: Bantam.

Kellogg, Marjorie. 1984. *Tell Me That You Love Me, Junie Moon*. New York: Farrar, Straus & Giroux.

Keyes, Daniel. 1975. *Flowers for Algernon*. New York: Bantam.

Lasky, Kathryn. 1986. *Beyond the Divide*. New York: Dell.

Marshall, James Vance. 1987. *Walkabout*. Portsmouth, N.H.: Heinemann Educational.

Mazer, Harry. 1982. *The Island Keeper*. New York: Dell.

———. 1986. *Snow Bound*. New York: Dell.

———. 1985. *When the Phone Rang*. New York: Scholastic.

Peck, Robert Newton. 1977. *A Day No Pigs Would Die*. New York: Dell.

Peyton, K. M. 1980. *The Flambards*. New York: Penguin.

Salinger, J. D. 1964. *The Catcher in the Rye*. New York: Bantam.

Schaefer, Jack. 1980. *Shane*. New York: Bantam.

Siegal, Aranka. 1983. *Upon the Head of the Goat*. New York: NAL.

Sillitoe, Alan. 1971. *The Loneliness of the Long-Distance Runner.* New York: NAL.

Speare, Elizabeth George. 1984. *The Sign of the Beaver.* New York: Dell.

Taylor, Mildred. 1983. *Let the Circle Be Unbroken.* New York: Bantam.

——. 1978. *Roll of Thunder, Hear My Cry.* New York: Bantam.

Westheimer, David. 1966. *My Sweet Charlie.* New York: NAL.

Wharton, William. 1984. *A Midnight Clear.* New York: Ballantine.

White, Robb. 1973. *Deathwatch.* New York: Dell.

Wiesel, Elie. 1982. *Night.* New York: Bantam.

Zindel, Paul. 1970. *The Pigman.* New York: Dell.

18 The Censorship
of Literature Texts:
A Case Study

Deanne Bogdan
Ontario Institute for Studies in Education

The best work done on the school censorship problem to date has been of a practical nature: advice to the warring factions, legal considerations, political procedures, and empirical evidence about the causal relation between words and human actions. In the case of censoring literary texts, though, we need more theoretical inquiry into what I call the "epistemo-literary" relationship between the reading and study of literature on the one hand and personal and social values on the other. This relationship affects both the censorship and selection of literature texts at every level of the curriculum. Teachers who question — or are challenged to justify — their use of materials, whether it is *Little Black Sambo* in kindergarten, *Flowers for Algernon* in junior high, *Merchant of Venice* in secondary school, or the literary canon itself in colleges and universities, are equally implicated.

Today the role of the reader is enjoying wide interest in a number of areas directly bearing on education. Reader-response critics validate reading as process; ethnographers chart individual reactions; cognitive psychologists measure behavioral effects; response-to-literature researchers devise instructional techniques; feminists challenge sexist language and masculine dominance in the literature curriculum. Nevertheless, increasingly worrisome crises in school censorship in North America indicate the failure of reading theory to address meaningfully the conflicting, deeply held beliefs about the educational function of the language we call literary. Opposing views of literary meaning or poetic truth and how they invoke the relationship between literature and life constitute a crucial though hidden agenda of the censorship debate. It is this aspect of censorship in the schools that will provide the focus for my analysis.

Drawing on the experience of one school district in Ontario, that of

Author's note: An earlier version of this essay first appeared as "School Censorship and Learning Values through Literature," by Deanne Bogdan and Stephen Yeomans, *The Journal of Moral Education* 15, no. 3: 197–211.

Peterborough County, I hope to demonstrate how the humanist position for the teaching of values through literature can be turned against English teachers and literature education when it is based upon a theory of language operating primarily on the assumption that literature directly portrays life. I will conclude with a different defense for the value dimension of literature, a model grounded in a theory of literary language as a hypothesis about life, rather than as a facsimile of it. While my example specifically addresses the senior level, I hope teachers across the board will find it applicable to their own situations and concerns.

The Peterborough County Experience

The book in question was *The Diviners* by Margaret Laurence. My discussion of the Peterborough County censorship controversy centers on the defense of the novel offered by the head of English at Lakefield District High School and on the rejoinder to that defense put forward by Renaissance Peterborough, a division of the religious fundamentalist group Renaissance International. The Peterborough debate, painful and protracted, raged at some times hotly and openly and at others covertly from 1976 to 1985. Its most visible target was the works of Canadian novelist Margaret Laurence, who has charted the powerfully mythic journeys of female protagonists toward consciousness. (Ironically, Laurence resided until her death in January, 1987, in the very school district that condemned her as a subversive and pornographer.) In defending her novels, Laurence disclosed a profound religious sensibility coupled with a personal conviction about the prophetic role of the poet. As she confessed in an interview, "The fundamentalists could say I was possessed by an evil spirit, . . . I can't argue with that. I have a mystic sense of being *given* something to write. I may not be an orthodox Christian, but I believe in the Holy Spirit" (Czarnecki 1985 p. 186).

   Anyone who becomes immersed in the array of briefs, depositions, and letters of support and denunciation that poured in as a result of both the 1976 and the 1985 censorship confrontations must come away acutely aware of the deep chord Laurence's works have struck in her readers. Whether it is a sense of outrage, fear, or affirmation, the feelings evoked by her poetic language in *The Diviners* are almost primeval. In reading the primary sources, one tends to empathize equally with all sides, with the mother who poignantly tells of her daughter's devastation when forced to read four-letter words aloud in class, and with the teacher who insists that students engaged with the

work are positively reinforced through "an exploration of self-aware-
ness, self-acceptance, tolerance of others, understanding of human
frailty, family responsibilities and honest relationships, love and compassion" (Textbook Review Committee 1985). Understandable also is
the position of the citizen whose resistance to knowing was so
entrenched that he insisted, "[W]hen you drink a glass of milk and
it's sour, you don't have to drink the whole thing to know, do you?"
(*Peterborough Examiner,* 26 April 1985).

The Diviners was reinstated in the curriculum in 1976 and again in
1985, along with three other indicted novels, J. D. Salinger's *Catcher
in the Rye* and Laurence's *Jest of God* and *The Stone Angel.* However,
the reasons for their retention ultimately had less to do with the
success of the apologias penned by Peterborough heads of English
departments in making genuine conversions among the members of
the Textbook Review Committee than with political manipulation. In
short, the jury, at least in the 1985 instance, was stacked in favor of
the novels' supporters. What seems to have been ignored in the latest
round of fire was that the 1976 trenchant fundamentalist argument
put forward by Renaissance Peterborough against the defense of *The
Diviners* went largely unanswered. As a result, a palpable disquiet
grips Peterborough English teachers, who continue to do what they
do best, teaching what they believe is great literature in the abiding
faith that reading and studying it is a moral endeavor. Looking hard
at some of Renaissance Peterborough's objections to the defense of
The Diviners may be one way of ensuring that their faith is not blind.

In his article "Liberalism and Censorship" Ralph Heintzman (1978)
writes:

> The bulk of recent commentary on censorship has been a crude
> mixture of knee-jerk reactions, unexamined premises, and the
> wielding of bogeys. This is as true of those who oppose it as of
> those who favour it, but it is more surprising and regrettable in
> the case of the former. The censorship debate has not been
> characterized by the careful thought and distinctions one would
> hope to find on such a sensitive and divisive issue, especially
> from the "intellectuals" whose special care it ought to be to make
> just such distinctions. (pp. 1–2)

Perhaps Heintzman is being unduly harsh here, if we take his term
"intellectuals" to include English teachers on the front line; after all,
courses in critical apologetics do not form part of their academic or
teacher training. Yet it would seem that professional survival today
depends upon writing a convincing "defense of poetry." In what
follows, I will examine some weaknesses of the 1976 defense of *The
Diviners* and some strengths of the Renaissance Peterborough rebuttal

in order to grapple with the serious challenges they both pose for the current state of school text censorship and literature education.

The sophistication of the procensorship argument, as advanced by Renaissance Peterborough, makes those of us who are against censorship think twice. No longer can the censorship problem be characterized only in terms of deficient reading comprehension or the rightist lunatic fringe. The Renaissance rebuttal to the teacher-authored defense, written by a professor of German literature, challenges teachers to clarify the entire process by which values enter into and are extrapolated from literature. The rebuttal also forces teachers to examine certain sacred cows of literature education, such as sympathetic identification, realism, and social relevance, within the context of their potential for psychological and social conditioning. Finally, it throws open for scrutiny the very premise upon which the study of literature in the schools has been traditionally justified.

Referential Meaning and Interpretative Literalism

Running throughout the letters of support for and the actual defenses of all four novels in question are appeals to the educational importance of vicarious experience and true-to-lifeness or verisimilitude. Statements such as "Students can relate to this novel" or "This book helps adolescents to see life as it really is" are made as though realism, sympathetic identification, and emotional absorption are self-evident guarantors for the sacrosanct nature of reading literature. It was these very epistemo-literary values, however, that were attacked by Renaissance Peterborough in denouncing classroom use of the novels. Both pro- and anti-censorship sides argued within the framework of a referential theory of language, which privileges the values mentioned above. I hope to show that the impasse resulting from the Peterborough controversy is a logical one that can be broken only by invoking a different theory of language, which reexamines the educational role of personal engagement with the text.

The reference theory of language assumes a one-on-one direct relationship between words and things, events, ideas, or values in the world to which words are thought to point. At its most primitive, truth-of-correspondence is a belief in the transparency of words and their power to reflect or reproduce "life as it really is." Those who subscribe to a narrow reference theory of language often tend to be interpretative literalists, who equate a literary work with the situations and things in the world that it is believed gave rise to the text (Ellis

1974, p. 153). In other words, a literary work is a "statement" that is judged by an interpretative literalist to be profane, ungodly, or pornographic on the premise that it reveals a profane, blasphemous, or pornographic "reality" in the world. Such an inference can be made only by omitting or virtually annihilating the concept of *genre*, literary values such as style, emphasis, and connotation, and the integral connection between literary form and content (see Ellis, p. 153).

Ignoring what Karlheinz Stierle (1980) calls the "self-referential nature of a fictional text" in which a poetic world is created unto itself, the interpretative literalists view a fictional representation of the world no differently from its actuality because they have no access to the hypothetical, "as if" quality of literature, to literature as the "representation of *possible* forms of organization for experience" (p. 103) (my emphasis). Under interpretative literalism the sour-milk metaphor, quoted earlier, does hold water, so to speak; for the interpretative literalist demands a textual meaning that is single and predictable and objects to that meaning if it fails to conform to a preconceived value system. When an espoused value is thought to be subverted by the text, the interpretative literalist often reacts, as in the Peterborough case, by deleting offending passages and referring specific readers to pages judged "unprintable" (Textbook Review Committee 1985).

Interpretative literalism trades on a misconceived idea of literary language as a narrow form of referential meaning, as "direct communication," as language that really means what it says, rather than as a kind of indirection dependent on literary context. In an attempt to overcome this misconception, anti-censors will often exhort the interpretative literalist to read a work in its entirety before condemning it. But such well-intentioned advice is usually of little help, for it begs the question of literary context. To reject literary language as direct communication in favor of it as a constellation of verbal symbols whose meaning is indeterminate and multiple requires thinking of the literary text as what Catherine Belsey calls a "constructed artifact."[1] Moving from the former to the latter model presumes a radical transformation of consciousness unlikely to be undergone by someone who is convinced that a dirty book is a dirty book is a dirty book. When this kind of change does occur, it must be prefaced by the *moral* predisposition to resist resistance to knowing.[2] For example, in Peterborough County the chair of the first Textbook Review Committee confessed his need for study and basic guidance in reading differently;[3] and in the more recent debacle a community representative did stress the importance of looking "at our own inhibitions before criticizing" (Czarnecki, p. 190). This augurs well for at least the possibility of educating the public to regard literary works not as guides to life, but as moving, powerful hypotheses about life, which bear much reflection and sifting through, as meditations rather than as depictors of moral propositions.

Censors habitually frame their attacks on books within the notion of literature as direct communication. What teachers must avoid is the temptation to buy into that fallacy in framing their defense of a particular work. This can be problematic, for they may despair of winning over the opposition on any other ground. A further difficulty lies in the fact that, while the literary critical background of the best qualified literature teachers militates against holding to a narrow referential relationship between literary works and moral and social values, increasingly nonspecialists are teaching English, and neither group is helped much by the educational administration. A clear grasp of the dynamics of literary creation and response rarely finds its way into educational documents. As a result, the professional mandate of English teachers moves them to accept a simplistic theory of literary language, one whose educational value is regarded primarily as that of role-modeling such virtues as "initiative, responsibility, respect, precision, self-discipline, judgement, and integrity."[4] Little wonder, then, that when a novel is met with allegations of profanity, blasphemy, and pornography, as in the case of *The Diviners*, its apologist should attempt to meet the moral objections on their own terms. The Peterborough English chair who wrote the most recent defense of Laurence's *The Diviners* described below deliberately downplayed *literary* values, and organized his rationale around the three areas of *moral* concern, "language, religion, and sex," which precipitated the outcry against the book's use in the schools (Buchanan 1985, p. 2).

Point, Checkpoint

The 1985 Peterborough defense (substantively unchanged from the 1976 version) is a hard-sell of *The Diviners* as a vehicle for transmitting the Judaeo-Christian moral and religious tradition. In support of its religious merit, the defender casts the book's protagonist, Morag Gunn, as a latter-day sojourner through Paradise Lost and Paradise Regained; and Christie Logan, the major male figure, as a contemporary version of John Bunyan's Muckracker. To counter the charges of "gutter" language and explicit sex, the rationale proceeds by way of an unabashedly moralistic interpretation of the novel's "message." The apologist directly parallels Morag's giving up swearing with her moral maturation and contextualizes the sexual exploits of all the main characters in terms of retributive justice for contravening the Christian code of ethics. On the view articulated there, *The Diviners* would seem to be an infallible self-help book for preservation of virtue in the young.

The problem is that it did not wash not only with the interpretative literalists, who could not or would not distinguish between strings of words and the "order of words" comprising literary context (Frye 1957, p. 17), but, more relevant to this paper, with the interpretatively enlightened censors. In the position outlined below, the religious fundamentalists play the politics of referentiality with greater skill than does the teacher-defender; as a result, they won the "moral," if not the actual, victory.

Despite its rhetorical slickness, the brief advanced by Renaissance Peterborough is argued from a more subtle definition of referential meaning than that held either by the interpretative literalist or the apologist for *The Diviners*. The fundamentalist group accepts the bid to read in context, but broadens the boundaries of literary context to include the sociological dimension of literature as well as the aesthetic. Consequently, these censors cull from the novel what they maintain is a more valid moral message than that of the Bunyanesque reading offered by the defense. *The Diviners* may well reflect certain values, Renaissance argues, but they are not those claimed by the literary-educational establishment. For Renaissance, the novel's theme of the road to Christian virtue is swamped by the muckraking needed to get there. Furthermore, according to the censors, the very literary terms of reference — realism, emotional engagement, and sympathetic identification (deemed by the anti-censorship faction as self-justifications for the moral value of teaching the novel) — indoctrinate students into believing that reality or life is primarily the seamy world of Margaret Laurence's Morag Gunn.

Building on the assumption that realistic fiction *does* project literary events as "true" representations of reality, the novel's detractors acknowledge just this power to shape attitudes toward life that teachers have traditionally claimed for it. However, they charge, as Plato did in banishing the poets from the Republic, that such power can influence for ill as well as good. By considering Laurence's whole canon (as any good critic would do) and by bringing to its logical conclusion the pedagogical implications of emotional engagement (as any good teacher would do), Renaissance turns these considerations to its own purposes. Ultimately it concludes that a curriculum overbalanced with realistic works fraught with transgression, self-conflict, and the darker underside of life necessarily skews students' visions of reality and thus constitutes its own form of censorship. Why, asks Renaissance, are Margaret Laurence's protagonists unremittingly drawn with such "a stunted idea of their own sexuality and their identity?" What, it asks, is the educational effect of such heroines? If realism does offer "a way of seeing, understanding, and evaluating human experience vicariously perceived" (by reflecting life as it really is), then "much of the direction of such a learning process [emotional engagement with that angle of vision] will hinge on the choice and treatment of reality" (Renaissance Peterborough 1977, pp. 2–3). Of course, the hidden agenda of the Renaissance group, like that of other religious fundamentalists, is that they want a say in which worlds are projected onto their children. This is a different issue. What concerns us here is how censors can use the very mechanism by which teachers tend to defend the teaching of values through literature — role-modeling virtues — *against* literary works. That these works might be classics or great literature becomes irrelevant to the moral issues raised.

The Renaissance Peterborough argument appeals to the sociology of literature. Not coincidentally, it is precisely the sociological dimension that is invoked by other groups such as feminists, multiculturalists, and nationalists who are as concerned as religious fundamentalists about what kind of ideology infiltrates schools.[5] Whether through book banning or revising courses of study, both the political right and left attempt to control the curriculum, and their positions on the relationship between the literature the curriculum and social conditioning disclose interesting similarities. Both sides repudiate aesthetic integrity at the cost of injurious stereotyping in individual works; both sides want to redress the balance of what they consider to be a lopsided picture of the world.

Solution, Resolution

I see no convincing rebuttal to the Renaissance position without the aid of literary theory to help unpack the relationship between literature and life. Literature teachers might respond that realism is not a "slice of life," but a form of literary convention that separates literature from life just as, say, fantasy or science fiction does. However, within the present anti-criticism climate in the schools, realism is not taught as Belsey's verbal artifact, as a literary genre that just happens to approximate what the reader feels to be "life." Too often literature serves simply as so much fodder for "life skills" within a pedagogy that fixates on emotional engagement with the text as though literary characters and events are real people living in the real world only, and not also confections of words that are literally made up. Afoot, too, is a naive psychologism that perpetuates the myth of the student as a "genuine primitive" (Frye 1976, p. 131), whose "free," "open," "spontaneous," precritical response is seen to be authentic and unprescribed merely because it is liberated from prepackaged, teacher-imposed interpretations and uncontaminated by the study of literary structure. No reading is innocent of reader bias.

One of the most problematic ramifications of thinking of literature as direct communication, as a verbal correspondence to life, is the danger of collapsing the distinction between literature and life. When that distinction goes unheeded in the teaching of values and literature, teachers are dangerously close to believing that the literary text is a Rorschach test that will elicit all the "right" human values in its readers. Renaissance Peterborough, I believe, has successfully challenged that belief. Lest I misrepresent my position completely, however, let me reiterate that my intention has not been to side with the censors in the Peterborough debate. Their assumptions about the reading process, the educational value and function of literature, and their relationship to education in general, I think, are wrong-headed. Yet so long as anti-censorship educators also think of literature and values only in referential terms, as role-modeling, they do not have it right either.

Rejection of the role-model theory of social conditioning does resolve the censorship dilemma to a certain extent by helping students to see that literature is not life. But the kind of aesthetic distance presumed by such an awareness poses problems for justifying the moral and spiritual value of literature. How can teachers maintain, on the one hand, that critical detachment from the text ensures that students will not be co-opted by its moral dicta and, on the other, that the educational value of literature lies in its capacity to alter their lives only for the better? In his book *Literary Education: A Reevaluation* (1983), British philosopher of education James Gribble recognizes this double bind and is willing to sacrifice engagement and its claims for moral improvement on the altar of detachment and its claims for moral neutrality. Gribble is content to risk "some form of aestheticism rather than to allow that a great work of literature . . . could be viewed in such a way that it (or what it 'presents') could legitimately be rejected in the light of a moral code" (p. 155).

I am not content to do so, nor are the literature teachers and researchers who believe in literature's potential for human development. To assert that language is not a transparent window through which we look at life or reality, that verbal constructs always mediate personal experience, is not necessarily to deny the emotional impact and imaginative appeal of literature. Plato did have one thing right when he banished the poets — literature does influence. That inhabiting other lives and other worlds vicariously can contribute to psychic growth, that readers knit up what is otherwise unknown through a powerful naming, conjuring, fabricating of fictional persons, places, and events is an educational reality not to be negated by what I am saying here. Reading literature contributes to psychic growth by inducing certain states of mind and then questioning them. Engagement suspends disbelief; detachment suspends belief. Both are part of psychic growth. But both sides of the censorship debate should recognize that psychic growth is inherently subversive to unexamined belief, for psychic growth entails some loss of certitude in what is being grown out of. Once the dialectical process of engagement and detachment is under way, there are no guarantees as to what may be brought to consciousness. Minds that become activated tend to activate themselves; once the lion has been awakened, there is no putting it back to sleep. This can be a real threat to parents and citizens who are deeply ambivalent about the power of independent thought to seduce youth away from traditional moral codes.

For teachers and educational leaders in the censorship issue, then, I think the key to the problem and perhaps to the solution is a more realistic view of the politics of the engaged reader, as well as clearer definitions of a literary text and a literary reading. Rather than a closed mirror on reality that leads the passive reader down a predetermined garden path to a set of beliefs or actions, the literary text by *virtue of its literariness* is open to manifold interpretations. These interpretations both accommodate and transcend the thrust toward sympathetic identification so essential to psychic growth. Part of the literature teacher's job, then, would seem to be to preserve the tension between engagement with the text as statement and detachment from it as hypothesis. As hypothesis, the text moves in a subjunctive, "what-if" world; as statement, the text engages the reader in something true and real, as anyone who has been entranced by a book will testify. Psychological projection is inseparable from literary knowing, but so is the withdrawal of that projection. That is why students need both the experience of literature as life and the aesthetic awareness that distances literature from life. The enjoyable reading of literature does give with one hand, and the study of its craft, historicity, and ideology takes away with the other. But it is just this capacity of literary language to work against itself that validates its educational significance as perhaps the best pedagogical tool teachers have for both individual growth and social criticism.

Conclusion

Reconceptualizing literature as open text, as hypothetical statement rather than as moral model, is one step toward defusing the indoctrinative aspects of literature. But it does not completely solve the problem. Teachers may claim that studying literature confers upon the student the power of moral choice by virtue of its capacity for widening perspectives and increasing the range of possibilities for belief and action, yet they cannot deny that certain kinds of literature stake out certain conceptual and emotional territories. One cannot live what one cannot imagine. That is why feminists seek to redress the scandalous underrepresentation of writing about and by women in the curriculum. They do not necessarily want to launch an affirmative action program in social conditioning; rather, they seek to bring to consciousness "possible forms of organization for experience" (Stierle, p. 103) disallowed by patriarchy and the male authorial voice.

If it is admitted that certain texts tend to define certain kinds of possibilities for belief and action, then what must also be acknowledged is the legitimacy of the fundamentalists' complaint that students are a captive audience in a prescribed literature curriculum, where the possibilities are defined and delimited by a central authority. Once the advantages and the limitations of referential meaning are acknowledged, the only way to escape the fundamentalists' charge of indoctrination is through a plurality of literary genres, themes, styles, and authors — and of critical approaches to literary works. Most readers — and writers — embrace referential meaning, whatever its limitations and qualifications. After all, the very act of reading for pleasure celebrates being manipulated by a fictional world. But to submit to the artistic manipulation of an author is also to adopt, at least for purposes of the fiction, the moral framework out of which the work is wrought. Even though a reader may transform his or her own values in the reading process, the grounds of that transformation are at least in part set up by the text. And so it would seem that the more varied the texts, the broader the base of reader identification and the greater the likelihood that literary experience will eventuate in a balanced view of the world. Providing a plurality of literary texts, then, safeguards students from the dangers of subliminal ideological seduction without impeding individual psychic growth. Providing a plurality of critical approaches to the text helps further the movement away from indoctrination.

Reading literature within the context of referential meaning by engaging with the text as true or real, is a necessary first step in the reading act, but one to be supplemented with the detached observation of that text as Belsey's "constructed artifact." Engagement presents an intuited sense of truth; detachment through criticism, a conscious healthy caution about the truth claims of any work of literature. Censorship battles do point up one of the most important premises of the educational value of literature: they remind readers to interrogate the text, even as they are moved or offended by it, to seek detachment along with engagement. This end can be achieved through the study of literary language as a language *art*, as nonliteral, ambiguous meaning, as indirect communication.

In the Peterborough County crisis, one of the suspect novels, *Catcher in the Rye*, was defended on just this basis. By coming to grips with the language of Holden Caulfield, the apologia argues, students are taught a lesson in the value of literary criticism as a life skill:

> We can see . . . in our consideration of the book that language consists of far more than its literal meanings, that it is replete with social and other connotations which must be taken into account by those who would be truly proficient communicators. In this way, the book offers many excellent opportunities for investigating the extent to which meaning is determined as much by context and tone as by the content of what is communicated. Thus, students may come to understand that, in the final analysis, effective communication requires a considerable sensitivity of spirit and flexibility of mind. (McAuley 1985, p. 4)

The above claim is more modest than the "search for truth"; but it is, I believe, more realistic, and in the end more honest. It may be objected that the position advanced in this paper merely weakens the case of English teachers by giving ground to the opposition. I do not believe this to be the case. For one thing, censors will probably regard the appeal to literary context as an *art for art's sake* moral cop-out, and the educational values — "sensitivity of mind and flexibility of spirit" — emanating from it as precisely those qualities that will take their children away from them. But the flip side of the censorship issue, the justification for the teaching of literature, is also at stake here. Literature itself, both as an art and as a discipline, is currently under siege not only from censors, but from sociology, post-structuralist criticism, linguistics, information theory, "tick-box" testing, and back-to-basics heresies about the redundancy of the literary in conceptions of literacy. All these influences, along with the ugliness of censorship battles, are forcing educators to reexamine the relationship between word and idea, image and action, literature and life. In the process, I believe, teachers can cast a more sober eye on their reasons for teaching literature. If so, English studies can only be the gainer.

Notes

1. Catherine Belsey (1980, p. 126). This distinction is, of course, not new; the two views of literature presented here may be seen as contemporary versions of Plato's and Aristotle's.

2. Studies have shown that increased familiarity with material judged obscene leads to more positive judgments about the material, but that those demanding censorship are reluctant to be exposed to further knowledge of the offending material. Thus a vicious circle is created "between the poles of refusal to be exposed and familiarity — those who associate obscenity with negative emotional response do not become familiar with obscenity and thereby continue to believe that it has a negative emotional effect" (Beach 1979, p. 142).

3. "I had to wrestle with this one. English is really not my field and there were some things I missed initially. I had to probe to see the significance of the book. I required a tremendous amount of basic guidance." Quoted from *The Peterborough Examiner*, April 22, 1976.

4. *Curriculum Guideline for the Senior Division, English, 1977*, Ontario Ministry of Education, p. 7. It should be noted that in the recently revised guideline the relationship between values and literature has not been rethought except to shift the emphasis on the normative power of literature study from personal growth to social growth: "The vicarious experience literature offers is a subtle and powerful force in building the character of a nation and its people. Literature is [still] an inspiring record" of human achievement, leading "to increased understanding among our many peoples by establishing a deeper appreciation of one another's experience."

5. See Galloway (1980) for a call for revision of curriculum with respect to contemporaneity, sex-role stereotyping, and Canadian content. For feminist critical concerns about the relationship between the ethical and the aesthetic, see especially Kolodny (1985, p. 150). For the relationship of realism to ideology see Coward (1985, pp. 227–30) and Belsey (1980, pp. 46–51, 126–27). It should be stressed that a major difference between fundamentalism and feminism with respect to literature and values is that, while fundamentalists appear to want to "guarantee" meaning, the most enlightened feminist critics, such as those quoted here, advocate polysemous or plurality of meaning.

Bibliography

Beach, R. 1979. Issues of Censorship and Research on Effects of and Response to Reading. In *Dealing with Censorship*, ed. J. E. Davis. Urbana, Ill.: NCTE.

Belsey, C. 1980. *Critical Practice.* New York: Methuen.

Buchanan, R. 1985. *Position Paper: Addressing Concerns Over Teaching* The Diviners *to Grade 13 Students in Peterborough County.* Unpublished paper.

Coward, R. 1985. Are Women's Novels Feminist Novels? In *The New Feminist Criticism: Essays on Women, Literature, and Theory,* ed. E. Showalter. New York: Pantheon.

Czarnecki, M. 1985. Margaret Laurence and the Book Banners. *Chatelaine* 58(October): 186–91.

Ellis, J. 1974. *The Theory of Literary Criticism: A Logical Analysis.* Berkeley: University of California Press.

Frye, N. 1957. *Anatomy of Criticism: Four Essays.* Princeton: Princeton University Press.

———. 1973. *The Critical Path: An Essay on the Social Context of Literary Criticism.* Bloomington: Indiana University Press.

———. 1976. *The Secular Scripture: A Study of the Structure of Romance.* Cambridge: Harvard University Press.

Galloway, P. 1980. *What's Wrong with High School English? . . . It's Sexist, Un-Canadian, Outdated.* Curriculum Series/43. Toronto: OISE Press.

Gribble, J. A. 1983. *Literary Education: A Revaluation.* New York: Cambridge University Press.

Heintzman, R. 1978. Liberalism and Censorship. *Journal of Canadian Studies* 13, no. 4: 1–2, 120–22.

Kolodny, A. 1985. Dancing through the Minefield: Some Observations on the Theory, Practice, and Politics of a Feminist Literary Criticism. In *The New Feminist Criticism: Essays on Women, Literature, and Theory,* ed. E. Showalter. New York: Pantheon.

Laurence, M. 1975. *The Diviners.* Toronto: McClelland and Stewart-Bantam.

McAuley, E. P. 1985. *Rationale for Teaching* The Catcher in the Rye. Unpublished paper.

Ontario Ministry of Education. 1977. *Curriculum Guideline for the Senior Division, 1977.* Toronto: Ontario Ministry of Education.

———. 1987. *Curriculum Guideline 1987: Intermediate and Senior Divisions (Grades 7–12).* Toronto: Ontario Ministry of Education.

Renaissance Peterborough. 1977. *Aspects of the Teaching of English Literature.* Unpublished paper.

School Board Votes to Continue Using Novels by Laurence. *Peterborough Examiner,* 26 April 1985, p. 1.

Stierle, K. 1980. The Reading of Fictional Texts. In *The Reader in the Text: Essays on Audience and Interpretation,* ed. S. R. Suleiman and I. Crosman. Princeton: Princeton University Press.

Textbook Review Committee. Peterborough County, Ontario. 1985. Unpublished brief.

Afterword

I began this book — several chapters and many months ago — with an extended analogy, comparing the work of literature with a construction site upon which readers in their various ways construct meaning. Like most analogies, this one can stretch only so far without breaking. For construction workers working at the same site produce only one building. It may conform more or less to the blueprint with which they began, but if the building is finished at all, it will be a single building, not several parallel buildings coexisting in the same space.

There is a sense, of course, in which many readers have contributed to our understanding of great works. However, individual readers, indulging their own idiosyncratic readings of the same text, will inevitably achieve dissimilar meanings. Though consensus may produce a communal interpretation, it will be apprehended only partially by any individual reader, and it will encompass only so much of any individual reader's private experience of the work in question. Has our building site, therefore, just disintegrated into a confusion of tongues, as at the Tower of Babel?

Writing twenty-five years ago, Northrop Frye concluded *The Educated Imagination* with an analogy of his own:

> The civilization we live in at present is a gigantic technological structure, a skyscraper almost high enough to reach the moon. It looks like a single worldwide effort, but it's really a deadlock of rivalries; it looks very impressive, except that it has no genuine human dignity. For all its wonderful machinery, we know it's really a crazy ramshackle building, and at any time may crash around our ears. What the myth tells us is that the Tower of Babel is a work of human imagination, that its main elements are words, and that what will make it collapse is a confusion of tongues. All had originally one language, the myth says. That language is not English or Russian or Chinese or any common ancestor, if there was one. It is the language of human nature, the language that makes both Shakespeare and Pushkin authentic poets, that gives a social vision to both Lincoln and Gandhi. It never speaks unless we take the time to listen in leisure, and it speaks only in a voice too quiet for panic to hear. And then all it has to tell us, when

we look over the edge of our leaning tower, is that we are not getting any nearer heaven, and that it is time to return to the earth.

So it is time to return to earth. What do we do on Monday? How do we teach our students the common language of human nature, the authentic vision of literature? First, we provide them with an array of texts and let those texts speak for themselves. We encourage them to respond actively to those texts out of the variety of their own experiences. We provide them not with finished interpretations that display our intellectual prowess, but with tools for shaping interpretations of their own. And, finally, we expect our students — in fact, we require them — to demonstrate a critical consciousness; that is, we expect them to use their experience to question the assumptions of the texts and to use the texts to examine their presumptions about human experience.

Thus, what begins as a transaction between an independent reader and an isolated text ends in authentic social vision, if we are fortunate. And what may have begun in this volume as a reaction against the autonomy of the text and as a celebration of the autonomy of the reader ultimately has led us beyond ourselves to a sense of social responsibility, to an awareness of the interdependence of many texts and many readers, each contributing uniquely to a reconstructed Tower of Human Imagination. Such a structure is a worthy alternative to the jerry-built skyscrapers Frye refers to. Like those skyscrapers, performances that pass for drama these days are often called "media events." They are built on the shifting quicksand of "communications technology" and the subtle manipulation of the unwary.

Through the continuing practice of diversity in response and interpretation, even the dialectic of critical opposition, readers of literature may yet hear accents of the common language of Shakespeare and Pushkin, Chinua Achebe and Tsao Hsueh-chin, Beatrix Potter and Virginia Hamilton, Lincoln and Gandhi. Now *there* is a summit meeting worthy of our attendance and our attention, a genuine media event.

We sow the dragon's teeth in fear and in hope that what we will reap will not be merely a "deadlock of rivalries" but an intellect and imagination armed to resist passivity and conformity, narrow-mindedness and arrogance.

One of Louise Rosenblatt's most influential books is entitled *The Reader, the Text, the Poem.* A collection of essays by Edward W. Said that asserts the importance of social responsibility in criticism is called *The World, the Text, and the Critic.* We might have called this volume *Readers, Texts, and the World,* merging the central concerns of both books. We chose instead, as our subtitle, the less ambitious *Readers, Texts, and Contexts.* Our shared thesis, if there is one, is that our classrooms will be impoverished if we neglect the experience of readers, the power of texts, or the claims on our attention of the social contexts from which literature springs and in which it is read.

Acknowledgments

In November 1985, in a meeting of the NCTE Yearbook Committee in Philadelphia, Margaret Early and Eileen Tway persuaded me to undertake the editing of this volume. Because of exigencies of scheduling (we were, in effect, already six months behind schedule) I agreed, but only if they agreed to back me up, to serve as *de facto* coeditors. Along with Jesse Perry, the other member of that committee, they have supported me in more ways than I had any right to expect. One of the genuine pleasures of this project has been this continuing collegiality.

This manuscript may have been reviewed and edited more times than any other book NCTE has produced. Though I take responsibility for whatever blemishes remain, I must express my gratitude to the writers who answered my call for manuscripts; to all the reviewers and editors, whose advice has been invaluable; to Don Zancanella, my research assistant, and Professor Linda Wyman, my friend and colleague from Lincoln University, whose reviews turned into continuing editorial conferences; to Tim Bryant at NCTE, who, in the role of liaison with the NCTE editorial staff, has been a model of patience and courtesy; to Beth Donnell Nelms, who — as usual — has balanced common sense with enthusiasm in her response to the manuscript at all stages and who, when a chapter on adolescent literature was called for at the last minute, pushed aside a stack of her students' papers, rolled up her sleeves, and made it work; and to our children, who for the past decade have provided us a live-in laboratory in adolescents' responses to literature and who — if they were to read what we write — would recognize themselves and groan.

Ben F. Nelms
Columbia, Missouri

Contributors

Marilyn Jones Andre currently teaches first grade at Robert E. Lee Elementary School in Columbia, Missouri, and has taught for some sixteen years in the Columbia Public School District. She holds a bachelor's degree and master's degree, as well as the degree of specialist in elementary administration, from the University of Missouri. Ms. Andre is a member of the International Reading Association.

Deanne Bogdan is an assistant professor in the Department of History and Philosophy at the Ontario Institute for Studies in Education, University of Toronto, where she teaches the philosophy of literature, literature education, aesthetics, and feminist criticism. Her research interests are in selection/censorship problems; the justification for teaching literature; aesthetic, epistemological, and ideological issues in literary response; and women's ways of knowing and learning. Dr. Bogdan is currently coediting a book on reading and response to literature. She has also contributed articles to *English Education, English Journal, Journal of Moral Education,* and *Journal of Aesthetic Education.*

James Butterfield has taught English in middle school at the South Colonie Central School District (New York) for the past sixteen years. He received his baccalaureate and his master's degree at the State University of New York at Albany. Mr. Butterfield has served as a consultant to the Capital District Writing Project (a site of the National Writing Project) and the Greater Capital Region Teacher Center, and to "A World of Difference" — a campaign coordinated by the Anti-Defamation League and designed to help reduce prejudice and discrimination.

Regina Cowin is a fifth-grade teacher at Sunshine Elementary School in Springfield, Missouri. She holds a master's degree in reading from Southwest Missouri State University and is working toward a doctorate in English education at the University of Missouri. Ms. Cowin has taught language arts methods courses at the University of Missouri and has conducted workshops in the teaching of writing. She has made presentations at meetings of the Missouri Writers' Project, the International Reading Association, and the Language Arts Department of Southwest Missouri. In addition, she has published articles in *The Reading Teacher* and *English Journal.*

Suzanne C. Davis received her baccalaureate in elementary education and her master's degree in curriculum and instruction from the University of

Missouri. She is currently teaching fifth grade at Robert E. Lee Elementary School in Columbia, Missouri.

Roseanne Y. DeFabio is currently principal of Saratoga Central Catholic High School (New York), where she also teaches a course in advanced literature. Previously she had a number of years' experience in the high school classroom, where she employed reader-response techniques and multiple critical approaches to the teaching of literature. She has given presentations at a number of conferences on the teaching of writing and literature and has contributed to a monograph of the New York State English Council, *Reader Response in the Classroom.* Mrs. DeFabio is a member of the Capital District Writing Project, the New York State English Council, and NCTE.

Margaret Early is chair of the Department of Instruction and Curriculum in the College of Education at the University of Florida, where she specializes in the teaching of English and reading. She previously was at Syracuse University, where she served as associate director of the Reading and Language Arts Center, head of undergraduate and graduate programs in English education, and associate dean for academic affairs. Dr. Early has also served as president of the New York State English Council, president of the National Conference on Research in English, and president of NCTE. She has, in addition, served on the board of directors of the International Reading Association and is currently on the executive board of the National Society for the Study of Education. Dr. Early has written *Reading to Learn in Grades 5 to 12* and is the senior author of the *HBJ Bookmark Reading Program.* She is the recipient of the NCTE Distinguished Service Award and the IRA William S. Gray Citation.

Bonnie O. Ericson is a professor in the Department of Secondary and Adult Education at California State University, Northridge, where she teaches English methods, secondary reading, and supervision of student teaching. She has served as a demonstration teacher in the California Partnership Program and as a consultant for the California Writing Project. Dr. Ericson has also conducted inservice workshops in secondary reading and writing, and has made presentations at meetings of NCTE and the International Reading Association.

Carol Decker Forman has been teaching high school English for fourteen years — twelve years in Troy, New York, and currently in Burnt Hills, New York. At New York University, she participated in a five-year research project (1977–81) dealing with problem solving and critical thinking in the arts. She has since been involved with research and curriculum development with the State University of New York at Albany and the Capital District Writing Project. Ms. Forman has published *Book Notes* on Dante and Steinbeck for Barron's, an article on the McCarthy Era for *Literary Cavalcade,* and two articles on critical approaches to literature in *Reader Response in the Classroom.*

Eugene K. Garber is a professor of English at the State University of New

York at Albany, where he teaches literature, composition, mythology, and literary and compositional pedagogy. He serves on the national advisory panel of the National Writing Project and is director of the Capital District Writing Project, a site of the national project. Dr. Garber has edited, with Walter Blair and John Gerber, *Better Reading I: Factual Prose* and *Better Reading II: Literature.* He has also published numerous pieces of short fiction in reviews such as *The Sewanee Review, Kenyon Review,* and *Proteus.*

Patricia G. Hansbury is a teacher of English at Canajoharie High School (New York). She has made presentations on reader response to literature at various professional meetings and has served as a judge for the NCTE Achievement Awards in Writing and as a regents item writer for the New York State Bureau of English and Reading Education. Ms. Hansbury is the coeditor, with Charles Chew and Roseanne De Fabio, of *Reader Response in the Classroom.* She is presently doing doctoral work in literary theory and composition theory at the State University of New York at Albany.

Nancy Y. Knipping is an assistant professor of early childhood education in the Department of Curriculum and Instruction at the University of Missouri. She teaches courses in early language learning and early childhood curriculum, and is currently researching the responses of kindergarten and first-grade children to literature. Professor Knipping has made national, state, and local presentations on literacy education, early childhood curriculum, home-school partnerships, and young children's response to literature.

James D. Marshall is an assistant professor of secondary education and English at the University of Iowa. He has taught high school English and was assistant director of the teacher education program at Stanford University. Professor Marshall has contributed many articles to *Research in the Teaching of English,* as well as a chapter in *Contexts for Learning to Write* (ed. Arthur Applebee). He has also made presentations at meetings of NCTE, IRA, and the Iowa Council of Teachers of English, in addition to conducting inservice workshops for high school and junior college teachers. Dr. Marshall is a consultant for the American College Testing Program and a member of the NCTE Committee on Response to Literature.

Ben F. Nelms is a professor of English education at the University of Missouri. He is director of the Missouri Writing Project and a member of the advisory committee to the National Writing Project. A former editor of *English Education* and current editor of *English Journal,* he has published articles on young adult literature, the teaching of writing, and English education in such journals as *English Education, Missouri English Bulletin,* and *English Journal,* as well as a chapter in *Literature for Adolescents.*

Elizabeth D. Nelms is a teacher of tenth-grade English at David H. Hickman High School in Columbia, Missouri. She is associate editor of *English Journal* and from 1984 to 1987 was coeditor of the *EJ* "Books for Young Adults" department. She is a teacher/consultant with the Missouri Writing

Project and teaches summer institutes on children's literature and the teaching of writing for the University of Missouri.

Ruie Jane Pritchard is an associate professor and coordinator of English education at North Carolina State University. She has taught English at both the junior high and high school levels, has supervised student teachers, and was supervisor and consultant for the Right to Read program of the Missouri Department of Elementary and Secondary Education. Dr. Pritchard has made numerous presentations at state, regional, national, and international conferences and has published articles in such journals as *Missouri English Bulletin, English Journal, English Education,* and *Written Communication.* She is a member of the editorial advisory committee for *English Education* and serves on the NCTE Standing Committee on Teacher Preparation and Certification.

Robert E. Probst is a professor of English education at Georgia State University in Atlanta. He previously taught English at both the junior and senior high levels in Maryland, and was supervisor of English for the Norfolk, Virginia, Public Schools. Interested in the teaching of both writing and literature, Dr. Probst has written *Response and Analysis: Teaching Literature in Junior and Senior High School* and was part of a team that prepared *New Voices,* a high school English textbook series. As a member of NCTE, Professor Probst has served on the Committee on Research and the Commission on Reading. He is currently on the board of directors of the Adolescent Literature Assembly and is a Colleague and faculty member of the Creative Education Foundation.

Doris Quick is an English teacher of some twenty-five years' experience and is chair of the English Department at Burnt Hills High School (New York). She is codirector of the Capital District Writing Project, the local site of the National Writing Project. Ms. Quick has contributed articles to *English Journal* and to collections of articles published by the New York State Education Department dealing with teaching practices in composition, improving the teaching of literature, and the writing processes of teachers.

Mary Hawley Sasse teaches college-bound and honors classes at Carbondale Community High School (Illinois), an NCTE Center of Excellence. She received her baccalaureate and her master's degree from the University of Wisconsin–Madison and her doctorate from Southern Illinois University at Carbondale. Dr. Sasse has published articles on creative writing, Native American literature, and censorship. She also contributes to an annual bibliography of composition and rhetoric. A past president of the Illinois Association of Teachers of English, she is currently chair of the Communications Liaison Committee and a member of the Publications Committee of IATE. Dr. Sasse has presented programs at state and national conventions, served as a SLATE Steering Committee member, and is currently chair of the NCTE Committee to Study Teacher-Peer Evaluations.

Eileen Tway is a professor of teacher education at Miami University, where she teaches courses in language arts and children's literature. She is editor of the children's magazine *The McGuffey Writer* and author of several articles and booklets on children's literature and writing, including *Writing Is Reading: 26 Ways to Connect*. She has served as chair of the Elementary Section of NCTE, has served on numerous NCTE committees, and currently edits "The Resource Center" for *Language Arts*.

Dorothy J. Watson is a professor of education at the University of Missouri, where she teaches graduate and undergraduate courses in reading education. For many years she was a classroom teacher and language arts supervisor in the public schools, and she has been involved in inservice teacher education programs around the world. Professor Watson is the 1987 recipient of the International Reading Association's Teacher Educator of the Year Award, director of NCTE's Commission on Reading, and past president of the Center for Expansion of Language and Thinking. She is an active member of local and national teacher support groups and sponsor of the Mid-Missouri Student Reading Association. Professor Watson is coauthor, with Yetta Goodman and Carolyn Burke, of *Reading Miscue Inventory: Alternative Procedures* and coeditor, with P. David Allen, of *Findings of Research in Miscue Analysis: Classroom Implications*.

Mary Lou White is a professor of education at Wright State University, where she teaches courses in children's literature and guides a graduate program entitled "International Literature for Children and Young People." She wrote the instructor's manual for *Children's Literature in the Elementary School* by Huck, Hickman, and Hepler, and she edited the 1980 edition of NCTE's *Adventuring with Books*. A former president of the NCTE Children's Literature Assembly, she is treasurer of the 1990 IBBY World Congress and serves on the NCTE Poetry Award Committee.

Sylvia L. White holds a master's degree in English education from North Carolina State University. She has taught English in grades 5–12. Ms. White has been named North Carolina Teacher of the Year (1984–85) and Wade County Teacher of the Year (1986–87). She has made presentations on various aspects of composition teaching at professional meetings in North Carolina and at the NCTE Southeast Regional Conference.